Forget

About

Location,

Location,

Location

Forget about...

"LOCATION, LOCATION, LOCATION!"

**THE DEFINITIVE REAL ESTATE INVESTOR GUIDE
FOR THE NEW MILLENNIUM**

Ozzie Jurock

¶ JUROCK PUBLISHING LTD.

*Canadian Cataloguing in Publication
Data:*

Jurock, Ozzie, 1944 –
    Forget About Location, Location,
    Location
    Includes index.
    ISBN 0-9684642-1-1 (pbk.)
    ISBN 0-9684642-0-3 (bound)

JUROCK PUBLISHING LTD.
• 1311 Howe Street
  Vancouver, BC V6Z 2P3
  Canada

Typeset, printed and bound in Canada.

CONTENTS

WE CREATE OUR OWN REALITY
Let's do some clear analytical thinking to allow us to grow
Writing creates thinking
Thinking creates pictures or images in our mind
Images create feelings and emotions
Feelings and emotions create action
Action triggers a reaction, which manifests in a
corresponding result.

LELAND VAL VAN DE WALL

Man has his future within him, dynamically alive at this
present moment.

ABRAHAM MASLOW

Chapter 1

THE BASICS

If basics were really basic, we wouldn't have to write so much about them.

This chapter is mostly about money and what to do with it. That's the real problem. What to do with money. (Let's assume that you want to do something with the money to make it more. If you don't, then I can tell you what to do with money in two words. Spend it.) Of course, there is a secondary problem if you don't have any money. If you don't have any money, you have to get some. But after you've got some then that brings you right back to the primary problem of what to do with it.

In this chapter we're going to talk mostly about what to do with money that you've already gotten. A little later in the book we'll talk a bit about how to use OPM (Other People's Money) to get some of your own. But right now the money in question is piled up in front of us and we want to do something with it to make it more.

This presumes that you believe that inflation is eventually coming back. If you think that inflation is coming back, then you have to do something with the money you already have to make it grow, or the effect of inflation will make it melt away like holding an ice cube in the palm of your hand. Not only do you want to preserve the purchasing power of your money but you'll be able, if you know how, to use the dynamics of inflation to make your money grow even faster.

However, you might be of the mind that inflation is permanently dead and will never come back or you might think we're going to have deflation. If that's the case, you'll want to sell everything, buy the highest yielding, longest term government backed bonds you can find and then use the leverage available in that portfolio to open an account to short the STANDARD & POOR 500.

The point here is that if you have some money you have to have an opinion to go along with it. The only person who can afford not to have an opinion about money is the pauper without ambition. And we're not just talking about cash money here; we're talking about all kinds of wealth. If it represents money, it is money.

And there is no shortage of people who will be more than happy to tell you what to do with your money. It's amazing how we're constantly exhorted and bombarded by an endless stream of financial planners, banks, trust companies – you name it – who want to tell us what to do with our money. And because most of us react best to fear – fear is the most popular technique they use.

The two strongest financial motivations are desire for gain and fear of loss. If you're selling to people with practically no money, you press the button labeled 'gain'. If you're selling to people with significant money, you press the button labeled 'loss'.

Scary claims are made. We are told that the pension plan we are depending on won't be there for us by the time we get to it. And even if it is, the purchasing power will be practically meaningless. You are presented with mental pictures of yourself: gray, wizened, bent with age and there you are with trembling hands warming up a can of dog food for your supper as the wind blows through the cracked window of your one room hovel.

They'll tell you: "If you have an income of $50,000 now, in 20 years when you retire you must have (because of inflation) a portfolio of $10 million to enjoy the same standard of living you enjoy today." And then based on this or that speculated interest or inflation rate, you'll be scared to death for the next X years as you progress along to age 65 and who knows how far beyond.

With the advances in medical science it might be possible that at some point in the future if you die without satisfying all your obligations to the government, they might just revive you and make you work off what you owe.

If you had listened to the experts who were dispensing the best advice available 20 years ago and locked yourself and your wealth into a plan which guaranteed to remit the then prevailing 'safe amount' of an income stream of $500 per month (a lot back then – pocket-change today) for the rest of your life, imagine the desperate poverty that you would retire to today. Stone soup would be a luxury.

Yes, we need more money now but who knows what this money will be worth tomorrow. Yes, we need more income, but who can possibly know the state of the world three months from now ... much less 20 years from now? Nobody knows for sure the 'what and where' of interest rates and inflation rates and the value of money. It's just not possible.

What we do know is that the *safety* that was inherent in the projected *big income* of 20 years ago is a pitiful joke today.

So we see that forecasting is never easy – particularly when it's about the future. Crystal balls crack, vaunted talk-show soothsayers wither and drop off the television scene and the books that were treasure maps wind up in the remainder bin at the bookstore. In the last three decades stock markets have surged up and crashed down. Certain mutual funds that looked like they were blue chips sprang leaks and sank while others soared like rockets only to burn out and fall back down. Through all of this the average folk watched their savings chewed away by insidious inflation.

However, in all the turmoil of this sound and fury, one asset has weathered the changes. Three decades ago, had you bought good quality real estate you would not be concerned about your future today. That real estate would have kept up with inflation, remained secure in value, and steadily appreciated. Sure, there would have been some temporary dips. There has to be because real estate is cyclical in nature. But one thing is certain – over the years, the base values have been steadily increasing. Back to that purchase 30 years ago – today it would be paid off and clear title – which means either a mortgage-free home (no more monthly 'rent' payments to the bank) and/or a steady rental income courtesy of your tenants.

Put into perspective, if you place a good portion of your assets into real estate today, you won't have to worry about tomorrow. It doesn't matter how wild or turbulent the economy or the marketplace. It's like riding a horse with one spur – if half the horse goes, the other half has to go along with it. No matter how deep or tempestuous the water, you're going to be floating on top of it.

Let's review something all of us already know. The Chinese have used real estate holdings for wealth creation for 2,000 years. All huge fortunes were either started or extended with real estate. Home ownership (the most common form of real estate holding) has been the single largest factor in the accumulation of wealth for the average North American, firstly because of straight appreciation due to inflation, secondly, due to the leverage involved.

This basic principle of appreciation holds true for pretty well any healthy major urban center. Let's take Vancouver, BC for an example.

If the laws of mathematics have not been repealed and if what has happened in the past and is happening in the present can and will happen in the future – you better sit down for this one (taking Vancouver, BC for an example) – in the year 2021 the average Vancouver home could sell for $7.1 million!

As radical as that number might be, just pause and consider the facts. In 1960 the average Vancouver home sold for $13,105. Thirty-eight years later in 1998 the average sale price was some $310,000. Almost a 2,300 per cent return. Not too shabby, but if you had put down a 10% down payment of $1,310 you would at this point be gloating over a 23,000 per cent return plus you would have a free-and-clear roof over your head.

On the surface, if we project this into the future it seems like an exercise in fantasy to arrive at a price of $7,119,420 for this same house. The question is, is this fantasy or is it a realistic application of 'doing the math'? If this kind of appreciation is going to continue, you have to be on the conveyor belt. If you're not, you're going to be left so far behind that it will be financially disastrous. And here we're only talking from the perspective of a place to live. This isn't even addressing the investment aspect of those monies outside the family home.

When you combine appreciation with leverage, you unlock the great secret of achieving the optimum result with real estate investment. And as you can see from the foregoing numbers, the 'lever' can lift you up or the 'appreciation', if you're on the wrong side, it can crush you down.

When your gain is measured on the capital invested, not the actual price of the property, some really astounding results come into focus. But the game is not as simple as it used to be. The goal posts move. The only constant is that everything is always changing. The secret of surviving and prospering is the ability to adapt to the changes.

The 1980s were very forgiving for the amateur. Benign with a capital 'B'. That 'B' could also represent 'Bucks' and 'Brainless'. Back then if you had a few dollars you could buy any piece of real estate, anywhere, and you would make money. Even if you could barely hear thunder and see lightning, it was almost impossible to make a big enough mistake. If you paid too much, it only meant that you had bought a little too soon. The clock and the calendar made you into a financial wizard. Thanks to inflation, prices soon caught up to you and bailed you out.

Still, there were lots of people in the early 1980s who managed to lose all their money in real estate. Those were the people who put their money into the wrong syndications, limited partnerships or real estate investment trusts. But we'll talk more about that later. In the late eighties fortunes were made.

But after the 1980s the real estate world became less forgiving. For some investors the times were downright terrifying. All of a sudden there was the sudden change. Markets fluctuated area by area both as to volume of sales and prices. Different real estate categories rose or fell without any apparent linkage to each other. You could see in one market area the average single-family detached home rise in value by 40 per cent while in the exact same market area downtown condos slumped in value by 12 to 20 per cent (Vancouver 1990-1995).

The people who tried to play by the old rules found themselves playing someone else's game. And most of the time they were handed their heads. Was it possible to avoid the dangers and yet at the same time prosper with the good stuff? Yes it was, but you had to put aside location, location, location, and instead you had to read the trends, position yourself as to the timing and then implement some new techniques.

To be successful real estate investors we must understand ourselves. That means we have to understand our investment objectives in relation to the risks we are willing and able to tolerate. But having done that we then must understand that aspect of 'ourselves' that is part of the New Consumer. The New Consumer is you and I. How everyone can be motivated is what has to be analyzed. Because that analysis is what will tell us how the New Consumer is likely to act and react in any given situation.

And the analysis is difficult because the 'talk people talk' is different from the 'walk people walk'. Buyers are liars. We say one thing and then go out and do the opposite. If you take a poll, people will tell you that they want service and human interaction in the satisfaction of their consumer needs. Then they blithely drive by the local, and friendly, corner store to the 'big box superstore' with the canyon of goods piled up to the ceiling.

They load up with a 27-year supply of pink toilet paper (it was such a deal), haul it out to their hulking off-road vehicle which costs more than a Cadillac but will never see a mud splatter in its life. Then they celebrate the $5 they saved on the toilet paper with a $6 expenditure for a no-fat double latte with an almond biscotti (in other words, coffee and a cookie).

The new consumer will fight to save, drive for miles, circle parking lots. Discounts are king. But he will also splurge $50 for a bottle of wine of 'fine vintage, with superb aroma tickling the palate'. There are lessons here for all businesses not just real estate. We all have changed. We kill to save on high volume everyday items (even if we must buy in bulk and go out of our way to get it) but we will spend big-time for something we perceive as unique, special and 'with it'.

If you had polled or surveyed these people to discern their intended consuming patterns, they would have drawn you a much different picture. What they say and what they do is very, very different. So you have to be careful when you're evaluating the prognostications of the demographers and the economists. That doesn't mean that you ignore them but you have to separate the myth from the reality.

When it comes to perception and reality for motivation, the perception becomes the reality. When it's a choice of myth or actuality to determine action; the actuality is always the determining factor.

One thing is for sure; we are different from what we were. The 'pre', 'post', and 'current' Baby Boomers want a certain type of home and a certain life style and the degree to which you can accurately read these trends will be the degree to which you will or will not prosper in your real estate investments. The savvy investors will ask the right questions and acquire the right answers before they make their investment decisions and take their investment actions.

The new consumer is concerned with living longer and healthier. A whole new philosophy of physical behavior is developing. We cram ourselves with oat bran, we devour lettuce and spinach by the bale, and we torture ourselves with jogging and calisthenics and other assorted masochisms. Some of us do it for an improved quality of life; most of us do it in a misguided and vain attempt to slow down the clock and the calendar. I once saw a man jogging in the park wearing a tee shirt that said, "Eat Right, Keep Fit, Die Anyway". Or as some Asian philosophers say, "Long life, short life, it makes no difference, they are all but a moment in time." Yet, we do not have the same dedication when it comes to cramming some real know-how into our heads. We rather have someone else do the thinking for us.

What we really need – in concert with exercising our bodies – is to exercise our minds and direct our thinking to understanding the basic principles of life. Do it and you will create the resilience, the self-reliance and the security that you are looking for which no financial planner can give you. In the words of Dr. Tomorrow: "In the past we were a nation of have and have-nots, in the future we'll be a nation of know and know-nots." Get onto the 'know' side of things. Life is a wonderful journey. A journey. You don't arrive somewhere and stay there. Make it an ongoing journey of personal growth of mind as well as body and no matter where the world goes you will be safe.

What does this have to do with real estate investment? Go back and reread the previous paragraph. It is one of the most important points of this book! Before you invest in property, invest in yourself. Time, thought, and taking action all help to create opportunity. Inertia, mental sloth, and the unwillingness to roll up your mental sleeves and do your own research keep you insulated from opportunity. When you do take action you will be much more likely to avoid mistakes and encounter fewer problems.

I know people who will spend more time analyzing the fine print on a can of tomato juice than they do reading the fine print on an investment prospectus or examining a house before they buy it.

These people are long on hope and gullibility, short on healthy skepticism. When someone comes up and offers them a 'slam-dunk' deal that will make them $100,000 overnight, guaranteed, they fall all over themselves reaching for the pen so they can sign up before it's all gone. It's the classic fairy tale of easy money with someone else doing all the work. You get rich and will never have to worry again. Sort of reminds you of that other fairy tale about three magic beans and a cow, doesn't it?

Remember what we said about people serving their own self-interest? If someone knows about a $100,000 overnight deal (and make no mistake, they do come along, not often, but every once in a while), they will never hand it over to an outsider. They do what you and I would do. They keep it for themselves or if they don't have the cash to swing the deal, they give it to their brother or their cousin or even their barber. The last person in the world they're going to give it to is you.

When you're approached with these kinds of scenarios, there is one element of truth: someone indeed is going to make $100,000 overnight. The $100,000 that's going to be made is your investment money and the overnight part involves a midnight scamper to places unknown.

Successful real estate investing is like anything else. It requires personal work, imagination and individual enterprise. But you've got to do the *important* work yourself. Read that last sentence about a hundred times. There is no substitute or way around it. I do not know of any successful investor in real estate (other than the homeowner, happily and unwittingly riding up the escalator of inflation) who hasn't learned the ins and outs of the business, who doesn't actively and consistently scour the market place, make offers, and when they are accepted, personally does the due diligence.

I knew a social worker who told me that all happy families are the same and all unhappy families are unhappy in their own unique way. Well, it's the same way with real estate investors. All the successful ones follow the same guidelines and all the unsuccessful ones find their own special ways to get into trouble.

The opportunities are everywhere and successful investors don't have to have any qualities that average folks don't have. And they don't have any esoteric knowledge nor do they know any secrets that are not available to mere mortals. However, and this is a biggie, consistently successful investors (and the operative word here is 'consistently' – just because you cut down one tree, doesn't make you a logger) have a different way of thinking. They are resilient. They are ahead of the crowd because they stay informed and they have the courage and the confidence to take action.

You do not have to be sponsored to join this exclusive group. Nor do you have to learn the password or the secret handshake. All you have to do is learn the basic principles and get started. Well, what are these basic principles?

Here is the basic outline, expanded later in the Ten Commandments we discussed in the introduction.

What?

What to invest in is the first question to ask. You have an entire spectrum of investment spread out in front of you. There are single family homes, condos, commercial properties, hotels, raw land and all the sub-categories and combinations that are possible. You have to make a choice. And here is where you have to ask some questions about yourself. How much skill and experience do I have? How much time do I have to devote to this? How much risk can I entertain? How much money do I have and what size investment can I handle? What is my time-line – long term, short term, what? After you've fleshed out this picture you view the categories of investments that have not been eliminated, put them in order of preference and then you go looking. In this, as with everything else, you have to have an opinion. Then, once you have an opinion, you have to make a choice and take action. We're going to keep coming back to this time and time again. You must have an informed opinion, you have to make an informed choice, and you have to overcome inertia and take action.

Where?

Once again, an embarrassment of choices. Downtown is close. Our own suburb is closer. What about the neighboring municipalities and small towns? Do I go out of Province/State? What about out of the country? Most of the time the closer you are to what you buy the happier you are going to be. But not always. There are times and there are trends when the best investment available is 3,000 miles away. You have to take each situation on a case by case basis and make your decision on the basis of the factors existing at the time. A good technique is to take a map of your area and put a pin where you live. Take a pencil and a piece of string and draw a circle with a two-hour travel-time radius, then do the same for four hours and then six hours. That's going to tell you how far you're going to travel and where your customers, when it comes time to sell, have to be or travel from.

Two hours you can go and come back in a day – you could commute. Four hours – you get there on a Friday night to spend the weekend. Six hours you're going to be staying for a week. Each area attracts a different investor group to re-sell into, each has its own pros and cons.

Here we have the same story. Scrutinize the options, make a choice, then go looking for opportunities.

When?

Timing is everything but it doesn't exist in a vacuum. There's no such thing as a bad piece of real estate. But there is real estate that you can buy too early or too late. Back in the days of runaway inflation if you bought too soon, eventually the clock and the calendar made you right. Those days are gone. If and when they return, then the game will change back. But now it's a different game from what it was. If you buy too soon it will cost you. Any money that you pay too much is profit that could have been yours when you eventually dispose of the investment.

Your timing has to be considered in the framework of all the other factors but especially the trends. If the trend is toward a particular category in a particular area, you might find it more difficult to buy at the price and terms that fit your formula. You might have to wait until trends change or until an opportunity appears.

That is why you have to be examining the market all the time because situations bubble up to the surface where someone is willing for his particular reasons to sell something you would want at a price that you would pay. But there's lots of competition for the good deals and if you would pay it so would lots of other people. You've got to be decisive and you've got to be quick – but you've also got to be right.

Why?

Your decision to invest in a particular property should be based on the economic, sociological and demographic considerations that apply at the time. But you don't just buy something because you'll make X amount of dollars on it. It has to fit within the framework of your investment objectives. The risk factors have to be in balance with what you can tolerate.

The only way you're going to be able to evaluate that is by doing your own due diligence. Some of this due diligence you're going to be able to get the agent (if there is one involved) to do for you. But the real important stuff, you're going to have to do yourself. This is one of the points where you will make or lose the most money. The deals you say no to are more important than the deals you buy. It's like panning for gold, the trick is to get rid of the sand.

You buy a piece of property because you get enough 'yes' answers to the questions you ask. You will prosper or suffer in direct relation to the number of the correct questions you ask.

How?

The monies you pay are part of it. The terms you arrange are part of it. The professionals you use are part of it.

This is where technique comes in, the technique of the nuts and bolts of getting from point A to point B. You can learn the component parts of technique from gathering information but you can only learn how to put those component parts together by doing it often enough until you know how. This is where the man with twenty years experience should have the advantage over the person with one year's experience. Yet, often we see investors making the same mistake over and over. What you don't want to be is one of those people who have one year's experience and repeat it twenty times so that after twenty years in the business you're still a beginner.

You certainly want to learn from any mistakes you make. What is much, much better is to learn from mistakes other people make. That is why the most successful investors are the ones who are the perpetual students.

How Much?

This is important. Remember that the price you pay is not just made up of the dollar figure. It is a combination of the dollar figure and the terms. You could pay twice the price of an apartment building if you could buy it for nothing down and pay off the mortgage at no interest plus half the net operating profit.

The common wisdom used to be: to buy a property, hold it a while as the appreciation mounted and then sell it to realize the profit from the inflation. In an inflationary continuum that's fine but if the inflation graph is a flat line, your profit is going to be contained in the price you paid. As an investor it is absolutely vital to first determine the current fair market value – and then buy below that fair market value. With taxes, real estate commissions in and out, closing costs, etc., the price you pay must be at least 12% below the current market value if you were to sell the next day. And that's just to break even. So buying at the right price is crucial.

And don't be afraid to offer the price you want to pay. You can buy anything that's out there but the seller usually just has this one property for sale. You know in advance that his asking price only represents his absolute wildest dream. You'll be amazed what sellers say yes to.

That's if you're a buyer. If you're a seller, you shouldn't be in a hurry to reduce your price unless you're in a hurry to sell. A seller is like a skydiver.

Let me explain: A skydiver can do anything that a bird can do. He can circle, he can swing right and left, he can go forward or backwards.

He does all of this while he is descending. The only thing he can't do that a bird can do is go back up. Once you lower a price that's it. It's a one way street so you should base your decisions accordingly.

Just remember the most important principle. You will make the most money the day you buy the property.

How Long?

This is different for everyone. It depends on the external forces of the marketplace and it depends on the internal forces of your own motivations and objectives. Are you a Keeper or a Flipper? Fortunes have been made with both approaches.

Every morning that you wake up you should consider every property you own and how much you could sell it for that day. Then you ask yourself this question, "If I didn't own this property but it was for sale and I had the money it represents, would I buy it today for that price?"

If the answer is yes, then you keep that property another day. If the answer is no, then you put that property on the market. In effect, every day that you don't attempt to sell a piece of property for its fair market value you repurchase it for that amount. Every day. No exceptions.

However, a lot of people only buy and never sell. Now, if you start with a few million you never have to look at a property again after you buy it and this will just work fine for you. But most other people (those that want to get the million) want to optimize their results and for them the examination and the evaluation procedure is a constant process.

Still, nothing ever stays the same. As we've already said, the only constant is change. The closer you watch the market the better off you're going to be.

What To Watch Out For?

Everything! The marketplace is filled with quicksand pools. You have to do all the necessary due diligence. If you don't, sooner or later you will make a serious mistake and it will be very expensive.

Part of the danger is in the property, but that's the easy part. The hard part is the danger contained in the people you deal with and external situations that can impact on your property.

People will only tell you what suits their purpose. Sure, there are laws, but the laws don't cover everything. And there are hidden factors. You could buy a property and then find that under certain circumstances you don't have access to it.

As many innocent property owners found in British Columbia and

Ontario there are properties where the roads leading in go across First Nations' lands that the natives can close anytime they want. If that happens you are stuck. There are properties with restrictive covenants in favor of hydro or railroads. You might not have known about it when you bought, or maybe you knew about it and didn't realize the importance, but if the buyer you're trying to sell to wants the title free and clear, you can't deliver it.

Or, you could buy a piece of commercial property that was a gas station for forty years with the ground so contaminated it could take you five years to clean it up enough to get a development permit. The examples could go on forever.

You can only avoid a danger before you buy. After you buy it's too late. Then the only thing you can do is survive it – at whatever the cost.

Who Do I Trust?

Most people are not going to make a full time career out of real estate investing and so they are not going to become expert in the multiplicity of areas where expertise is required. Therefore, they are going to have to rely on some outside experts. Even the full time practitioners have to select specialists when they come to areas where they don't have the knowledge they need.

If you're talking about Lawyers, Accountants and Insurance people, people who you are using for implementation, it's a relatively simple process. But if you're talking about people who you are using to help you make value judgments, the selection process becomes very complex and absolutely critical.

Remember that people can always be depended on to serve what they perceive to be their self-interest. When your self interest and an advisor's self interest are at a variance, guess which one he will consider the most important?

This is another place where you make or lose (and especially lose) the most money. Ask any group of real estate investors, or for that matter any group of any kind of investors and they will all tell you the same thing. Almost all the optimum result situations where they made the most money came from them doing their own due diligence; almost all the money they lost they lost because they listened to the wrong people.

Track record is an indicator but it's not enough by itself. The company an advisor is associated with is no guarantee. You have to know how he is getting paid and how much he is getting paid and by whom. You have to know if his objectives are close enough to yours so that your trust will be well placed. Your objectives and his objectives are never going to be identical (unless your advisor is a Mother Teresa), but you want them to be close.

This is an area where you usually get to make one mistake. Because if you do make that mistake, that investment capital is gone and it takes a long, long time to replace that lost money with fresh investment capital. Be very, very careful!

If?

One of my mentors from my early years in the business told me, "All the money I've made in real estate I've made by saying yes. All the money I've kept I've kept by saying no." After you gone through the process of asking the foregoing nine questions you take all the answers and examine them to answer the tenth question and that is, 'If?'.

When in doubt, say no. Opportunities are like streetcars. There's another one coming along every ten minutes. As long as you're in the market place and examine what's available you're going to have more opportunities than you will have time, money, or energy to deal with.

So be cautious – remember, if you see something that seems too good to be true, you're absolutely right! But not too cautious – you can't get results without action!

~

In Essence

Ask all the questions. It's not the things you don't know that kill you. It's those things you assume to be true that aren't.

Do your own due diligence. You will not only pay for the mistakes you make but you'll also pay for the mistakes that you allow other people to make for you.

Be patient. There is no shortage of opportunities. They come along in a constant stream.

Once you've made the decision to act then take that action. Nothing happens until you take action.

Chapter 2

TIMING

Reporter: I understand you're a very successful comedian.
Entertainer: Yes, I am.
Reporter: What is the secret of your succ.......
Entertainer: Timing!

As with stand-up comedy and practically everything else in life, timing is everything. In real estate investing, the degree to which your timing is accurate is the degree to which you will achieve optimal or minimal results. It is very often the difference between success and failure. Yeah, but – and I hear this all the time – what about Location, Location, Location? To my mind this is the worst cliche that exists in the market place today. While there are countless examples to the contrary, everybody trots out the Location principle as the guiding light to successful real estate investing. Poppycock. Developers, realtors and reporters repeat those three words ad nauseum, yet they have nothing to do with value appreciation. Sure, some locations are better than others and location for a lot in Toronto is worth more than compared to a lot in Saskatoon; but in any given market for the average investor (or homeowner for that matter) it is far more important to understand the principle of timing.

Take a suburb in Vancouver, say Burnaby. You bought an average bungalow – in any location – in that fair suburb in 1989. You would have paid about $260,000 for it. You ran it into the ground, didn't cut the grass and in 1995 you sold it to me. I paid the then prevailing $400,000 value; you made a hefty profit. I cleaned up the house, finished the basement and cut the grass diligently and find that in 1999 it's worth

$350,000. I lost, you gained – same location. The same is true had you bought a house in Toronto – any location – in 1985 and sold it in 1989 – you were a hero. Had you bought the same house – same location – at the peak in 1989 you were a bum. This is true for New York if you bought in 1984 – hero – and sold in 1988 – bum. If you bought in 1988 and sold in 1995 – small hero. If you bought in Manhattan in 1995 and sold in the spring of 1998 – big hero (prices rose 30% in 2 years). Yet – probable bum – if you bought in 1998! The same applies to San Diego, Los Angeles, Phoenix and Calgary – or HongKong, Tokyo and Berlin. Your problem is never location, it is timing. Whatever area you live in as you read this, check your marketplace. You will find the same principle at work there. Forget about location, location, location and start to think about timing! What stage is the real estate market cycle in my area? What influences the cycle? What are the principles? Remember that real estate markets are never national always local and so are the cycles.

So you say, "Good! I will learn what I have to learn about timing and then I will know how. Where do I start? What are the rules?"

Well, it used to be easier to identify in the past. Timing wasn't as important because the dynamics never changed. Today's dynamics change constantly. As we go into the new millenium we are more likely to move into small towns, have greater population flows, new job creation at home and a hundred other factors that may affect value. We expect this to continue and the changes – in fact – to increase in velocity. Just when you think you have it figured out the rules change.

For example: Let's say I take you onto the tennis court to teach you the game of tennis. I hit the ball to you in a certain direction with a certain amount of force and the ball travels from my racquet in a straight direction on a certain trajectory at a relatively constant speed. Easy enough. You have normal eye/hand coordination and normal motor skills so if we practice this for a while you will learn the timing involved with tennis.

Now you go out to play tennis but you find yourself playing in a game where the ball angles left or right in mid-flight. The trajectory suddenly goes up or down. The speed of the ball changes in mid-flight to either a faster or slower rate. You would find yourself playing a game where the timing that you had learned when you were being taught the game was of little or no use to you. In fact, you would be running to where the ball was not going to be and to add insult to injury you'd be getting there either too soon or too late.

With real estate investment it is like that surreal tennis game we've just described. When you look at the market you are looking at a snapshot in time. That's the way it is at that moment but in a month or a year it might be very different.

One of the problems we have is in our education. All of our teachers prepare us, regardless of what the subject is, for a world that is not going to exist by the time we get to it. They take a snapshot in time of the world as it is in the present and they prepare us for that. When we go to use that information, we find we're in a different world.

If you are in an inflationary real estate cycle, the rules are relatively simple. You buy a piece of property utilizing leverage, you wait a certain amount of time for the property to appreciate, then you might sell for a profit and buy something larger or you can borrow on your increased equity and buy something in addition. What could be more simple?

However, if you're in a flat-line segment of an inflation cycle, you have to buy below fair market value to establish your profit at the beginning. You have to give greater importance to cash flow considerations.

Fine, for both scenarios. But what happens if you buy in an inflationary cycle and then it turns flat-line? You have to shift your focus every time the market changes. It's like riding a bull at the rodeo. Every time the bull does something different you have to change your position accordingly or you're going to be thrown very forcibly to the ground, stomped on, and gored unmercifully. Another example of sport imitating life – except life is more cruel.

The marketplace is continually changing, therefore what we have to do is learn to read the changes, interpret what the changes mean, and adapt ourselves to them.

First question. What are the determining factors? Here we come to some good news. The component parts, the determining factors, are not complex or difficult to deal with. You look at migration, affordability, inventory availability, inflation, the environment of growth and the demographics of an area.

Of course, there are dozens of others that affect the shades and subtleties but those are the main ones. Remember this isn't as complex as rocket science or brain surgery – it just pays better.

Let's look at the list of timing indicators:

• Migration

- Affordability
- Inventory availability
- Inflation
- Environment of growth
- Demographics

These aren't in any particular order of importance but they are all important in the order of things. Each factor has a bearing and an impact on the other factors and all of them affect the price of property. Look at all of them and you will get a clearer picture of how to determine the timing of your real estate investment.

Migration: People have to want to be there. So the migration has to be an inward migration if you're looking for prices to go up. What is it that makes the price of real estate go up? It is a demand for the use of it.

Usually, the formula is that population increase equates to value increase in the price of the real estate. But it's not just the number of people, but the number of people into a relatively small area. If you move a thousand people into a thousand square miles, you have a density increase of one person per square mile. But if you move a thousand people into ten square miles, your density increase is a hundred times more and will impact on the prices accordingly.

People have to want to go there and they have to have an economic reason or a sociological reason to go there. In the 1930s Las Vegas was a wide spot in the road where you stopped for gas. You could have bought the whole town for practically nothing. Look at it now.

You'll find some of the most expensive real estate in the world in Las Vegas. Go ten miles into the desert and you can buy all the land you want for a few hundred dollars an acre. Will that land ever be worth what the land in downtown Las Vegas is worth? Not likely because who wants to go there?

When you see a marked increase in inward migration you know that the timing is getting right for an increase in prices. The why of the inward migration is very important. It matters why the people are coming. If the government built a dam and created a lake, that lake is going to be there for a long time. However if somebody is building a hoola-hoop factory, that is a different story. When the fad is over the people will be gone. In Porcupine Plain or Shell Lake, Saskatchewan you can buy a building lot for one dollar. The catch is, you have to live there. In 'anywhere downtown' on the waterfront a lot is priced at a million dollars. The catch is, everyone wants to live there. This is the only time where location – in the grander scheme of things – matters.

How do you know where to go for the facts? Your StatsCan office federally and/or provincially, department of immigration all publish the relevant numbers. In fact, StatsCan provides winners by city and place and projects the future. Get the numbers over time and you'll have an idea about your area's prospects.

Affordability: There is a curious factor about people. All of them, virtually without exception, like to sleep inside. You will die from exposure before you die from anything else. You can go a long, long time without food, a slightly lesser time without water, but exposure will take you off long before you die from hunger or thirst. Once you've got air to breathe there isn't anything more important than shelter. And that shelter has to be affordable.

If property in an area costs less than properties in comparable areas, but there's a demand for the use of it, it's probably time for it to be going up. If property is selling for less than its replacement cost, then it's probably time for it to be going up. If prices are equal to replacement costs and there are no vacancies, then it's probably time to build some.

Value is an important consideration but affordability is much more important. Your customers have to be able to pay or they will either go someplace else or they will do without. What you buy has to be affordable to the end user. So this is what you look for. Federal Agencies publish affordability ratings, so do all major banks.

For instance in 1995 Canada Mortgage and Housing Corp. (CMHC) published a ranking of all major North American cities. Vancouver came in third in affordability after Honolulu and San Francisco, Toronto 23RD and Calgary 47TH. Easy to form the basis for an opinion with those numbers. It isn't the only number to look at, but this one together with others may help you to pick a city.

Inventory Availability: Here's where the law of supply and demand kicks in. If there is an oversupply in a particular category in a particular price range, then prices and values are not likely to increase; in fact, they are likely to decrease. So you watch the statistics on the available inventory. When you see those numbers start to move in either direction, you act accordingly. This is where timing is important and fortunately, can be measured fairly accurately.

There is also a correlation between affordability and inventory availability. When affordability becomes a problem, people will compress downwards. Instead of a house they'll settle for a condo or an apartment. Instead of a three-bedroom they'll settle for a two-bedroom and use the den or the computer room as sleeping areas, if need be. People will double up. Recreation rooms will become in-law suites. When this happens the more expensive accommodation becomes stagnant, forcing an upward pressure on the less expensive accommodation.

All the statistics are available. Local Real Estate Boards, major Real Estate Brokerage firms all publish relevant monthly and yearly numbers. Some boards publish running totals of 5 years and more. Make sure you know the source and do your own interpretation. You have to stay on top of it. If you don't, you're going to be playing in that tennis game we were describing.

Inflation: Inflation comes and goes. Every time it comes there spring up three schools of thought:

"It'll go up forever."
"It's going to stay where it is now."
"It's going to go the other way, we're in for some deflation."

When inflation disappears and the graph shows a flat line, three schools of thought spring up:

"Inflation is dead, it's going to be like this forever."
"No, it's coming back, you'll see."
"No, it's deflation and with it the end of the world is at hand."

You can gather your facts from wherever they are available but after you've done that you have to form an opinion. This isn't like religion where you decide on a moral philosophy and then go out and carve it in stone. This is an ever-changing continuum, soup that is boiling and bubbling and nothing is ever where it was the last time you looked. The difference between 'too soon' and 'too late' is timing! If you watch the trends as they change, you'll be able to time your actions for optimum results. In the late nineties there are the most dire predictions of a return to the dirty thirties. Analogies abound about terrible times ahead.

No one has the finite crystal ball. The world has changed and is continuing to change; the nineties can be frightening, but so were the eighties and the seventies and the sixties. In 1969 I couldn't give away brand-new $19,900 full basement homes, in 1974 the U.S. stock market crashed by 40%, in 1987 by 28% and gloom descended on real estate markets in sympathy. In 1981 and 1982 in Canada and 1988 to 1992 in the U.S. real estate values did crash. Mortgage interest rates did hit 16.5%. Throughout all turmoil there were those predicting a return to inflation and those predicting an abject crash into deflation. All sounded so reasonable and so possibly right. Yet, had you listened to all the doom and gloom of 1961, 1974, 1981, 1982, 1983, 1986 and 1988 and not bought real estate you would have done a serious disservice to yourself and your family. If you are banking on deflation, the odds aren't with you. Inflation not deflation returned time and again.

Environment of Growth: This is the toughest one to read because here we are dealing much more with what's in the headlines on the front page of the newspaper rather than the statistics we find in the articles in the business section.

Are people coming in because there are jobs? Is industry making major investments? Is this a one-industry town? What are the prospects for the future? Will the new highway add to this area by getting people faster to this town or will it bypass the town, condemning businesses to die? Is the local government relatively easy to get along with? Is the federal government reasonable with taxation? Do management and labor get along? Can an investor expect a fair return for the capital invested?

These are the factors that contribute to an environment of growth. If times are good, that's good. But even if times are bad, if they are starting to get better there can be more potential in that than if times are good.

When learning the game of soccer, my coach told me I only had to know one thing and that was, "Run to the ball. Wherever the ball is, you run to it!" With real estate investment you run to the environment of growth. You go to where it is or where it's starting and you avoid the places where it is not.

And you watch for changes. It is the changes that tell you when the time is getting right to either buy or sell.

Demographics: The buzzword of the nineties now is the question of demographics. Clearly, economic forces change with changes in demographics. During World War Two when a lot of able-bodied men were away in the army, the maternity wards weren't very busy. Well, boys will be boys and girls will be girls. When the war was over and the boys and girls got together again, everybody made up for lost time. The result was the baby boom of the late 1940s. As these boomers reach various ages and the demographic bulge they create enters the graph and passes through the time line, there are very important changes in the marketplace.

All of a sudden joggers and tennis players and aerobicizers become golfers. In a few more years those golfers will become lawn bowlers and mall walkers. What this means to you is that the size, depth, and desires of any segment of the market is measurable and predictable.

As with almost everything in life, there are two schools of thought. One school of thought says that the baby boomers have hit 50, they've already bought their single-family homes and as they die off so will the need for single family detached housing. Or, as the kids grow up and leave home the boomers will want to divest themselves of that house in the city and go someplace less urban and more pleasant.

That would mean that fewer housing starts would be required. Instead there should be a glut of houses all hitting the market at the same time creating a situation where you have too much product and not enough buyers.

Now the other school of thought says something different. It says that there will be a whole bunch of these boomers who are going to be active longer and stay in their homes longer. No old age home for them. Besides, it used to be that the kids left home at 19, now they come back at 22. Then they leave again at 24 but then they get divorced and come back with two more kids. So, there isn't going to be a shortage of bodies to fill those extra bedrooms.

Anyway, the immigration from outside the country is going to keep the cities filled, so you're not going to see downward pressure on the market from that factor.

Which one of these schools of thought is right? Maybe both. Maybe neither. It doesn't matter. Go back to the basics. There are no experts. The public is always wrong.

Remember this, demographic forecasts are one thing. I know how important demographics are for long range projections. We report trends as well. But to individual businesses working in the 'today' they rank way down on the list of important things. Business is concerned with economics (what is the general local business environment), operating practices (how do you successfully compete in this market), sales and marketing (how well do you service your customers) and then, maybe demographics. There is no difference to real estate investors. Local conditions always override long-term projections. Futurists are more often wrong than not. In 1970 the 'Club of Rome' predicted that we'd run out of oil by 1990 and oil prices would soar. Today, we have a glut of oil at 20-year low production prices.

As long as you let them be general enough, the futurists can make a very good case for themselves. But when you pin them down to specifics, it doesn't look so good.

For example: One futurist says that in a particular urban area in the next 25 years the population will increase by somewhere between one million and three million. But if you ask him, "Which is it, one million or three million?" The answer you will most likely get is, "I haven't the faintest idea."

Also, one of the best selling Canadian books of 1996 claims that the population of Canadians under the age of 15 is now some 772,000 fewer than it was 30 years ago. If that is correct, it is just as important to understand that Quebec has 552,000 fewer, Ontario some 10,000 more, but that BC and Alberta have some 274,000 more young people under the age of 15 than they did 30 years ago. In any case if the demographers of 1994 were right, why are real estate values rising throughout Canada and the U.S. in 1998?

Be that as it may, the above are the determining factors. But how does the average person learn to read them? One of the short cuts is to take the contrarian view. The contrarian view is the supposition that the public is always wrong.

It flies in the face of logic but it's true. The public *is* always wrong. Take the situation with pre-builder land. Pre-builder land is the piece after the next piece to be built on. Let's go back to that land around Las Vegas that we were talking about. You have a piece of land that has been worth practically nothing stretching back to the dawn of history and nobody wants it. Suddenly, there is a demand for the use of the land, prices start to go up, and when they've gone up enough, everybody wants to jump on the bandwagon. They say, "Hey, now is the time to buy!" But they're wrong. This isn't the time to buy. This is the time to *sell*.

The time to buy was back when the prices first started to go up.

It always amazes me. Real estate markets go up and they go down. At the peak the press proclaims things are never better and they will get better yet, but at the bottom they are never worse and will always get worse yet. For some reason we believe that if 6 buyers wrestle each other to the ground in the living room of the vendor and one emerges victoriously and pays $20,000 more than the place is worth at a 12% interest rate, it is a good market. When the buyer can make the $20,000 (buying it cheaper) at 6% interest, somehow it becomes a terrible market. Same place, same city, same property – yet somehow worse.

The fact is that changes have happened for some 50 years. Markets rise with demand until they get overheated, then they fall until demand is dead ... then they rise again to complete another cycle.

How is someone supposed to know when the changes are coming? The changes are heralded by a change in the numbers in the statistics. Trends continue until they change and you can read the beginning of those changes in the statistics. Now, usually by the time you see a report on the changes those changes have already occurred. What you have to do is go upstream from the news reports directly to the source of the numbers, those various boards, bureaus, and agencies and get the news while it's still new. If you're internet literate you can go right to the web pages involved and be right in on the beginning. Or you can get an unbiased, independent 'real estate only' newsletter and fax publisher to do it for you (hint, hint, wink, wink).

Is it possible to predict the length of a trend? If you could only get a copy of tomorrow's newspaper, you could make enough money in one day to last you the rest of your life. It's not possible to know exactly but historically, real estate cycles go in 4-year swings. A single swing is from peak to peak or from valley to valley.

But that's a very broad perspective. The large companies and various government agencies allow for a 3-18 month swing when they are doing their forward planning.

It's interesting that we find this four-year cycle repeated in other situations. For example, you should always try to time your mortgage to come due during a U.S. presidential election year, because – like magic – the interest rates will always be lowest in an election year.

Once you study the statistical factors and the numbers involved you'll be able to apply a stop-loss factor in your real estate investments.

The same way you would use a stop-loss if you were trading in commodities or stocks, you should apply that principle in your real estate dealings. Naturally, you want to let your profits run as long as they are going forward but if things start to change, you want to limit the retrogression as much as possible.

A good way to do this is to watch the inflation rate. Historically, house prices have always risen on par with or slightly ahead of the inflation rate. So, as a rule, not always but as a rule, your profit rate will be tied to the inflation rate.

However, during the late eighties and nineties governments around the world, particularly in North America, made changes on how they calculated the inflation rate. For example, in the United States, tax increases and house price increases both new and old, have been taken out of the index. In Canada only new home prices are a factor. From the late 1990s on there have been greater margins for error in trying to read indicators for the purpose of predicting trends. You can run into some misleading factors.

For example, in 1998 real estate values were rising by over 9% per annum throughout the United States (12% to 14% in California, 21% in Manhattan) while the official rate of inflation was reported at 1.5%. Calgary home prices rose by 13% and in Toronto by 7% in 1998. Yet we have an official .5% inflation rate environment. So we can't compare these unadjusted factors in a straight line. What it really means is that it will pay you to keep an eye on these indices. Just make sure you are always multiplying apples times apples.

And there are signposts from outside the real estate area. You have to be aware of what's happening politically and economically both on a broad scale and also on a local focus. Changes never happen in a vacuum. Everything impacts on everything else. The more information you have the more likely you will be making the more informed decision. Governments do matter to investors. Ontario and Alberta turned up and BC down because of their new governments. All investors need stability and certainty for the lifetime of their investment, but particularly real estate investors.

So what of the experts? They are only guessing. Futurists are never right except by accident. Historians are never wrong except on purpose. We've already said that if you had tomorrow's newspaper you could make millions. If you have yesterday's newspaper, you can wrap fish in it.

Except! Contained in yesterday's newspaper are changes that have already started and if you get to them soon enough, interpret them correctly and then act on them, you can do yourself some serious good. It's not necessary for you to have the entire wisdom of the world at your fingertips. It is not required for you to master the intricacies of economics to be able to predict if the aging baby boomers are going to be concerned about their retirement funds, or whether all of this retirement money is going to exert a downward pressure on interest rates therefore making cheaper money available which in turn facilitates the development and purchase of new housing.

That should interest you but it isn't necessary for you to be able to predict it. When it happens you'll read about it in the paper while you drink your morning coffee. What you should really be focused on is what is happening in the specific segment of the marketplace where you are concentrating your attention. Remember that this is going to vary from person to person according to their age, their pocketbooks, their tolerance for risk, and a myriad of other factors.

It's like the stock market. You don't buy every stock that's on the board. You select a category and from that category you pick a few stocks. These are the ones you watch. Same thing with real estate. After you've decided on your categories – i.e., detached houses, condos, apartments, urban, rural etc. – keep a close eye on that which you're involved in and regard the rest of the market with only a general interest so as to be able to know if and when it's going to be prudent to switch categories.

You have to be able to read the changes or you have to have someone read those shifts for you and report so you can act accordingly.

∼

In Essence

We have to read changes, interpret their meaning & then adapt to them.

The public is always wrong.

What makes real estate increase in price is a demand for the use of it.

You don't have to know it all – just knowing enough about your specialty will make you rich.

Chapter 3

TRENDS

The trouble with trends is that they go in one direction for a while and then they stop and go the other way for a while and then they stop again.

It used to be so simple because the rules never changed. And because it was simple any dummy could make a fortune. All you had to do was buy a piece of property in a good location and then keep breathing in and out and after enough breathing in and out you could sell it for a big profit and then do it all over again.

If you try to do that in a relatively non-inflationary or low inflationary market, you can make some very serious mistakes. Now, you have to watch the trends; and the direction of the trends will tell you where your money should be invested. The previous chapter was about timing. In this chapter all the categories are the same but the focus is on trend. Where there is a movement in the trend of any particular category, there will be an opportunity to take advantage of or a danger revealed to be avoided.

I once asked one of my mentors what was the difference between a danger and a risk. His answer was illuminating. He said, "A risk is a negative variable that *might* occur. Once it *has* occurred then it becomes a danger." The careful observation of real estate trends will very often pinpoint the negatives before they occur and allow us to avoid them and pinpoint the positives in time for us to take advantage of them.

First question: What are real estate trends? Answer: The change of any factor that has an effect on the price of real estate.

As we stated in the last chapter, perception is that the real estate train to price appreciation is driven by the location, location, location engine. We argued that timing was more important. So is the identification of new trends.

For instance, if one wanted to invest in Surrey, BC in 1992, it was far more important to understand both the principles of timing and trend than the one of location, location, location. The popular 'location' espousers actually knocked Surrey – "living in Vancouver means you never have to say you are Surrey" – it was not the recommended place to be. At the same time, condos on Vancouver's waterfront were touted in great sweeping pre-sale blitzes. But, between 1986 and 1991 the city of Surrey grew by over 68,000 people. More growth than all of the Atlantic and Prairie Provinces (excluding Alberta) combined. The trend was for huge population growth. In Vancouver condos were built like hotcakes, slapped together, blown out. Buyers snapped them up – they had to be good, because they were in a 'good location'. By 1995 had you bought such a condo you were down 15% and more in value on your purchase price of your 'well located' condo. Had you bought a building lot in much maligned Surrey – anywhere – you would have been up by some 150% in value, as the average lot price soared from 1991 to 1995 from $55,000 to $160,000. Your $5,000 downpayment soared by $80,000 in value. The trend of huge inward migration drove values and locations be darned. Trends matter. The fallacy here was that the trend of people moving to the 'wrong' location didn't matter, the trend was huge, values followed.

You have to question yourself as to what is your opinion. In everything to do with real estate you have to have an opinion. Ask yourself some questions:

What is the trend and does the trend matter to real estate investors?
Is this trend real or is it a fallacy?
Which way is the trend going?
Is it likely to continue in that direction?
How far will it go?
How long will it last?

Whether you gather the data yourself or rely on an expert is not as important as asking the questions and making sure that you have answers. And you just don't do this once and then forget about it. No. You have to ask these questions over and over about every factor and every category concerning every piece of real estate that you look at from now until they carry you off in that box with the six silver handles.

Be careful to separate trends that have an impact on price (what we investors are interested in) and trends that have no impact on price at all. There are many accepted fallacies as far as real estate price appreciation goes. It isn't just the location, location, location fallacy. We have dozens of other fallacies in the market place.

Here are some generally accepted fallacies:

Interest rates drive markets higher. Not.

You see it announced everywhere: Interest rates drive the affordability and thus real estate prices. For some reason our press projects the prospects of stronger real estate prices because of lower interest rates. Yet history shows, that while interest rates do make an impact on affordability – you can buy higher priced homes at lower mortgage rates – they have nothing whatever to do with price appreciation. In 1979 the average price in Vancouver was $78,000. By May 1981 that price soared to an average price of $180,000. At the very same time 5-year term mortgage interest rates soared from 9.75% to over 16.5%. From 1995 in the same city interest rates have been reduced a total of 36 times to a 44-year record low 6% 5-year term. Yet, values fell from February 1995's average price of $345,000 to approximately $280,000 by the end of 1998.

Interest rates do NOT determine value. It was the perception of investors and homeowners (remember the wrestling in the living room?) that things would always go higher in 1981. "High interest rates be darned," they said. "I don't mind paying 15% if I make $50,000 profit," they said. At other times, even record low interest times, low interest rates be darned, they say, "I won't buy."

So do not accept that prices go higher because of low rates but study how do lower rates affect the trend. Buyers that would normally have held off for a couple of years before making the plunge are motivated by the low rates to move into the market. But there are only so many bites on the carcass. If these buyers come into the market earlier, they are drained from the future. If rates stay low, this reach into the future is increased – wallets and purses will stretch even further with the result that sooner or later that pool is going to dry up.

Actually when the interest rate trend changes and rates begin to rise, values change higher with the rising rates. Buyers, previously sitting on the fence jump in worried they might miss the bandwagon. However, if interest rates rise too far (as in 1981) the engine of interest rates/affordability will indeed sputter and die.

All foreign immigration is good for real estate. Not.
It isn't only important to know that there is immigration, but what kind of immigration. If you are looking for price appreciation in an upscale area, strong refugee immigration doesn't help much. More important to know is the component of investor class, entrepreneur class, family class type and refugee immigrant. One brings money, creates business and jobs, the other needs federal subsidies. For example, of all the business and entrepreneur class type immigration from 1990 to 1996 into Canada, BC received over 61%. Clearly, that was a positive powerful trend to reckon with.

Trends that will continue to matter:

Trend: Inward migration does matter.
Yes, I know we already discussed this under timing. But let's assume you have the right kind of immigration. Why is inward migration so important? Because the people staying in any given area already have a place to sleep. Drive around your town. Observe all the benches at the bus stops and in the parks. Notice that they are never crowded with prosperous looking families and individuals who are sitting there with their suitcases and furniture piled up around them wondering where they are going to sleep that night. That has already been looked after.

The people already here have a place to sleep and a place to work and facilities for entertaining themselves for the other eight hours a day. But new people coming in need all those accommodations and that in-migration is going to have an effect. So you examine that trend. And you ask yourself the above questions because you've got to form an opinion.

For example: From 1986 to 1991 Vancouver, BC's population grew by 16.5% or more than double the national average. From then until 1997 it grew at over 2.5% per year. Only the average number arrived through the maternity wards, the rest were migrants. People who, for whatever their reasons wanted to be in Vancouver. (Keep this thought in the forefront of your consciousness because it is very, very important.)

The reason itself isn't as important as the fact that there is a reason. But that doesn't mean that the reason is unimportant, it's just not *as important*. You still want to know what those reasons are so you can keep an eye on them and in that way you'll be able to watch and predict the trend.

Anyway, while Vancouver is not expected to keep growing at that rate; even with falling population growth rates the predictions are that by the year 2020 the population of Vancouver will grow from its current 1.9 million souls to just over 3 million. This is a very strong engine indeed. These new arrivals bring in fresh hopes, skills, and money. All of which drive up existing housing prices.

Migration, both in and out are factors that have to be watched. Vancouver's biggest real estate collapse came in 1981/82 and followed on the heels of a time when 4,000 people a month were leaving.

Every community has its own growth rate. BC doubled the national average of 1.2% and grew by 2.6% annually from 1991 - 1997. But inside BC there were great variances. Kelowna in the Okanagan grew by 5% per annum; Courtenay on Vancouver Island grew at a whopping 8%, Whistler at over 10%; yet other areas fared far worse. Find out the growth rate and projected growth rate on the area you wish to invest in.

How to identify inward migration trends?

You get population statistics from StatsCan, Immigration Canada as well as the CMHC office in your area. Every community in Canada is surveyed every five years. Last statistics were compiled in 1991 and then again in 1997. Get them for your area. Look at the quantity and quality of immigrant from offshore as well as inter-provincial migration numbers.

There are other yardsticks. A friend of mine who is a very astute real estate investor said in those years you could gauge an exodus or an influx just by counting U-Haul trailers.

His thesis was you go to the highway and count the number and note the direction of the U-Haul trailers. If they were coming into town, good times were on the way. If they were heading out-of-town, that was a storm warning. Or, he said, you could go to the U-Haul trailer parking lot and look at the license plates of the trailers on the lot. If there were lots of license plates from other locales, you knew things were booming or about to boom. If the parking lot was practically empty, you knew there was an exodus in progress.

I've always felt that this was an ingenious barometer of what was going on. I'm sure that somewhere in the government there is a department with thousands of square feet of very expensive office space and hundreds of employees and millions of dollars of budget all devoted to gathering information that they could obtain by having one person stroll down to the U-Haul lot. But that's a whole different crusade.

Trend: Supply and demand makes a difference.

Supply and demand is not any single pair of factors. It is a continuum. There is the money supply and the demand for it. There is the customer supply and those customers' ability and desire to consume. There is the product supply.

None of these factors exist in a vacuum. They are all interrelated. Not only are they interrelated but they vary also from time to time and from place to place. In one part of the country things can be completely different. For that matter, you can move a couple of blocks in a city and things will be more different than if you moved across the country. You can have single family, townhouses, condos, and rental apartments all in the same block and the supply and demand factors will be completely different for each one of them.

But the basics don't change. If there are more buyers than sellers, clearly there will be upward price pressures. Prices will adjust to the number of units on the market against a given number of buyers. It always has been this way and it will continue to always be this way. It's just that it never stays the same which is why you have to continue watching for changes in the trends so you'll know whether to be a buyer or a seller.

Often, even if you identified the trend of population growth correctly, you still have to watch the supply coming in. Like you, astute builders and developers watch the same statistics. Increased population means more building is necessary. In a competitive world their rush to capitalize may be your rush to your financial grave.

In 1994 we identified the trend of population growth for Courtenay in our newsletter. Prices were low, cashflow was high and people moved in droves to the Comox Valley. By the summer of 1994 we put Courtenay on investor alert. Did we expect the population to shrink? Did we not think it was a great place to live? None of that had changed, but as our newsletter is only concerned with making money for our subscribers, we felt that the influx of developments trying to cash in on the population growth boom was far in excess of even that great boom. Thus, investor alert.

Another example is Whistler, BC. Even though the population growth trend was clearly giving the go signals, we placed Whistler on Investor Alert in February of 1997. If you ever wished to be intensely disliked – by non-subscriber investors – put a ski resort on investor alert. Yeah, but don't we realize that it is a great mountain? Indeed. Yeah, but isn't the population going to keep on increasing? Indeed. Yeah, but hasn't Whistler been rated the number one resort in North America. Indeed. To us while the population trend said buy, the supply and demand trend screamed sell. The condo and condo hotel building boom was outstripping any sane population/ski visitors/tourist growth increases by a wide margin. Whistler's resort association forecast room nights to soar from 1.2 million nights to 2 million nights in 3 years. Thus, investor alert. Thus supply and demand are a trend to watch. Oh, and we were right to alert subscribers, both communities saw values crash AFTER our warning.

How do you get the numbers? Get the local Real Estate Board statistics, Canada Mortgage and Housing statistics. Other forecasts and predictions. There is always plenty of warning for the astute.

Trend: The new consumer.

The new consumer and the New Job growth that has to be there to accommodate him or her.

When we talk about the New Consumer we're not talking about someone who either comes into an area from someplace else and who is looking for what has come to be described as a low paying McJob. And we are also not talking about people who grow up out of the kiddy pool into the low paying McJob market. Rather we are talking about companies and individuals who come from some place else, set up shop in a new area and create high-quality, high-paying, and sorely-needed jobs in the business and manufacturing sectors.

The world is changing. The old, monolithic big business has to move over. StatsCan reports that 81% of all new job growth comes in companies with fewer than 20 employees. In BC over 15,000 home businesses were formed in 1997. The big companies are making room for all those small, flexible, export-hungry new firms of between 50 and 300 employees. I call these the 'mongoose businesses'. (The mongoose always beats the cobra because his reflexes are so fast and his reaction time is so quick that for him the cobra seems to be moving in slow motion.) It's this quicker reaction time and flexibility that give the small business the advantage over the big guy.

As consumers, we've changed. We are more discontented and much less placid than ever before.

We don't trust our governments and dislike our politicians. In Peter Newman's famous words we are so disenchanted that, "even if our politicians tell us they lied, we don't believe them."

Who to trust? Police are more concerned about giving the average guy a speeding ticket than getting junkies off the street. Judges seem to make ever-incongruous decisions letting rapists and murders go with a slap on the wrist and even our priests – goodness me – cannot be trusted. Senior executives read in the paper that their company is lean and mean and they know why. They just laid off 10 people and wonder whether they are next. At night they doodle on a pad with their wife and muse about moving to a small town. A better environment. We are stressed out, debted out, and out of sorts. We are much less patient with pat answers and panaceas that don't work. We are not nearly so gullible and malleable and susceptible to the tricks and techniques of those people who would take advantage of us if they could. As the questions of the world get more complex we are demanding more simplistic answers.

And there is much more variation among the new consumers. You can't paint our portrait with the broad-brush strokes that you could use in the past. Some of us want to live in highrises but some of us want a place to plant our flower bulbs, our barbecues, and our roots.

As technology develops so do the choices of lifestyle. The fax machine, the computer, the satellite dish, and the cell phone have given everyone seven league boots. The physical locale of the business has become much less relevant. Those who want to are going to be able to locate in small towns and outlying areas. This footloose new consumer is a brand new engine indeed.

So we will watch this consumer and see where he goes and what he does when he gets there. The trend of the new consumer will tell us what to buy and where to buy it.

Today's real estate investor, if he wants optimal results, has to keep a close and continual watch on these trends. Any one of them has the power to lift prices up or down. And of course there are all the possible combinations and permutations that are maxi-trends and mini-trends depending how they affect the market.

You want to watch the trends because there are three main things you are looking for. You want to know what category to buy, when to buy, and where. That's how you're going to make money. But you also want to continuously study the trends because you also want to know when it's time to run for the hills. That is how you get to keep the money after you make it.

We looked at some of the old trends of inward migration, affordability, supply and demand as well as the larger question of whither inflation? But there are also some new trends. We will expand on all of these trends in the following chapters.

Let me give you some 'for examples':

Trend: New Government.

When governments look like they are going to change, this could herald an altering in trends. Ontario and Alberta were basket cases in 1993. In 1999 they were thriving. BC was a thriving province in 1992, in 1998 it struggled.

Trend: Out with Government.

With our continued disenchantment of all things political and by extension, all things government, we will continue to force government to downsize. Knowing this new trend it became easy for our newsletter to place Edmonton and Ottawa on investor alert in 1995, Victoria in 1996. But the same holds true for any community totally dependent on government services. Today's tough voter will force government to downsize everywhere. The only exception are communities that will administer large outside amounts of cash such as the several hundred million dollar native land claim settlements that may benefit the city entrusted with the administration.

Trend: The Superstore index.

The Big Mac of real estate. A few years ago, some students at the University of Cologne came up with an ingenious way to predict the relative strength of worldwide economies. The Big Mac Index. They used the price of the Big Mac and could (pretty close, actually) conclude the various strengths of a number of countries economies. If it cost $2.95 in Berlin, $9.00 in HongKong and $3.15 in Toronto, it was easy to draw an economic parallel. In real estate you may call it the "Superstore index." Whenever you get wind of Costco, Canadian Superstore, Wal-Mart and others opening a store in a given location, it stands to reason that the future growth of the community will be strong. These stores open where their research (they have more money than you do for research) shows that the community they open in will thrive. They can't afford to have only the white hair brigade as shoppers. They already bought all the hammers they are ever going to buy. Where they go, active families live and will continue to move to. Thus, a pretty good trend indicator are the superstores.

Trend: Where they play, real estate will stay.
In many places in Canada gambling is now a fact of life. While I am not particularly fond of it, casinos – first class casinos – can add value to markets. Casinos attract new employees, new visitors. They all have to stay somewhere. Windsor and the whole Niagara Peninsula rose in value by over 20% following the opening of the casinos.

Trend: The great move out-of-town.
While Vancouver outgrew the national growth rate by more than double, some small towns grew and still are growing at 4 times to 5 times the national rate. Small towns are an art form all by themselves. They can contain terrific opportunities but sometimes, because of their size, certain changes can contain the seeds of a lot of volatility. If they are 'single industry' towns, a plant closing can have a very drastic effect. Strikes in that industry can devastate the economy of a town. Or, if they are 'government towns', where the government is a major industry any shift in that continuum can bring major changes. Or, a military base shutting down can have a significant downward effect on prices. (More in Chapter 21)

Trend: Resort Buying.
With the new found wealth many can now buy that second vacation home or even their future residences in special resorts: places like Whistler or Sun Peaks in BC, Mont Blanc in Quebec as well as other types of destination resorts. Generally speaking, do not expect to gain profits if all you have is a chairlift and a parking lot. Look at the capital investment, look at the general ambiance. The second home buyer has choice; he'll pick style, class and ambiance every time over roughing it.

More than any other kind of real estate you MUST understand the different real estate investment classes offered. Even at Whistler with an average price increase of 300% over 5 years, some investment classes lost money. (More in Chapter 21)

Trend: Downsizing companies need smaller spaces.
There is a strong trend towards mini warehouses with an office component built in. As we have smaller companies, many move to their own 1,500 sq. foot to 3,000 sq. foot space. Rent them out or build them for profit.

Trend: The greening makes for fewer changes in industrial zoning.
If you own a heavy industrial zoned property hang on to it. No municipality will grant new zoning for the (perceived) environmentally unfriendly heavy user. As companies downsize and diversify all industrial property (well located; yes, location close to freeway, rails and employees makes a difference here) will benefit. Formerly fringe city industrial turns into service office/industrial.

Trends: Downsizing families mean new storage needs.
Mini storage parks will be money makers. Huge cashflow, minimal overhead (deluxe storage means you provide a light bulb to illuminate the four concrete walls) and a real estate play to boot.

Trend: New jobs for a New World.
The computer age is destroying some jobs and creating others. Thus CMHC's E.M.I.L.I. will destroy the regular CMHC appraisal business (E.M.I.L.I. can appraise in 7 seconds). The computer and the internet will make home buying a uniquely different experience (see Chapter 20), it will totally change the profession of the Realtor, the broker and the banker. In the future you will make money on information only in two ways: you originate the information or you interpret the information. This will create the need for new professions: joint venture specialists, troubled property specialists, mortgage brokers, resort-only professional property managers. Specialists will reign. The home renovation business in Canada will surpass all new construction business within 6 years (it already is bigger in the Atlantic provinces). All these trends have an application also for the investor. We know of one 'troubled property specialist' that ends up buying all troubled properties.

Trend: Technology.

Have you noticed that your wallet is getting thicker? No, it' s not more cash, it's more cards. We get a plastic card for everything. Every store, every bank has one. Cards for parking meters, for the phone, for your groceries. But worse, we are being weaned off our personal contacts ever so slowly but surely. We are being trained in many subtle ways. Pay your parking by credit card, it's a $1.10 per hour. Use an attendant it's a buck and a quarter. Transact by bankcard it's fifty cents a transaction, use a teller it's a dollar. Even your grocery discount can only be obtained if you have a card. No card, no discount is the new motto.

And then there are cash cards. Everything goes electronic. Why the proliferation of cards? Cards keep track of who you are, where you live, what you buy and how often you do it. Even the government loves a cash-less society ... hard to do underground transactions, easy to track expenditures and match them against – unreported – income.

On the real estate side of things – you haven't seen anything yet. In 1995 there was hardly a property advertised on the internet. Today there are over 6 million listings in North America– many properties featured several times on different providers. As computer packages crash in price through $500 (projected for mid 1999), *everybody* can own one. The ramifications for the real estate industry are enormous. In the future you either originate the information or you will interpret the information ... there will be no other way to earn income from information.

The proliferation of information will be astounding – making sense of it, even more so – but creating excellent new opportunities for interpreters. Already the real estate brokerage has downsized by over 40% in 8 years. This will continue. Real estate commissions will crash and what income is left will shift to the selling agent from the listing agent.

Appraisers will disappear, replaced by computerized programs, conveyancers will be replaced by automated title insurance, dozen of current professions will either have to change dramatically or disappear altogether. New jobs – some already here today – will take their place in the very near future. The new cry "adjust or die" will be the call of the day. For the astute real estate investor there will be untold new opportunities to find deals and more importantly to find buyers, where access was closed off in the past.

Above all, when you identify a trend and you wish to buy into it, shop the market and bargain hard. If it's not a deal of a lifetime, you go on to the next one because when there's a superabundance of sellers and a shortage of buyers it's not going to be good for the sellers. As Sancho Panza says to Don Quixote, "If the stone hits the bottle or the bottle hits the stone, it's going to be bad for the bottle." Same thing here.

Everyone should make a little sign and paste it on the bathroom mirror where you have to look at it at the beginning and at the end of every day and several times in between. That sign should read:

You make the most money the day you buy the property!

Trends will tell you what to do and when to do it. For optimum results you have to become a student, and hopefully, someday, a master of trends.

∾

In Essence

There are true trends and fallacies.

There are old standby trends and there are new ones to watch out for.

Trends are cyclical and the investor has to keep watching so as to know what to do.

No factor exists in a vacuum. Every factor has its impact on every other factor.

The basics don't change. If there are more buyers than sellers, the price will go up.

Today's market is more complex and the people in it are more knowledgeable and sophisticated. You have to keep up or get left behind.

Technology will become the new wild card of real estate riches.

Chapter 4

THE SMALL INVESTOR/THE LARGE INVESTOR

F. Scott Fitzgerald made the observation that:
"The rich are different from you and I."
To which some astute commentator inserted the addendum:
"Yes, they have more money."

'Big Investors' and 'Small Investors' have some similarities and many differences. No matter which category you find yourself in it's important to know the best way to thrive and even more important to know the best way to survive. Almost all the 'Small Investors' want to grow to the point where they can make the transition to being a 'Big Investor'. Almost none of the 'Big Investors' want to become 'Small Investors'.

It brings to mind the old joke, "If you want to come home from Las Vegas with a small fortune, all you have to do is go there with a large one." Well, very few 'Large Investors' want to make the transition that way.

Most people reading this are going to be little investors and so, of necessity, we focus more in that direction and because there are more small deals than there are big deals. But when we talk 'small' and 'large' we are not just dealing with the number of zeros. We are also talking about investment objectives. The small investor and the large investor sometimes have very different investment objectives.

The small investor starts off with the problem of getting enough money for that first deal. That's the hard part, getting the first olive out of the bottle. This is why so many small investors run into trouble with the 'flavor of the month scam investment'.

An uncle of mine once explained to me why crime doesn't pay.

Crime doesn't pay because no matter how many mistakes a neophyte policeman makes, eventually he can get to be a professional policeman. The crook, however, every time he makes a mistake he goes to jail for a period of time so it isn't likely that he will have enough time on the job to become professional. As a result, law and order, becomes by definition, a contest between professionals and amateurs.

Well, you know what usually happens in that case. Daymon Runyon once wrote, "The race is not always to the swift, nor the battle to the strong – however, that's the way to bet." And that's the way it is with real estate scams when it comes to the small investors (see Chapter 13). The scammers almost never get sent to jail so after a time they can develop a proficiency at their profession. But the small investor gets wiped out and has to go back to go, acquire more investment capital, and start all over again.

These scam investments are seductively attractive to the small investor.

It allows him to participate in a market where he wants to be because he's been conditioned to want to be there. For his whole life he's had pounded into him that the ownership of real estate will keep him warm and safe and so he better get some. And everyone has a friend or a brother-in-law who is always bragging about all his wonderful 'deals'. And so our small investor can hardly wait to dive into those shark infested waters because the sharks are never a reality until you've been bitten – and here's the amazing part – sometimes you have to be bitten several separate times before the sharks become a reality.

So with his appetite lashed to a frenzy he approaches the market and he finds it a very daunting proposition. And because he usually doesn't have enough money to do it by himself he opts for being part of a group with the professional management that usually goes with that kind of investment. All too often this is where he makes a fatal mistake and there goes whatever little capital he had and he's out of the game. Well, you're reading this to find out what to do and what not to do so the first thing you don't do is: don't give your money to someone else if you're going to lose it. How do you know this in advance? Keep reading.

For example, as this is being written there is a company that has just been shut down by the regulatory authorities. They were a mortgage company that took $250,000,000 (that's sure a lot of zeros, isn't it?) from 10,000 separate investors and each and every one of those 10,000 investors thought they were going to be warm and safe. It remains to be seen whether anyone will see a dime of their money back.

All of these 10,000 separate investors were small investors. Small investors are not knowledgeable enough or experienced enough to protect themselves and they put their faith where it was misplaced. That doesn't mean that large investors are immune from these kind of mistakes. The moment you put in the element of faith and trust into an investment you set the wheels of disaster in motion, if those wheels are there in the first place.

There is an old Sicilian saying, "God protect me from my friends – I'll protect myself from my enemies."

But let's say that we are not going to get embroiled in a syndicate type investment but instead we're going to deal with individuals in individual pieces of property. For our purposes, in this chapter, a smaller investor might be a person buying a second home. Or it could be a person buying a recreational property. It might also be the investor with no cash. Generally, a small investor buys one or two units; whereas a larger investor might be a person looking for cash flow to supplement other business income or who is looking for a development and so buys land either to develop right away or to hold until the time and circumstances for development are more propitious.

One thing that the small investor and the big investor have in common is that a single mistake can wipe them out. And it's a very unforgiving world out there. The big difference is that the larger investor is usually better insulated by lawyers and accountants than the small investor, simply because of the economy of scale of the amount of money involved.

Of course, there is more emotion involved with smaller investments and smaller investors. And I'm not just talking about the emotion of greed. True, greed and fear are the two most prevalent and dominant emotions involved in the process but there are lots of others that come into play.

Smaller investors have two main objectives: First, to make a capital gain and secondly, to have someone else pay the mortgage down.

In the first instance, the key is to make the most money on the day you buy the property. This is absolutely essential. It is a cold, harsh, realistic world out there and you will not be forgiven if you buy wrong. That is why it is so important for the smaller investor to know his market extremely well. He has to look for the undervalued situation. He has to look for special circumstances such as divorce situations, foreclosures, auctions, a willing seller and so forth.

He has to be on the lookout for houses where executives have been relocated, and that as a result of this have been vacant for a while. Companies that own these kinds of property are sometimes willing to take a significant deduction off the price just to get it out of their hair. Bear in mind that if you are, say, a computer company the last thing you want to be dealing with is a piece of residential real estate and whoever is making the decisions will probably be more interested in moving that file folder from his in-basket to his out-basket than in getting the optimum fair market value for the property.

This is where the small investor actually has an advantage over the large investor. He's like that mongoose against the cobra. He has speed and agility. He makes his own decisions and can make them much more quickly and is more likely to be dealing with properties that are large enough to be interesting to him, but not large enough to be of interest to the large investor.

If the smaller investor knows his market well and has a clear understanding of current values, he can put this knowledge and understanding to very good use. But he has to be in the market place every day and he has to step up to the plate with a constant stream of low offers. And the operative word here is, 'low'. In fact, if you're not being turned down on 9 out of 10 of your offers you're not an investor. As an investor you have to get used to being turned down to make sure you don't pay too much.

It's just like adjusting a carburetor. You wind in the air screw until the engine starts to miss and then you back it off half a turn. What you want to be doing is burning as much air and as little gasoline as possible.

If the smaller investor is buying for cash flow thereby having someone else reduce the mortgage, he may have to adjust his location objectives. Buying a $300,000 townhouse in Vancouver and renting it out for $1,200 doesn't make any sense from the cashflow perspective – you have to hope for capital gain. Buying a $110,000, 15-year-old bungalow with a basement suite in Edmonton makes perfect sense. With a minimum down payment and the best mortgage rate your payments likely still are below $900 per month. But income can be $900 - $1,100 from the main floor and $400 or so from the basement. We have seen small investors return 30% cash on cash returns from 1994 - 1998 and these kind of opportunities are still available. If he wants to buy in BC, he will have to restrict his activities to the smaller towns. Generally, in a climate of low inflation and low interest rates he can find these investments in the Interior of BC, Vancouver Island and other various locations in Ontario and Alberta.

While our statistics show that generally the smaller investor has *always* more capital gain in single family home than in an apartment, it is certainly possible to build a portfolio of apartments in smaller towns, low, low down payments, low mortgage payments and relatively high rental income. What the smaller investor wants to look for is apartments in the $35,000 to $65,000 range where the city has a good employment rate, vacancies are low, and where the city is experiencing growth. (Study Chapter 21, there are some pitfalls.)

As time goes on, all of these numbers are going to change but the principles remain valid. The various geographic areas' desirability will ebb and flow but the principles we're discussing here won't change.

As this is being written you can quite easily go outside the large urban areas and buy a $50,000 unit with a rental income of $600 per month and this will pay mortgage, taxes and strata title fees. And here comes a very important point. Once the investor has this kind of property he becomes like a cork floating on the water. Inflation – deflation – it doesn't matter. Somebody else will pay down the mortgage for him. All he's got to do is keep breathing in and out and the clock and the calendar will work their magic.

Mind you, not everyone's investment objectives are served by the buy and hold philosophy. Some people and particularly people that understand the principle of timing, prefer to locate the viable situation and do a buy, mark up, and flip. It doesn't matter because the dynamics don't change.

There are also special deals that a small investor can benefit from. The key here is to identify an opportunity from special circumstances. If we were to call a spade a spade, we'd describe this as cashing in on someone else's misery. This process has been described as, 'Grave Dancing'. Whether you are buying to hold or looking to flip, the main thing is that you have to be in the market every day that you expect to do business because these situations never stay around very long. You have to act quickly. You have to be the mongoose!

The smaller investor who buys for the purpose of having the mortgage reduced thus allowing him to build an equity portfolio often has relatively little cash. 'Grave Dancing' only works when you have enough cash to solve, or at least reduce, the troubled person's troubles. And flipping without cash only works if your timing is absolutely bang on. It's profitable if it works and although it can be learned, it can't be taught. I don't recommend this activity for the beginner.

Let's talk about another class of small investor. This is the person who has bought a number of income producing properties over time. I call this person, 'The Paper King'. He goes and buys a condominium in a small town for, say, $28,000, (yes, you can still do that!) he fixes up the property with some cosmetic application of paint and some cleaning up; and now he has a very presentable condominium that didn't cost him very much money.

He then looks for a young couple in that area who have the attributes that he's looking for. Those attributes are lots of character and no cash. They are employed and they look good enough to him so that he sells them the property for nothing down. Yes, he gets credit reports and if they just had their TV repossessed – forget it. He may sell it for, say, $32,000 and he then carries back a second mortgage on the financing which covers any money he's had to put into the property for down payment, fix-up, and his mark-up on the selling price.

And he just keeps doing this over and over and thus he is able to build a significant portfolio of mortgage paper. I know of one of these Paper Kings who continuously builds a portfolio up to around $1.5 million and then goes to a mortgage company and discounts the paper. He may take a 10% or 15% discount for those mortgages, the lender gets a high yield and everyone gets what they want out of the transaction. The key lies in finding the right "no-money down" buyers. Good people, with no money but wanting to own. People that will make the payments.

This works very well as long as the properties are in the lower price range and as long as his own ability to value and judge character is up to the task. The closer the small investor is to the market the better this technique is going to work for him. You've got to have principles that work and you have to stick to those principles. And you should be prepared to either hold or flip, depending on which approach is best at the time. You can flip without your own money in the deal but for the longer-term hold, you have to have a certain amount of investment capital.

Take the principle of "you make the most money on the day you buy," and add the skill of finding the right buyer (if you carry back a mortgage) or the right tenant ... and you will be a successful real estate investor, no matter how small or how big you are and regardless of where you buy and what the timing is. Your mortgage gets paid off by someone else.

The question always comes up, "Ozzie, where does one go to learn this? Are there schools, are there books?" While this book hopefully goes a long way towards clearing "the fog of dreaming" and putting you on the road to reality, there are no schools. You can't learn this kind of stuff from books.

Yes, there are courses. If you buy a course, do be sure to buy a Canadian one. Most colleges, real estate boards and even financial institutions offer some sort of a basic course.

However, most late night TV U.S. courses have little application in Canada. Remember also, that if these late night courses work so well for the writers, why are they selling courses and not making millions buying real estate? What you need is something more ongoing, not a one-shot tape, book, course.

There are a number of investment clubs throughout BC, Alberta, Ontario, and the U.S. that give advice. What you have to watch out for is that you're not being sold something at the same time.

A lot of these organizations remind me of what I've heard about meetings at various addiction therapy groups. Somebody stands up and says, "I bought a new condo with no money down and got the vendor to carry back a first mortgage and the first mortgage payment was three months down the road!" And the entire audience erupts in frenzied applause. Then someone else rises to his feet and says, "…and I bought a condo in another town…" and when he's finished cataloguing his triumphs, again the audience erupts in frenzied applause. It gives everyone present a warm glowing feeling of belonging to an elite group that knows how to create wealth.

Some of these clubs charge as low as $10 per month as a membership fee and just meet once a month. Some charge $200 to $300 per month for finding investment deals. Now, clearly the small investor has to be very careful of where he puts his trust and following that, where he puts his money.

Consider, at $200 a month – two years of this and you have the down payment on a house. Also, if the club sells you its own real estate – run. You are not being taught, you are being set up – to buy their stuff. And yes, there is my weekly *Jurock's Facts by Fax* which actually scours out 'no money down deals' or 'what looks good to us deals' for subscribers. And yes, there is our monthly *Jurock Real Estate Investor* newsletter that analyzes towns and suburbs, the legals and the internet deals and where the government sells land and where the auctions are. And, yes there may be other newsletters.

But that still doesn't teach you the feel for a particular property and the feel for the people you deal with everyday. No book, no newsletter, no club can teach you that. The only thing that teaches you is to get out and do it. Take a look at some of the 'how to' chapters in this book and then get into action, write low offers and get familiar with a certain area. Visit tenants that want to rent from you where they live now (to find out how they'll treat your property in the future!) and gradually you WILL develop your own feel for property you should buy and the people that are in the circle of the real estate investor.

Let's talk a bit about the larger investor. The larger investor has totally different objectives. A larger investor may buy a tract of land that he wants to develop. To buy land and to be able to subdivide it into lots has been the single largest money maker for the large investor and the large development corporation.

Historically, land developers have been rewarded beyond any proportion to their original investment, capital, or know-how. How? Simply by buying land to subdivide. Or, in the case of the railroads, receiving the land ancillary to other business activities.

More than any other investment, the vacant land investment, or land banking has to involve two major factors. The first factor is that you have to buy right. The second factor is that your timing has to be right. Several very large corporations have been sunk by their land banks because their timing wasn't right.

If you buy at the peak of the market, you have nowhere to go but down. What happens is that in an active market one can get caught up in the hysteria. You think that it's going to keep going and when it doesn't you find yourself incurring large losses.

But when it works, it's beautiful. When a larger investor has that skill in negotiating with the owners for their land and also the ability to thread his way through the maze at city hall, and the acumen to deal with the public hearings plus being able to unwind all the red tape – then that investor is going to reap the commensurate rewards. And these are unusually high rewards, sometimes in the 1000 per cents – and higher!

Naturally, it goes without saying that those who do not have these skills do not reap these rewards. There doesn't seem to be a middle ground here. You either win or lose. However, the larger you get, the less risks you are usually willing to take. At a certain point larger investors start looking for portfolio diversification. Even large investors who are in other fields want to have some real estate in their portfolios and they look for income producing properties such as apartment buildings, small shopping centers, plazas, small office buildings, etc. The most lucrative of these has quite often been the regional or small shopping center. Not only does it provide a cash flow in the 7% to 10% range but it also appreciates in those areas that have population growth.

Although values depreciate in areas where people are leaving they can also decline where there is an over ambitious anticipation of absorption. Take for example the situation where a developer is building a new office building. While he is constructing his building and wrangling with city hall, a period of three years could pass. Market conditions have shifted. His building is half out of the ground but he has no choice except to complete the structure, even though he is going to be putting more unwanted space into a market that is enjoying good population growth but glutted with office space.

Vancouver had spectacular residential value appreciation (over 60%) from 1989 to 1995 but office building values collapsed by 40% (from $279 per foot at the top down to $179). Another example where simple location, location didn't apply. Vancouver was a good location for real estate investment in 1989, wasn't it? Not if you owned the wrong kind such as downtown office buildings. Whistler is a good location? Not if you own the wrong kind of real estate.

Still, for the larger portfolio they remain important. They will become increasingly important as the Real Estate Investment Trusts (REITS) continue to absorb quality income producing property, (the operative word here is, 'quality'), without regard of return on money invested.

It is money available to invest in real estate that makes values rise, not income. If stock markets stay stable, we can look forward to good capital gains on quality buildings through the late 1990s and into the 2000s regardless of market conditions. If they don't, sell.

These mid-size regional shopping centers and small strip malls go between $800 and $3 million. In cities such as Vancouver and Toronto this number will go up as high as $5 million. They are very popular with the mid-size offshore investors who want to be able to see and touch and be as close to downtown as possible.

The really large investors, that is the pension funds or REITS, have different investment objectives. The pension fund is much more interested in diversification. In Canada, pension funds have less than 5% in real estate and almost all of that is in the commercial sector. They would have more in residential but elements like landlord tenant acts and renters groups dampen the enthusiasm for this area.

REITS are a relatively new kind of large investor. They spring up in good times and you hear a lot about them when things are humming. When the market goes the other way, they seem to go dormant but they're always back when the action springs up. They started in a big way in the early 1980s and then got clobbered in the Savings and Loan debacle. But right now they are back and they are back with a vengeance. In Canada some $6 billion went into hotel type REITS, condo type REITS and commercial property type REITS in 1997. That number is far reduced in 1998, but clearly that amount of cash is driving values. (For more on REITS see Chapter 17.)

Larger investors more often buy real estate wholesale and sell it retail. Therefore, in a vacant land scenario, clearly you buy it by the acre and you sell it by the foot. In the industrial areas many larger investors will buy a site and rather than building one large edifice for one large user, they put up a group of mini-warehouses from 2,500 to 4,000 square feet. Then they sell them off to individual owners.

It used to be that these kind of warehouses would only have a 5% office component. But with the downsizing and new company creation, things are changing. Warehouses now have between 15% and 20% office components and small companies find it possible to downsize into these smaller facilities and move the whole company there. Rather than have an office downtown and a warehouse in the suburbs, a small company can move into their own strata title warehouse (but it's not called that – it's called an office complex). There usually is a loading dock in the back where trucks can pull up. It is a very acceptable place to do business. To call these new complexes industrial parks is really a misnomer. It would be more accurate to call them office parks.

A larger investor can make a much greater return by selling small pieces of the development to the end user. And the same thing is happening with some older office buildings downtown where buildings have been converted, or actually built, with this owner-user in mind.

Also, larger investors benefit from the greater understanding of industrial property in general. In most major areas of Canada, industrial vacancy rates are well below 4.5% in 1999 and values of industrial land are continuing to rise. While some smaller astute investors can play, you generally need more cash and staying power. Today, existing heavy industrial zoning is money in the bank. No city council – unless they want to live with environmentalists camped out on their front door – will grant new zoning. And while everyone waffles eloquently about the need for more diversification they don't want it in their own back yard. Larger investors have done exceedingly well identifying this trend. There is also the question of new type industrial/office park providing spaces needed for biotechnology. Special use parks are springing up everywhere – usually connected to universities, but also independent.

We're seeing more and more of small, three story buildings where there are strata title stores on the ground floor and condos or apartments on top. The large investors are going to be doing more of this, it is profitable, city councils in big cities like it – better use of space overall and the like. It's quite prevalent in Europe and expect to see a lot more of it here.

In Vancouver there are a number of buildings that have retail strata on the ground floor, strata title offices on the second and then 2 or 3 floors of residential. While we believe there is limited depth-of-market appeal, they have done well for the developer or larger investor. But we do not recommend to buy such a unit for the small investor as owner or user. Contradiction? Well, the Strata Titles Act applies to the WHOLE building. If you own a commercial space and share it with tenants you are liable for all the leaky roofs, tenant violations of a normal residential building and much grief you didn't bargain for. Also, you have a lot less security. We expect to see a lot of disputes arising from these kinds of situations in the next 5 years.

You may find another such contradiction when we talk about hotel type syndications. For the larger developer it is a gold mine. Marketed well, professionally pre-sold and market blitzed it is sexy, fast and highly profitable. Sexy, because you can 'lease' a brand name such as Hilton or Marriott, fast, because I have seen 80 units blown out in a week and profitable … think about it. But I have yet to see one that makes money for the small investor. More in Chapter 17.

The new trends a larger investor should look at are mini warehouses, trailer parks and mini storage. All of them have a real estate appreciation play. All of them are cash cows. All of them are really low overhead and none of them have tenant laws. A true new millenium play. Take mini storage. As people move more out-of-town they need more storage space. Minimum construction, a fence and a 15% cash return. Basic space is a concrete cubicle. Deluxe means you offer a lightbulb.

The main similarity with the small investor and the large investor is they both want more money. The main difference is that the smaller investor has to run more risks to accomplish this.

~

In Essence

A big investor can survive a small mistake but a small investor can't survive a big mistake.

Investor clubs for small investors can contribute to your knowledge but you want to make sure someone isn't selling you something.

No matter what your size, if you're not being turned down on nine out of ten offers then you are not really an investor – you pay too much.

Times change and circumstances change. Both large and small investors have to be prepared to change with them.

The closer the small investor is to the market the better his strategies are going to work. His agility (like the mongoose) is his advantage over the large investor.

There are new opportunities for the small and the large investor.

Chapter 5

UNDERSTANDING YOURSELF

Everyone agrees that honesty is the best policy – for other people.
You can only understand yourself to the degree that you can be
honest with yourself about yourself.

This chapter is titled, 'Understanding Yourself'. Actually, the title of this chapter should be, 'You Can't Understand Real Estate Investment Principles Until You Understand Yourself'.

I suppose you could understand the principles from some objective frame of reference if you didn't understand yourself but that would be like being able to name all the tools in a tool box but not being able to fix anything with them. You'd know enough to get started but you wouldn't know enough not to hurt yourself. And that's what we're going to talk about in this chapter – doing yourself the most good. A concept that carries with it the built-in accompanying principle of doing yourself the least harm.

The principal message I'm trying to get across here is that you have to take a good, hard, serious look at yourself. And you have to do that from a variety of perspectives – financial, intellectual, and temperamental.

Our emotions are an important part of the equation. Quite often we hear the words 'foreclosure' or 'auction' or 'sealed bid sales' and we get all excited because we've heard all sorts of stories about opportunities in those areas. And we get so excited by the opportunity that we lose sight of the other factors that are involved in the equation and those factors are 'work' and 'risk'. I find from my own experience that almost every foreclosure that I participated in where the due diligence was done correctly (at least to my satisfaction) took almost a year before the deal crystallized. Judges usually bend over backwards whenever they can in the direction of the people who are being foreclosed on. You might have to work on ten foreclosures before you actually close on one. Do you have the temperament for that?

This is also a good place to ask yourself if you have the temperament to evict a mother of three small children who has been deserted by her husband. If you do have that temperament, I wouldn't want to know you but the point here is that these situations do come up in this business and it's important for you to know in advance what you have the stomach for and what you don't. You might find yourself unwillingly sponsoring a private charity of your own.

As you can see, it is vitally important to know what kind of a person you are. You want to know what situations to steer towards and which ones to steer away from. Some people take a visceral delight from the roller coaster excitement of certain kinds of deals. Good! They should find as many of them as they need. On the other hand there are people who couldn't bring themselves to play liar's poker to see who was going to pay the lunch check. None of this is, in itself, either good or bad. But it is important as it relates to you and it is important to know in advance.

And the reason it's important is that the more honest we are with ourselves the more likely we are to match ourselves up with properties that will be what we expect. We will stand less of a chance of encountering all kinds of surprises. Almost all the unanticipated unhappiness in real estate investment comes from wishing instead of planning.

After many years of observing the human condition and relating cause to effect I agree with some of the grand thinkers of our age that we 'become what we think about over time'. If you look at the results you have in your real estate investment activities and in fact the results you have in all of your life's endeavours … reflect and think. You will find that your results show what you think about most of the time.

So, be careful what you think about. Having had the privilege of managing literally thousands of people I find that most of the time, people act without thinking. We act on our beliefs. And our belief system is formed by what we think about most of the time. We become what we think about. Worse, people are creatures of habit. So what we think about becomes ingrained in us. Remember that every single qualification for success is acquired through habit. Personal success, business success, success in real estate investing. People form their habits, and habits form their futures. If you don't deliberately form good habits, then you unconsciously form bad ones. Today as you read this, you are what you are, because you have formed the habit of being your particular kind of a person and the only way you can change yourself is through changing your thinking and with it your habits.

You were born rich, you were born with everything you need. Albert Einstein said "Imagination is more important than knowledge." You have great imagination. Use it. Do some thinking, do some dreaming. Too heavy for a real estate investment book? Well, if you want to be a successful anything, you have to learn about yourself, you have to make some changes, if you don't, the penalty is 'just' a dreary life. However, if you don't know yourself in your real estate investment dealings, the penalty is a damage to your wallet in addition to the dreary life.

I want to cause you to think in a new dimension about your life, your mind, your ability, your talent and your imagination.

The challenge is to think. Habits are very hard to break. But YOU know what you are doing and what you are not doing. You also know what you ought to do!

We all have the best of intentions. Someone said: "The road to hell is paved with good intentions." You aren't the first person in the world with good intentions ... but it isn't enough. To 'intend to do it' is really meaningless. To actually DO IT is everything. And it all starts with trying to understand yourself, thinking in a new dimension about just what kind of a person you want to be.

The mandate of 1999 and beyond is learning how to keep learning. A new world.

George Bernard Shaw said "2% of the people think, 3% of the people think they think, and 95% would rather die than think."

Everything we ever want out of life is already here. It doesn't have to be made from somewhere, it is already here. If you are looking for a mate, the mate is already here. If it is money you want, it is already here. If it is a real estate portfolio you want it is already here. The kind of people that you like to work with every day of your life are already here. You become what you think about, you attract into your life what you think about. The oldest sayings in the world tell the truth of it:

Smile, and the world smiles back. Cry and you cry alone.

Happy people attract happy people. Miserable people attract miserable people.

Birds of a feather flock together. Like attracts like.

The rich get richer, the poor get poorer. What goes around comes around.
Real estate investors that have money problems get involved with other real estate investors that have money problems. Owners of problem properties keep buying other problem properties. Real estate owners with tenant problems keep attracting problem tenants. Like attracts like. Most people go through life with pre-conceived ideas in their heads ... and then they are bewildered why they always attract what they occupy their minds with.

To some extent, failures are very successful because they are consistent. People who are sick all the time are successful being sick all the time. Thinking is our only privilege, it is also the only thing we have total control over.

Remember, the majority of people like to do what everybody else is doing so that they can belong. Think, dream, plan and travel on your own road. Observe that everything stems from yesterday's dreams. Today's results stem from your dreams of yesterday. And the size and direction of the result is directly related to the size and direction of the dream.

We also are contrary creatures. We say one thing but then we do another. We pay lip service to the concept of what we think we should think and then we go ahead and do what it is that we really want to do. People act on emotion and then they justify it with a rationalization. Read that last sentence again. It's very important. You see, this is the hard chapter of this book. This is where you get the seven league boots of real estate investment but to do it you've got to take an agonizingly hard look at yourself.

Please, please, please do not read this and think that we're talking about someone else. We're talking about you.

It's hard to figure out what we really want. People buy real estate in all kinds of places, sometimes all over the world. And when they are asked what it was that they found as compared to what they started out looking for, the answer is very often that what they finally bought was much different from what they started out looking for.

For instance, in Vancouver, BC many people buy at the Whistler ski area because they have a mental image of themselves getting personal use out of the unit. They go through all kinds of pictures in their minds of all the wonderful times they are going to have there. All of these wonderful times are going to be paid for by the investment aspects of transaction and it's going to be just wonderful. The reality, of course is that the high occupancy periods are the most desirable times but it will cost very dearly to use those times for yourself. So they end up renting out the unit. Those wonderful mental pictures stay where they started – right there in the imagination.

The question is, would they have paid the same amount for that property if they had looked at the deal with the cold, hard, objective eye of the investor rather than the emotion laden, romantic perspective of an owner-user. Of course not. The misunderstanding of not knowing your motivations and therefore coming to the wrong conclusions about the projected results translate into the difference between success and failure. One would be miles ahead to buy a piece of rental property way below the market and use the profit to rent someone else's condo in Whistler for two or three weeks a year and let that owner worry about it the rest of the time while your slum property is sending you a cheque every month all year long.

Or people say: "I invested in real estate." When asked, what they bought, they say: "Oh, I bought a great Limited Partnership deal in the States." They have a vague idea that they "ought to own something" but don't want to learn the what, where and how to do it and so they follow some guru or some 'get rich quick' scheme.

Everyone will agree that personal investment in real estate requires work. What usually comes as news is that the first work has to be done on yourself. First, you'll want to define your investment objectives. What are you looking for? Is it cash flow? Do you want mortgage reduction so as to build up an equity base? Do you have staying power? Are you in for the long haul or are you a flipper? Do you enjoy the rough and tumble that comes from personal interaction with people or would you rather have passive situations where you'll be left alone?

You want to define and delineate these questions about yourself because the answers to them will determine the kind of property you buy.

For example, let's take a situation where you have $20,000. In one scenario you're a flipper who wants to turn over a property right away for a quick profit; and in another you are in for the long haul because you want to build up equity. In the first scenario you would look for a property that you could buy for well under the market and then look to resell at a quick profit. In the second scenario you would use your $20,000 for four $5,000 down payments on four condos that you would keep and rent out into the indefinite future. This second scenario works particularly well in inflationary times. The first scenario works particularly well when you find a motivated seller that has to sell and whose time is a more critical factor than price.

But this is just not dollars and cents. This is matching up the investment to your temperament. If you don't handle property problems well, but you're looking at a property with problems because that's where you find the motivated seller then you are not going to be a happy camper. If you don't handle people problems well and you require eight hours of untroubled and uninterrupted sleep at night, then those four condos in the low rent district are not for you.

You need to ask yourself what kind of investor you are. What level of involvement am I willing to engage in? What am I good at? How much time do I have for this? What can I tolerate as far as money risks and people problems go? How will this impact on my family?

Of course, if your answers are: "I want no involvement, I'm not good at anything involving conflict with people and I can't drive a nail straight or balance a cheque book, I have no time for anything and I have a zero tolerance for money risks," then the only real estate investment for you is a REIT.

And the questions you ask yourself should not just be general, broad brush strokes. You have to be specific and you have to be detailed.

In terms of knowledge you have to know where you're starting from. If you're just starting out, you have a lot to learn. How much time and effort are you willing to devote to this activity of learning? How much reading are you willing to do? Will you take courses? Will you go to seminars? What are you willing to do to fill in the blanks?

Also, this business is not just about real estate. The factor that gives real estate value is that people use it. How am I with people? Do I have the temperament to get tough with tenants if it's required? Or, will I keep putting myself in their position and wind up treating each one as a private charity case that I am responsible for? That's not to say that the humanitarian approach is bad. It's very commendable. All we're saying here is that you have to do the analysis so you'll know what game you're playing.

What about my investment objectives? Do I have a long term or a short term outlook? A short term outlook is where you look to buy extremely right so you can sell almost immediately. I know a man who has made a fortune in the California market and every purchase document of his is made out in his name or 'Nominee'. That way he can sell the property before he closes on it. A long term outlook might be where you buy a piece of land with second growth forest and you literally grow yourself your million dollars – that would be a long term outlook in the extreme. There's nothing wrong with extremes. Flipping the property before you close is an extreme at the other end of the time scale. What you're trying to do is understand your investment objectives so you can then match up the investment to the objective.

Your age is a factor. Your investment objectives at 25 are not your investment objectives at 65. At 25 that property with the second growth forest is the absolutely smartest thing you could do. At 65 you may hesitate before you buy green bananas. Unless, of course, you're 65 and you're buying the second growth forest property for your 5 year old grandchild. What the investment objectives are is not important. What is important is that you have delineated them and that you understand them and that they are your own.

In real estate investment there is no past and there is no present. There is only the future. Even if you buy for cash flow, it is a cash flow that starts tomorrow and extends into the future. So what you want to do is sit back, relax and take a look at what your dream is. Because today's realities stem from yesterday's dreams and tomorrow's realities are going to be determined by today's dreams. Whatever you are today, whatever you own or whatever you don't own are the results of what you imagined and envisioned in the past.

You might want to bear in mind the philosophical adage that one should be careful about what one wishes for because you just might get it. However, dreaming and wishing are different. Dreams contain the element of planning. Wishing contains the element of miracles. As we've said before, it's all right to believe in miracles as long as you don't depend on them.

Project yourself into the future. It is five years from now and you are a successful investor. First of all, what does that mean to you? We have to define the term. Do you have a portfolio of income producing real estate? Are you the owner of a 1,000 acre ranch? If you stumbled across that magic lamp and the genie gave you a wish, what would it be? And the next step in this dream analysis is to ask, "What did I do to achieve this?" Because you are the genie and the lamp is the life that you have to live. It's all there for you, all you have to do is do it. So, what did I do? Did I continuously trade my way up? Did I buy and hold and let the user of the property pay off the mortgage? Was I the hare or the tortoise?

It doesn't matter what the dream is as long as you have one. Imagine that the you from five years into the future is reporting to the you here in the present, what steps were taken to get from where you are now to where you want to be in that five years. Yes, there is a "Future Best You" real estate investor.

All of this comes back in a circle to understanding ourselves. If you don't go through the exercise of identifying exactly what kind of person you are, then you're going to be working with misconceptions.

There is nothing worse than thinking you are a person who has a great appetite for risk and finding out that you've become an expert on what's on television at three in the morning because you can't sleep due to an investment that's keeping you awake.

If you don't have your true nature specified and understood, it is going to be more difficult for you to buy real estate successfully over the long term. Note, I didn't say impossible, I just said more difficult. And the difficulty is in the perception not in the reality. Shakespeare said, "There is nothing either good nor bad, but thinking makes it so." It's true.

For example, you get into some income producing real estate so that someone else will pay off the mortgage and the equity build-up adds to your net worth. Then there is a downturn in the market. Properties are selling for less. If your objectives were confused, you might lose heart and sell out and if in a few months, there is an upturn putting the market back where it was, you will be on the outside looking in. If you understood, and had it as part of your strategy to have someone else pay down the mortgage, then it wouldn't really matter what kind of a market this was happening in. This can be achieved in all kinds of markets. If the object of the exercise is to go from point A to point B in a canoe, then it doesn't matter how deep or how shallow the water is as long as you're clear of the rocks on the bottom.

It is most important to realize that in real estate investment, like all investment the old adage, 'know thyself', is a critical factor. It is the rock that will either anchor you or break you. So when you are doing the self analysis as part of the formation of your plan of action you have to search your soul. And I mean this literally. I cannot overemphasize how important it is that you ask yourself the hard, straightforward questions about your motivations. You have to be completely, utterly, truthful with yourself. If you don't, you're going to come up with partial answers and incorrect answers and for this you will pay a very dear price. No matter what labels you put on things to make them look different you will only be fooling yourself. The reality will always obtrude.

If your answers are not candid and honest, you will not have the results you are looking for.

You have to keep asking the same questions over and over because as you grow and change, the answers to the questions will grow and change. What abilities do you have? Are you good with a hammer and a paint brush and all those other things for hands-on renovation? What about your temperament? Do you have a tolerance for risk? What does the term itself mean to you? How many long distance collect calls of "my toilet is flooded!" can you take without cracking.

Financially – how many months of no income from tenants can your temperament support? In a little while, in Chapter 7, you'll be asking yourself how many months of no income from your tenants will your pocketbook be able to support.

The questions are simple, the process of interrelating them complex, but they must be answered to your own satisfaction before you buy. (I have seen hundreds of people change their lives dramatically once they grasped the concept of "understanding oneself", and particularly their real estate investment lives.) I feel so strong about this, that I offer you a FREE tape of a speech I made called "17 success secrets of top producing people" just for the asking and the shipping cost. Call 1-800-691-1183 for shipping instructions.

So, really take a look at your personal weaknesses and strengths. Ask some of your friends and relatives what they perceive your strengths and weaknesses to be. Here you have to be a little careful because you might not like what you hear. You may wind up with a shorter Christmas card list. But even so, what you are looking for is truth. Ask a former business associate, or a current one, what they perceive your strengths and weaknesses to be. You'll probably get the most truthful answer from the former associate.

Now admittedly this search for self-knowledge that leads to self awareness is not easy. If it were, more people would do it and the opportunity to excel would not be as marked as it is. Sure, you can live your whole life without it. And if you are unaware of what you're missing, you won't notice any difference. The people who notice the difference are the people who know the value of self-knowledge and do the work that is necessary. The difference they notice is that they pass the people who don't and they leave them far behind in the dust.

But the awareness has to be there. If the awareness isn't there, then there's nothing to talk about. It's like trying to describe colors to a blind man. There simply is no frame of reference.

Do the work. Create the difference. You'll see how that difference will work for you.

∾

In Essence

Understand yourself, there is only one you in the universe – and many think this is a good thing too!

You attract what you think about.

2% of the people think, 3% of the people think they think, and 95% would rather die than think.

You can't get useful answers about self knowledge if you don't ask the right questions.

The most important factor in knowing yourself is not in knowing what you know but in knowing what you don't know.

Chapter 6

THE THREE WAYS TO LOSE MONEY IN REAL ESTATE

Don't go around saying the world owes you a living; the world owes you nothing; it was here first. – MARK TWAIN

There are a myriad of ways to make money in real estate and it can take a lifetime to learn the applications of all of them. There are only three ways to lose money in real estate – Greed, Ignorance, and Bad Luck – but you can put all of them into effect the first day.

Let's talk about those ways to lose money in real estate. And here's where this book can probably be of the most use. There are shelves full of books on how to make money in real estate. If you want to get some idea of just how many there are, go down to the main branch of your library and take a look at what they've got. You'll be amazed. There's no shortage of material on how you make money but there isn't nearly enough time devoted to the loss side of the equation.

It's important because there are three main tiers in the process. There is the actual money involved, there is the time it took to make that money and the time it will take to replace it, and there is the emotional strength that is sapped in the loss process. When people talk about real estate losses and when business writers write about real estate losses, everyone concentrates on the money factor and practically no mention is made of the time factor nor the emotion factor. Well, we're going to cover the whole spectrum.

We have discussed the fact that the investment in the single family home will outperform the town house investment most of the time, and townhouses outperform condo suites. We have talked about high rises versus low rises but all of these comparisons are focused on the making of money. When we make these comparisons we are attempting to measure the various degrees of increase of value. Which area of investment is going to give us the most increase in a given time period. We've got a couple of hundred pages where we can talk about this. Let's take a few minutes and talk about losses. They fall into two main categories: category number one is where you should (and could) have known better; category number two is where you were just at the wrong place at the wrong time.

For example: You bought your dream home in January in Vancouver and in February your boss comes into your office with a big smile and informs you that you've been given a promotion. You're taking over the Halifax office in March. You put your newly acquired house on the market and to nobody's surprise it doesn't bring what you paid for it.

You knew when you bought this property that you would have to own it for at least five years to outlive the vagaries of the market place and be in profit. After five years it wouldn't matter when you bought it, you could expect to be in profit. But all of a sudden you become what we call situationally or circumstantially disadvantaged and you're going to lose money. Or, if you had looked ahead and foreseen this possibility you would have had this dealt with in your employment contract and so the loss is your company's, not yours, but nevertheless it's still a loss.

People get caught up in all kinds of situations and most of the time they *should* have known better because they *could* have known better. This, of course, excludes the time when you are walking down the street and there is a cataclysmic earthquake, the ground suddenly opens up and swallows you. The general rule is, "If you could have known better, you should have known better!"

Of course, all of us are blessed with perfect hindsight – or "it is so easy to forecast what happened with 20/20 hindsight." But, what we want to talk about here are some of those situations and circumstances that could have been avoided had we but used some of that very uncommon common sense. In a later chapter we'll talk about what to do when the unavoided or unavoidable problem actually happens.

We so often see people take their hard earned money – and it is hard earned, collected over a lifetime – and without much thought, give it to someone who promises them a better world. To me that falls into the category of ignorance. Why would you, having never gambled much in you life, take your hard earned money and give it to a total stranger simply on the promise of performance in the future?

We have said time and time again that track record (which, by definition, is in the past) is no guarantee of future performance but yet we see, almost on a daily basis, new companies coming on the scene making the most outlandish promises and people stampede to hand over their money. And these are brand new companies with no track record at all!

Now we're not talking rocket science here. We're talking about very basic common sense. A company comes along and says they are going to earn you a certain per centage return. The number doesn't matter. It could be 15% or 18% or 24% – one thing that is always constant is that the number will be high enough to be attractive.

Here comes a concept that will be new to you. Practically nobody knows about this one. What these people are appealing to is that little (or maybe big) kernel of larceny that exists somewhere in your soul. Gasp! That's right, Larceny with a capital 'L'. The fact of the matter is that it is not possible to cheat an honest man! That's a fact.

You see, an honest man knows that there is no such thing as a free lunch. An honest man knows that anything to do with money is a zero sum game – which means that whatever one person wins some other person has to lose. So in a world of 6% or 7% returns a promised return of 25% should have all the appeal of fish that has been lying on the dock for about three days. But what happens?

Our larceny overrides our common sense. Our larceny allows someone to press our greed button. And so we don't ask even the most simple questions and we throw our money into the fire.

For example, we take the following situation. It's hypothetical but it's typical.

A company puts a big ad in the financial section of the newspaper that on a certain date they are having a seminar in a hotel where they will tell you how you can have an investment in real estate that will pay you 24% with complete safety. All you've got to do is go to this seminar where you will find this particular financial Holy Grail.

So you go to the seminar. Someone stands up there on the platform and tells you how they are going to buy something at one price and sometime later they are going to sell it at another price. If you will give them the money to make this possible they will pay you 24% for the use of your money. You are interested so you fill in the card with your name, address and phone number. A few days later you get a call from someone in the organization and you arrange to go down to their office to discuss things in a little more detail.

You and your spouse attend at their office, a very swanky office, indeed, deep carpets, rosewood paneling, expensive furniture, computers humming, phones ringing, employees hustling and bustling hither and thither. It looks good.

You sit and get more of the pitch. You're not really getting a lot of substance. What you get is mostly meringue, but that's okay because all you really care about is that number they keep throwing at you – 24%. Their Offering Memorandum (OM) also reads that commissions total 10% - 17%.

Yet you still hand over your life's savings. Am I making this up? Is this (the part about handing over the life's savings) a figment of my imagination? I wish it was. If I had $1 for every person I know about who has done this, I'd be able to fill my house with the cash.

So you hand over the life's savings and you go home and wait for the cheques to start coming in. And they come in for a while but one day they stop. You contact the company and you get some explanations. Then you contact the company again and you get some excuses. Then one morning you pick up your morning newspaper and read that the company you gave your money to has been handed a cease and desist order by one of the several government agencies that are supposed to regulate them, and the yogurt is starting to hit the fan.

You make more phone calls, get more explanations and more excuses. Since it is less painful to believe now than not to believe you elect to believe that everything is going to be all right. But as weeks and then months pass, with more articles in newspapers on how the company is defunct, you start to realize that the second mortgage you had that was supposed to be like a letter from the Lord is really so far removed from having any actual equity that you might as well have done the whole deal on a handshake. The reality of your situation starts to seep into your consciousness and you go into the same shock as if someone close to you had just died.

There we have just one scenario, in broad brush strokes, from start to finish. Okay, that is what did happen. The question is, what should have happened? How could this tragedy have been avoided?

Let's go back to the newspaper ad that started the entire process. 24%? First common sense question: How can they pay 24% when first mortgage money is 7% and second mortgage money is 10%?

If the basic tenet of business that risk has to equal return is valid, then doesn't it stand to reason that the reverse of the equation has to be just as valid and return has to equal risk? Therefore, if they are offering me a 24% return, are they not also asking me to undertake a 24% risk? But let's say I ignore this particular red flag and still attend the seminar. The newspaper ad that brought me in cost X number of thousands of dollars. They hired that big ball room in the hotel, they gave me brochures and they paid a speaker to stand up at the microphone and do his dance. This also costs X number of thousands of dollars. All of this money has to come out of my investment dollar before it goes to work. Who's paying for all this?

Let's say I also ignore this other red flag and I attend at the office. All that rent. All those expenses. The salaries for all those people. The commissions to all those salesmen. If I ask the question, "What does this all cost?", and if I get anything that resembles a logical answer I should be able to conclude that a prudent man shouldn't be putting his money into something like this.

The next question I should ask is, "What is this property that I'm investing in worth today?" And more important, "Says who?" Is there a valid independent appraisal? And was the property acquired at arms length or are there wheels within wheels of interlocking companies with undisclosed fees and commissions and markups?

A prudent man would deduce that at best 25 or 40 cents out of every dollar was coming off the top before the money was going to work, at worst – well at worst it could be a lot worse. Because even without any hidden costs it means that the 60 cents that was left would have to earn over 100% in order for you to get back $1.24 at the end of one year.

And what about track record? How long have these people been in business? You will find almost without exception that the company is new and that they have not had even one cycle of successful endeavor. By that I mean that they don't have a list of investors that went into a project and came out the other side with a profit in hand. What they will point to is a bunch of people that are currently receiving the promised results. But close examination would reveal that the old money is being paid by the new money. Just as you as today's investor are going to be paid with the money from tomorrow's investor. And everything goes along just fine right up until it collapses.

It's almost always a Ponzi scheme. As a matter of interest, Ponzi was a man, early in the century, who convinced people that he could buy postage stamps in one country and sell them in another country at a higher price and that way he could pay investors very high interest on a weekly basis. People would line up to give him money and then to test him they would ask for the money back at the end of the week. When he paid them the money they would take it and rush to the end of the depositors line to put it back in.

No one knows for sure how many millions (and remember, this was back in the days when a million dollars was a serious amount of money) of dollars Ponzi took from his victims – you have to call them victims, it would just be too inaccurate to call them investors – but when the whole pyramid eventually collapsed Ponzi was sent to jail and ultimately died in abject poverty.

The deal we've been describing isn't any different from Ponzi's deal. Not in kind, not in degree, and not in the intent of the perpetrators.

But let's take a slightly different focus. Let's say all of this is so new to you because you've been wrapped in cellophane for the last 40 years and you don't have a frame of reference for any of this. You don't know what questions to ask, so what do you do?

You do the same thing you do in every other aspect of your life. You don't make your own clothes, you don't cut your own hair and you don't repair your own car. You go to a professional. I am at a loss to understand why people will spend all kinds of money on everything under the sun but will not buy any of the readily available expertise in the financial fields.

Any knowledgeable financial advisor who could hear thunder and see lightning would be able to assess this situation at a glance and tell you to take a pass. You could pay someone $200 for an hour of their time or you could take a course at the local Real Estate Board, attend a teaching seminar (as opposed to a selling seminar) or even get a book out of the library.

But ignorance isn't the problem. Larceny and greed are the problem. Ignorance is just the fertilizer that encourages the growth.

The majority of people have the delusion that the government is protecting them from their own ignorance. Nothing could be further from the truth. The government is just there to prosecute wrongdoers when they bob to the surface. You're going to have to protect yourself.

Ignorance isn't an excuse; it isn't a defense; and it certainly isn't the basis on which some government agency is going to give you back your money. As we've already said, if it was possible for you to know then it is your responsibility to know. And most of the time even the most basic of precautions are all that is necessary.

Hopefully, by the very fact that you are reading this book – if you were ignorant, you no longer are. But there are basic principles that we apply to real estate purchases that everyone ought to know because they are readily available.

Most important of all is the appraisal of the property. Appraisal is based on comparisons to sales of recently sold properties that were similar in nature. You should have at least three of these to compare to the property you are considering. You should have three that just sold, three that are still on the market and three where the listings expired before they sold but were recent and similar.

The operative words here are 'recent' and 'similar'. That's a basic appraisal stance that is used all over the civilized world. Recent means that the comparables used for most properties should not be older than 60 days (in a hot market sooner, the only exceptions are rare out-of-town or special property situations where older comparables must do). Similar means, that the properties used to compare yours to should be similarly located, same style, size, etc.

This might seem like a lot of work but it really isn't. Any knowledge-able real estate practitioner should be able to get you this information with a few key strokes on his computer.

And all the appraisal tells us is if the price is right. But you have to go deeper. Where does the property stand compared to the immediate neighbors? Is it the better house on the poorer street and not the other way around? One is a much better investment than the other.

Or if you're looking at a unit in a strata building you must get a copy of the last 12 months of strata council minutes. We have hammered at that to our subscribers for 6 years. Strata councils usually wash their dirty linen at the council meetings. If they don't want to give them to you, walk away. You need to know, what roof repairs are pending, what's breaking down, who's breaking in and what monies are in the contin-gency funds to cover it all. Talk to people who own units in the building. Talk to tenants who rent in the building. You've got to walk the walk.

If you think this is a lot of work and not worth doing, then you'll be making a very basic mistake. Think of whatever it is that you do for a living and consider what you have to do to make a thousand dollars. Because the money you are investing is earned one dollar at a time but when it's lost it's lost in handfuls. You owe it to yourself, if you're going to be a prudent investor, to spend the time needed to protect your investment dollar as much as possible.

You've got to ask those questions and make those comparisons and do the necessary research. If you want the returns and the safety that a professional investor gets, you're going to have to do what a professional investor does. You've got to ask questions – make comparisons – dig and research until you know as much as it is possible to know. And don't expect all of this to come easy at the start. It's difficult at first because it's unfamiliar but after three months of looking at specific properties in a specific area your veil of ignorance will be gradually lifted and you'll be able to make your own valid value judgments.

The real reason that cheats and charlatans can push the greed button in so many people is that the vast majority of the public are not capable of making their own value judgments as to value so they have to abdicate that function to someone else.

When I look at the debacle of various mortgage companies and funds that have gone down in the past and those that are in the process of going down even as I write this, I am filled with sadness for all those thousands of people who have lost millions of dollars and it is all so unnecessary and all so easily avoided.

And the way it is easily avoided is by learning the questions to ask and being able to recognize when the answers are valid. When you do this you become your own expert. Then you're in a position to utilize the real experts in the real estate world to help you maximize your results.

In investment there are two principle emotions that are always at war with each other: fear and greed. Fear of loss and greed for gain. Greed is the most powerful and also the most dangerous. Fear will only cause you to lose opportunity but greed will cause you to lose capital. And because human beings are the way they are, greed will overcome fear almost every time.

Still, we've all got some common sense and if we put that common sense to work, our gut feelings can keep us out of a lot of trouble. I'm a great believer in gut feelings (once you're grounded in a certain amount of basic knowledge, of course). There is a maxim in this area that it doesn't matter how many good deals you turn down – what matters is staying out of bad deals.

I can't overstress the importance of greed. With hindsight we look at any of those Ponzi schemes and we say, "Well, who would go into that – it is obviously not a serious investment vehicle." But 10,000 investors wrote them cheques! They wrote the cheques because the story sounded so good.

Here's an important point. The story is *always* good! Let me repeat that: the story is always good. They don't stop working on it, they don't stop polishing it, they don't stop revising it until it is good. It doesn't have to be accurate, it doesn't have to be factual, it doesn't have to be true. It only has to sound good.

If you take it at face value, you take the chance of being taken. That's three 'takes' in one sentence. Remember it. What you've got to do is 'due diligence'. You've got to corroborate the elements of the story. If your findings don't match with what you've been told, you just keep walking.

So they show you a proposition – it may be a specific property – or maybe they are just going to go out and look for one. They show you a business plan, they give you a history of the company and biographies of the principals, and it all always looks good. Naturally! They aren't going to show you anything that doesn't look good.

And yet if you start digging below the surface you'll find that the people in charge have a history of business failures, bankruptcies, and even instances where the people in charge have been in jail for theft and fraud.

The most important points to corroborate is 'the basic premises'. Because once you accept basic premises you're going to accept almost everything that logically flows from those basic premises. Here's just one example. If the premise is that the people are honorable and know what they are doing – and you accept that – then you will probably accept what they say about the property being worth what it's being acquired for.

You've got to corroborate the premise before you extrapolate from it. If you learn nothing else from this book, your time and money have been well spent.

In another area of investment possibility (especially for the beginner) we see a number of investment clubs that teach the principles of no-money down property buying. Quite often these principles work. You definitely can buy property with no money down. However, sometimes people who have barely enough money to meet their own mortgage payments will get caught up in their enthusiasm and instead of buying one property and walking before they run will jump in and buy five properties just because they are available.

In many cases, the club has acquired a block of these properties and is piecing them off to the club members. What happens here is that the club member gets caught up in his enthusiasm and just keeps adding zeros to his projections until the number is big enough to make him feel warm and fuzzy and then he goes for it. Again, it's the greed thing.

It might have been a good idea to take one property, keep it a while, build some equity and then get another one. In the meantime, if you were a beginner, you would have a chance to get more experienced, and therefore more comfortable with the vagaries of the property market with its legal costs, taxes, operating costs, tenants skipping out owing you rent and plumbing that malfunctions.

On the subject of 'nothing down' – it only works if inflation is on the rise and if you're timing is right. That's your basic premise in this matter. You have to be convinced beyond any doubt that the real estate market is going to inflate.

One of the big dangers with property is that the size of the mistake you make doesn't have to be very large in order to be fatal. For example, I know about seven different investors in British Columbia who at this writing are caught up in a trap of their own making. Their lives have been transformed from comfort and ease to sheer misery. They bought too many properties for their specific circumstances. Although the monthly negative cash flow is only between one thousand and three thousand each, it is enough to break them.

With each one of them it was a combination of ignorance and greed.

Which brings us to the third element of loss in real estate and that is the element of 'Bad Luck'. Bad luck is where you did your due diligence, you hired good people, you worked with good people, you had a good project located in a good area but still lost money. In most instances this is more a matter of timing than anything else.

In the early 1980s you could have put your money in with some very fine people, who had great successes in the past and without anybody doing anything criminal – nobody had any bad intentions, nobody was out to cheat you, nobody took unreasonable up-front fees – but the timing was such that markets literally collapsed. Everybody got swept up with it. That was an example of bad luck happening to you.

And it happened to everyone from the largest real estate companies in North America to the smallest individuals. The only people who were immune were those with fully paid for property or those who were in between deals and were sitting with cash. (Guess what they did with that cash once the market bottomed out?)

Bad luck comes in all kinds of packages. Sometimes you find that the good investment property you bought, all of a sudden has been rezoned or put under some non-conforming covenant of some sort that reduces value. Generally speaking you can avoid bad luck simply by owning the property outright in your own name. If you own the property clear-title, it is usually just a matter of waiting it out. But if you're relying on the upward motion of inflation and you're highly leveraged, then there's a glitch in the market – your financial survival will depend on your staying power.

Where bad luck really kills you is when you're in bed with someone whose situation is worse than yours. Such as a developer who gets caught by the ticking time clock of interest on his mortgages. For instance, you may have put money in with a good developer who had the best of intentions, at a good time, with a good business plan, only to find that when you come to market the units they don't sell as per the projections. All the profits get eroded because the market conditions stretch out the sales period.

The most frustrating thing about being caught in this kind of circumstance is that you can't do anything to help either the developer or yourself. You are just like a skier or a snowmobiler caught up in an avalanche. You are swept along by the economic forces at play and you're going to get just as buried.

Ignorance, Greed, Bad Luck. Correcting the first, controlling the second, will help you avoid the last.

~

In Essence

You can't cheat an honest man.

There's expertise for hire to help you make valid value judgments. Use some of it.

People think the government is protecting them from their own ignorance. Nothing could be further from the truth.

Chapter 7

THE PERSONAL REAL ESTATE
INVESTMENT ACTION PLAN

*Samuel Goldwyn said that a verbal promise was not worth the
paper it was written on. I say that an Action Plan which is not
written down is not worth the paper that it is not written on.*

The keyword here is in the chapter title: 'Personal'. Any investment
plan that is not personal to you is like wearing somebody else's tailor-
made suit. No matter what you do, it isn't going to fit as well as the suit
that you have made for you. If you want optimum results, you've got to
do things right. And when it comes to real estate investment it all starts
with the personal plan.

In real estate, or any other investment, the average person looks for
'formula' solutions. And we try to take the short cut of finding somebody else's solution rather than one that we devise for ourselves. Most
of us go through all phases of our lives looking for somebody else to
give us the answer – some guru to follow. We want to be relieved of the
responsibility for the decision making. We search around for somebody to trust and when we think we've located such a person we cheer-
fully hand over all our money and then hope that he will do a good job.
If they do, we are prepared to love them forever – or until they are
wrong at which point we are immediately prepared to hate them. It's
like they say in show business: "You're only as good as your last show."

Such a course of action is fraught with danger. And the way to avoid
that danger is relatively simple. Note, that I didn't say, 'easy' – I said,
'simple'. All you've got to do is to sit down with a piece of paper and list
some of the serious questions.

You have to ask yourself what is it that you're trying to accomplish. Are you buying for cash flow? Do you need to make an investment that brings you a cash on cash return or are you more interested in building equity?

Those two questions seem like an oversimplification but it's really very complex. It's like an onion with a series of underlying layers. Each time you peel one away you reveal the one below it.

For example, if you have $1,000,000 to invest and you need cash on cash you're going to have to buy a property with the terms arranged so that it will have a mortgage on it small enough to yield to you the cash flow that you require. If you have no need for cash flow, you can buy a larger property with a larger mortgage and let the tenant of that property pay off that mortgage. In that scenario your return is in capital appreciation rather than a cash on cash return.

However, there are all kinds of variations. Your objective might be to create a portfolio of mortgage paper where you buy a property for a low down payment, turn around and sell it to a suitable purchaser for also a very low down payment and take your profit in the form of a second mortgage. By doing this repeatedly you would build a portfolio of second mortgage paper. As we discussed, I know of many 'average Joes' who over a period of time have built up one and two million dollar portfolios. Or, you plan to buy one property a year until you achieve a pre-determined monthly income from rental.

It is interesting how many times the basic concepts of real estate investments keep coming up. There are really just a few basic concepts. It is the various combinations and permutations of how they interact that are infinite.

And the next question to ask is where are you in the current cycle of investment? Or rather, where do you put yourself in the scheme of what is happening in the world? And – this is vitally important – it is you who puts yourself in any particular position and you do it with your opinion of what you think is going to happen. Also, the things you want for yourself give different colourings to various situations.

For example, can you see more inflation on the horizon – or less? What are your personal objectives? Are you acquiring a property for a specific purpose? If so, will the property serve that purpose? You might be of the opinion that a property might be rezoned. Or, you may have read in the paper that a new highway is going in or a new highway intersection will be close to the property that you are going to buy. If you can spot a trend before it happens or when it just starts, then it can result in a very handsome payoff for you. In each and every case you have to decide what your opinion is and then you have to act on it.

Once you have your opinions delineated you have to take them and mold them into a plan of action. It will be more than just a simple plan of action. It will be a Personal Real Estate Investment Action Plan! Remember where we said that today's realities stems from the dreams, or the lack of dreams of the past. Those seeds that you planted in the past are what you're harvesting today and it all started with a thought. That is why I am pressing so hard on this point. It is crucial to realize that whatever your today's dreams are is what your expectation of the future is. Sure, it's metaphysical but it is almost like a mathematical formula – if dreams are connected to a plan and the plan is connected to action, then the action will be connected to the reality.

It's easy enough to evaluate. Based on what you're doing today you should be able to gauge what your result is going to be tomorrow. If you don't like what you see, then now is the time to make the changes. We're talking about you. And you are the world's greatest living expert on the subject of you. You, Ltd.!

Remember, as unlikely as it seems, in all the past universe there was never anyone exactly like you, in all the futures there will never be anyone like you - and some say it is a good thing too! But seriously, you are unique and that uniqueness deserves a very personal tailor made plan for your best possible future.

Imagine that five years from now you are the guest of honor at a testimonial dinner that your friends have organized for you. You are rehearsing your speech in front of a mirror. Did you achieve the income stream of $10,000 a month? Did you create the $500,000 portfolio in real estate? The thought is father to the deed!

Once you have the dream in focus, create a set of steps that will move you towards your goal. If income is the goal, you'll want one kind of real estate. If it's growth, then you will want another. But in any case you'll want to do it step by step. And each step that you take should move you that step closer to your goal. I call this 'the doctrine of the next specific'. In any course of action there is one specific action that is the most important thing to do and therefore it is that action that should be done next. If you apply this to your action plan, by definition, you will always be working on exactly what you should be working on.

Always review and always re-examine. Review and re-examine your basic premises to see if they are still valid. You should do this at least once a month because nothing ever stays the same. The sooner you recognize a change and adapt to it the further ahead you are going to be.

That's one of the chief advantages of the written action plan. You know where you're going. If one way gets blocked, you are better able to find another. And remember, when you make a change in the plan – write it down so the change becomes part of the new plan.

The problem with old sayings is that they are all trite. And because they are trite most people tend to ignore them. However, pause and consider that the only way an old saying can last long enough to be trite is if it's true. Now, the old adage – "We don't plan to fail except where we fail to plan" is as true as truth can get but because it's also trite the true meaning of it tends to get lost. Don't let that happen with you. Take it to heart.

The best way to start any specific learning process is to get an idea of where the holes are in your knowledge. Before you can start with the first steps in the action plan, before you acquire that first property, you have to know what the terms in the documents mean. What's an option? A lease? A vendor takeback? What's a deferred down payment? A balloon payment? An abatement? A foreclosure?

Do some reading. Take a night school course. Get some good unbiased real estate newsletters. Listen to tapes. The information is there. You've got to go and get it.

The person who acts, even if he's only 90% or 95% right is usually going to be further ahead than the person who waits to be 100% sure. Remember, if you wait for all the traffic lights to be green between your house and your destination, you'll never leave your driveway.

Temperament is a very important part of the equation. Perhaps you are a renovator at heart. If this is the case, it also helps if you are a renovator in hand. If that is the case, then clearly you are going to have an advantage when purchasing rundown properties for the purpose of revitalizing them and availing yourself of the added profit inherent in that function.

The renovation field has become so large that senior forecasters are predicting that in some areas it will be as big as the total new home construction business within the next five or six years. It is important to match up your activity with what's going on in a particular marketplace.

In any case, remember what we are doing here. We're making a list so as to be able to make a plan. Get it down in writing.

The next big question is what kind of game do you want to play? Are you clear on what your risk tolerance really is? Almost nothing is worse than thinking that you are sitting down to one kind of game and then finding that you are in a totally different one. If you have purchased a property and you find out after the fact that you have to feed it $500 a month because what you are grossing after expenses fall short of what the mortgage payment requirements are, or you can't rent it, or the tenant leaves you with a lot of repairs – can your personal financial position support that?

Try to get these factors jotted down on paper. Take as much time as it needs. The answers will tell you what kind of properties you can buy. You need to be able to match up your investment objectives and your temperament in the properties you buy. This is really a case where it's 'different strokes for different folks'.

If you don't need cash flow and want lots of safety and at the same time would like to build equity then you might want to make a larger down payment on a smaller property and let all the rental income go towards paying down the mortgage. But if you think that inflation is about to come back then you might want to go for maximum leverage and buy the biggest property you can find for the lowest down payment and for that, if you're going to avoid negative cash flow, you might have to go further afield geographically to one of the smaller towns in one of the more active areas.

There are all sorts of variations and permutations and geography is very important. As this is being written we are seeing deals in some cities – Edmonton, Calgary, Kamloops, London, Kitchener – where $110,000 houses with basement suites are being bought for 10% down with the main floor renting between $700 and $900 and the basement suite for between $400 and $600. This yields a very handsome return in the way of positive cash flow. But location is always very important. Pick up that house and drop it down into a more expensive city and your $110,000 wouldn't buy you anything.

It's possible you wouldn't be able to touch this house for under $300,000. If the maximum rental was $1,700 or $1,800, it would result in a serious negative cash flow.

The objective should be to construct a set of goals so that we will have a plan or a template to follow. And again, you've got to write these goals down. Goals and plans that are not written down are nothing but musings. I know, I know – you're different. Sure you are.

According to Tony Robbins, at Stanford University in the 1950s a study was initiated where students were followed for a 20-year period as to their goal setting habits. Only 7% of these students consistently wrote down their goals. Like magic, those that wrote down their goals and objectives ended up being the heads of companies and the leaders in their industries and professions. They were the Chief Financial Officers and the Chief Executive Officers or were the owners of their own companies.

Although there were some outstanding successes in the 93% group, the majority of them were just average. Obviously, while there are always exceptions, the lesson here is that if you don't want to be 'just average' you're going to have a better chance of excelling if you put your goals in writing.

Naturally, just writing the goals down is not enough. After you've made the plan you have to put it into action.

The key to the whole thing is in action. We spend an infinitesimally small amount of our time acting and all the rest of it in reacting. We react to situations, we react to circumstances, we react to other people's actions because we feel we have to. All of these reactions involve us doing the best we can at the time and almost all of them are adaptations. But the real change, the real forward progress comes from taking action and the best kind of action is the action that is planned.

Planned action has a goal. You can't hit a bull's-eye without a target. Once you've planned an action from the initiation to the goal, you must form it into an action plan. There is one factor that is common to all successful action plans. They are all written down! If you don't write it down, it isn't an action plan. It is merely a component of the dream. You have to get it down in writing. You dream of it, then you create a goal from your dreams. You create an action plan, you write it down, and you commit yourself to it. Then, every month you measure your results, you change, you adapt. Then you re-commit yourself, you do it again … you measure your results again … you recommit again … Yeah, I know – nag, nag, nag!

Most people do not like to write things down. Most people don't achieve a fraction of their dreams either. Almost without exception, the really successful people I know are list makers. They need a result measuring stick. The writing down defines and crystallizes the dream into the goal. Once you have your action plan written down you have something to measure yourself by. You know when you're proceeding in the right direction; you know when you've strayed off the track. You know if you're on, behind, or ahead of schedule. You can consider each proposed action in the light of the action plan. Is this next step going to be a forward step along my action path or is it going to be a detour to the side? Nothing creates a tangible frame of reference like putting your action plan into writing.

Part of your action plan is going to be a crystallization of your investment objectives and part of that section of the plan is going to be a cataloguing of your preferences. Once you've done this it's easy to evaluate the situations that come your way. Consider a proposition and say, "Yes, this takes me a step forward along my path and it fits into my action plan," or, "No, it doesn't." Then you either act on it or discard it.

Remember:
"I want to make a lot of money" is *not* a goal.
"I will work hard" is *not* an action plan.
"I will buy one property under $60,000 with no money down. The income must carry all expenses. I will buy it between October 1, 1999 and December 31, 1999." That *is* a clearly defined goal.
"I will have an income of $5,500 per month by January 1, 2008 and I will achieve it by buying 11 properties by January 1, 2004. All properties must cashflow $500 per month by January 1, 2008," is a clearly defined and measurable goal. This forces you to actually write down how you intend to get the monthly income.

The planner is ahead. He knows that following the plan leads to success. Understanding what he wants to achieve and having a road map practically guarantees it. Why don't people do it? Because it takes discipline. You watch great athletes and you see discipline. You look at top producers and you see discipline. Discipline moves you to a different level of consciousness and the difference is good habit generation. I can show you the greatest business plan in the world that will take you right from here to where you want to be, guaranteed, but I can't make you do it. You have to have the discipline to start for yourself.

But I won't judge you if you don't do it. You are doing what your goals are … not deciding to do something, means you made a decision. Energy flows to where your concentration goes, to where your focus goes. A good action plan creates a laser beam focus on your objectives. Just the exercise makes you stronger.

Ask yourself. What are you concentrating on? What are you giving your energy to? What are you giving your focus to? What are you surrendering to? What is your alignment? What do you talk about? What do you complain about? Remember it is all a form of energy ... and energy flows to where your concentration goes!

Where do you go to get the information you need? Join an inexpensive investment club. They are all over the place. The library and the book stores are full of books on the subject. Buy an independent real estate oriented newsletter. There are all kinds of information out there just for the asking and for the taking.

Once you've done sufficient preparation the next step is to get out into the field. Nothing will take the place of personal, hands on examination of the real estate. Nothing will give you a more accurate frame of reference than doing this part of it yourself. If you don't believe this and if you have other ideas of how you want to do this, stop reading right here. I can't help you and I can practically guarantee that you will make some horrendously expensive mistakes.

So we're agreed. We're going to get out into the field. If you plan to deal with 'by owners', fine. Learn about it. Do it. If you plan to deal with a Realtor, fine. Do it. Connect up with a quality Realtor. In fact get on the list of a number of quality Realtors who specialize in a lot of different areas. The operative word there is, 'specialize'. Tell them what your parameters are and be specific and be definite. Your personal action plan once written down makes it clear what you can and cannot buy. Once a Realtor knows what you want he won't waste your time, or his, with anything that is outside your area of interest.

For example, you could tell the Realtor that all you want from them are divorces, executive transfers, foreclosures, auctions, or any circumstance that will motivate a seller to give a 'deal'. Or you want all 'no or low down payment' situations. Then, once you have the relationship with the Realtor, see that you respond quickly to whatever he brings you. Once the Realtor perceives you as a player who will give a quick No if the answer is no and a quick Yes followed by quick action if the answer is yes, you will be on his A list.

You see, this Realtor is exactly like you. He classifies all his properties in order of importance. The easiest to sell is at the top of the list. He also classifies all his prospective purchasers in order of importance and the ones most likely to buy are at the top of that list. You want to be on that list so that you can see what he has as soon as he gets it.

When times change, specifics change – but the basic principles always remain the same. If you're reading this in Dallas or Toronto just substitute the cities and towns in your area. The principles and the elements involved won't alter.

The planning is just the first step. Or rather, the self-assessment is the first step and the planning is the second step. But the next step – whatever it is, the next step is always the most important step because if you don't take it nothing happens and if it's a misstep that's where everything fails. The next step is deciding where to buy in relation to the prices possible and the tenants available. After that the next step is to do the due diligence.

This is the point where a lot of fortunes are made or saved. If you ask someone who's supposed to know what his or her opinion is and call that due diligence, then you are probably on the road to ruin.

Real personal action plans include details like this:

I will perform research for the best city to buy in between November 1, 1999 and February 1, 2000.

I will get the official CMHC vacancy statistics survey for the target cities by October 31, 1999 (this is published every October for every city in Canada for every class of property 1, 2, 3 bedroom condos or houses etc.).

I will get the StatsCan and the Provincial stats for population growth rate projections to show what the expected population growth is in the city I selected by October 31, 1999.

I will get school board statistics to see if grade 1 registration statistics are increasing or decreasing in the area by October 31, 1999.

These four simple steps by themselves will tell you what kind of a tenant base you can expect to have. Whether it is an area of young families or retirees. That way you'll have an idea of what to expect from various kinds of rental properties in these areas.

There are all kinds of help out there just waiting for you. Stationary stores have forms that are designed for evaluating rental property. If you can't find what you want, go to the library. The libraries' shelves are filled with books on the subject and in those books you'll find just the right form that you can adapt to your own needs. Or ask your Realtor for an evaluation form that he uses and use that as a basis.

There are very few things in this business that I am as sure of as this: If you sit down with yourself, analyze your objectives and then write them down – and having done that, create a written action plan on how you can achieve your objectives – you will have a useful measuring stick. A compass that will take you to where you want to go. It doesn't have to be perfect because you're going to be continuously fine-tuning it as you go along.

It's like walking a tightrope. You are continuously making adjustments in your balance. And you will be continuously making adjustments to your action plan.

But please, don't have a great written plan and then shove it in a drawer and forget it. It has to be something that you are continuously working on, and adding to, and adapting.

The person who does this will progress further and faster than people who are richer and smarter and better connected. It is the most important single thing you can do.

～

In Essence

Your action plan helps you determine what kind of a game you want to play.

Energy flows to where your concentration goes.

One of the single most important factors to delineate is just what is your risk tolerance.

You've got to know where you're starting from before you can map a route to where you want to go.

The next step you should be taking – whatever it is – is the most important step.

Your action plan doesn't have to be perfect from the start because you're going to be fine-tuning it as you go along.

Chapter 8

THE IMPORTANCE OF DOING IT YOURSELF

If you want a job done right then do it yourself. If things turn out badly, at least you'll know who to complain to.

It is my observation that most of the successful, top producing people that I encounter in my business activities are very structured. Often they have very big dreams; sometimes their dreams can be described as grandiose. And in my view there is nothing wrong with that. We need to have big dreams. I've yet to meet a top producing person or a successful top producing investor who dreams of driving a Volkswagen. They all want to have that larger car, the bigger house. Dreams drive us.

And almost all of the time it isn't the money per se. The game is what's important to most of these people. The money is just the way they keep score. One should be careful about dreaming too small a dream because that's all you might get – along with the limitations involved in small dreams. You might leave a lot of chips on the table just because you aimed too low.

The other aspect of this is that once you're in the game and playing it successfully, it is the same amount of work and risk to go after the larger goal.

It is also my observation that generally, successful real estate investors are logical and reasonable. You find as a matter of course that the larger the investment, the less emotion is going to be involved. Thus, the investor buying a hotel or a shopping center – if he's a big enough player to be playing in this game – is going to understand yields and cash flow and cap rates. He is going to have a very clear view of the specific goals that he wishes to achieve down to the last per centile.

For example, let's take an investor named John who has a million dollars in cash but who's not interested in taking any inordinate risks. That being the case then his options might be the following. (And this is totally subjective and personal to John.) Everybody has their own scenario in these matters. John might keep 3% in the bank, 5% in bonds, maybe 6% in a shopping center. That shopping center represents the amount of 'risk' that John is willing to allow into his portfolio. For some people this would be too high, for others it would be too low, but for John, just like the baby bear's porridge, it is 'just right.' The operative factor here is that John has to decide these ratios for himself.

He measures the problems and the exposure of dealing with tenants, weighs these against the upside of the income and the capital appreciation and whatever tax benefits there might be for him and then comes to a go or no-go decision. He can seek all kinds of advice from all kinds of experts and consultants but the actual decision has to be made by whoever is writing the cheque.

The degree to which he filters out his own subjective emotion is the degree to which he will improve his chance of making the right decision. When it comes to a shopping center everybody agrees with this approach and subscribes to it. For some mysterious reason when we come to residential investment property like a single-family home or a condo apartment or a house with a suite in the basement all sorts of emotional factors start to seep in. We shouldn't allow that because if we take the same approach to the small investment as we do to the large investment we are going to be less likely to make a mistake.

What is the goal? What is the upside? What are the risks? Do I really want to do this? Is there something better I could be doing with this money? You ask and answer these questions and you'll be much further ahead than if you don't. But again, this is something that you have to do for yourself.

The careful investors on the larger end are always asking questions. They want to have written copies of leases for their tenants. They study these leases with their lawyers. They want to understand the zoning requirements. What are the parking restrictions? What can they do in the future? What are they precluded from doing? In other words, what are the options?

You should do the same thing even if you're buying a single-family home as an investment. Ask questions. If the answers you get don't match the facts or if you just don't like the answers, then find out why.

And you do all of this before you buy because afterwards it's too late. In real estate investment, the money you don't lose is twice as important as the money you win.

It is equally important that you don't rely on anyone else for this function unless you trust them implicitly. This trust has to be in regard for their ability as well as their integrity. If you go into a brand new neighborhood, find a brand new salesman and then accept everything he tells you, you might as well just pile all your money on the table and set fire to it.

For example: You find a very acceptable subdivision in a small town some distance from where you live. You purchase a property that looks good. The price is right. What you don't know is that your unit is built on clay and your basement is likely to flood. Every owner with a unit like yours is going to have problems. All the prospective owners who did their due diligence are invested some place else and don't have this problem. The difference is doing what needs to be done – and doing it yourself.

It is very important to inspect the property yourself. Very often we delude ourselves with the idea that we don't have the time. The 'inspection factor' is of vital importance. The most money ever lost even for the big guys is on properties that were not personally inspected. Even when it involved investors buying 100 and 200 unit apartment buildings.

If you think you don't have time for personal inspection think of it in this perspective – if I told you that in a park in this property where the houses are built on clay, under a rock, there was $50,000 in cash that you could have if you went up to get it yourself do you think that you could find the time to go and get it? Basically it's the same thing.

Nothing is more important than the personal inspection. If you are such a captain of industry that you can't find time to inspect it, don't buy it. Wait until you can. And this is particularly true if we're talking about a long distance purchase. Quite often it might look very good on paper and we might even have pictures, but when we get there we find out that the backyard looks out over a gas station. You could be looking out over a garbage dump. There can be environmental problems.

I have a developer friend who bought a property from pictures that were shown to him. The pictures showed a beautiful view of a screen of tall deciduous trees. The reality was that when the leaves fell off the trees it revealed the city works yard with all the heavy equipment sitting there rusting away – not a pretty sight and nor a pretty site. Had he inspected the site personally he would have been aware of this.

Our number one principle is that you make the most money on the day that you buy. And the amount is dictated by how effectively you do your due diligence. Any Realtor can provide you with comparable statistics. Check out the comparables as well. Remember that you're not just inspecting the subject property but you are looking at it in the context of its comparables.

Professional Realtors in an area represent a tremendous resource. The key word here is 'professional'. You want your Realtor to be a practicing professional and not one that practices on you! Talk to a number of them. Find out what are the general circumstances of the area. Get an idea of both the advantages and disadvantages so that you can decide whether the subject property fits your formula.

If I were to buy a single home for an investment, I'd look to buy the cheaper home on a more expensive street, but never the most expensive home in an area of cheaper ones. There is a 'leveling dynamics' where more expensive homes get pulled down and less expensive homes get pulled up towards a median price in any particular block.

We've all seen cases where someone overbuilds in an area and puts up a mansion in a fairly good neighborhood and then can't re-sell it because people who buy mansions want to live in a neighborhood with other mansions. Still, that mansion, even though it can't be sold, will have a positive effect on the less expensive houses on the block.

Absolutely everything has an effect on value. The factors of freeways, road noises, gas stations etc., all affect value. A quick trip to City Hall is always advisable. Most planning departments are a wealth of information just for the asking. Are there major zoning changes contemplated? Is there going to be a change in any of the streets? The key here is not to take anybody's word for these things.

The motivation of the people giving you the information is an important factor. You are much more likely to get accuracy from someone at City Hall or at the municipality office than you are from someone who is trying to sell you something.

What you don't want is to have a four-lane highway coming down the road towards you and then in a year or two winding up in your front yard. Still, changes are sometimes beneficial. A new shopping center, golf course, or some other kind of development might turn out to be a big benefit. If you know about these things then you can cut your cloth accordingly.

Developments like new highways will open up some areas and throw others into abysmal darkness. With real estate, as with any other commodity, you have to have an opinion. For example, if it is your opinion that the government is going to downsize its activities in a particular 'government town' then you wouldn't be looking to buy property in that town.

Will Rogers used to say that the secret was to find out where people were going and then get there before them and buy the real estate. Conversely, if you see people leaving an area – for any reason – that's not a place where you want to be buying. Real estate values are determined by a demand for the use of the property. If people are leaving, you are not going to make any capital appreciation.

Build your deals small. Buy one, buy another, but keep upgrading your deals. Whatever the size of your deal is today think of it as small.

But, if you want to get into a larger deal, ink this principle: "The only project I will invest in are the ones where if I lose, I will lose small but if I win I will win big." Never invest where you can win small and lose big. Remember: lose small/win big or lose small/win small. Never lose big/ win small or lose big/win big.

Remember also that you need to structure your deal properly at the start. You do not need to do projects for the experience. Any time you enter into negotiations to buy a property you want to make sure that you buy yourself enough time in your subject clauses in your purchase agreement to give yourself the opportunity to investigate the title completely.

I know of one case where the utility company had an easement over a piece of property and the owner had to remove a three-car garage. In another case someone bought a large tract of property for a subdivision development and found that one of the homeowners on an adjoining development had built a tennis court on his property. It was a windfall for the new owner of the tract but it was very distressing for the owner of the tennis court.

We repeat it so often it is like a mantra – you make the most money the day you buy your property. The time you take in doing your own due diligence adds to that factor in a direct relationship. The only time you might get away without doing your own due diligence is when you are in a time and in an area of high inflation where you are flipping properties by getting in and out in a very short period of time.

But flipping is a game that should only be played by the very brave and the very experienced. It is based, in part, on the 'bigger fool theory'. The 'bigger fool theory' is where you say, "I am a big fool to enter into this deal but a bigger fool will come along and buy me out at a profit." And this is all well and good until we come to the 'last fool' in the line. He's the one who winds up with no one to sell to at a profit. Think of it like a game of financial musical chairs. When the music stops there is a scramble and the losers are the ones who can't manage to grab a chair.

It's easy to see that this is a game for the experienced, the quick, and the brave – it also helps if you are using someone else's money. I don't recommend it for the uninitiated. I only mention it because it is a part of the real estate scene from the past and who knows how many years will pass before we see it again?

Nothing takes the place of doing you own due diligence. Don't take shortcuts. Remember that it's real money – *your* real money – your real after-tax money that is being put into the deal and will be lost if you make a mistake. It is important to keep the reality of the money in focus. It's the awareness of the reality of the money that keeps you in focus.

An example of this can be found in the gambling casinos. They do everything they can to depersonalize the money. As soon as you put money on the table they take it and stuff it into a slot to get it out of sight. They replace it with chips and they give diminutive names to the chips. A five-dollar chip is a 'nickel'; a twenty-five dollar chip is a 'quarter'. People don't realize what's happening to them until they go to pay their bills at the end of the month. Make sure you keep the reality of the money in focus.

Every time I think I've seen the limit in human naiveté someone comes along and pushes the envelope a little further. In one of my lectures I commented on this importance of doing the due diligence oneself and in the question period that followed one of the men in the audience asked, "You mean I should inspect it even if it is in the United States?" It turned out that this man who was considering investing between $60,000 and $100,000 or more was balking at a $500 expenditure to do his own inspection!

Go see the property. Quite often that graceful palm tree in front of that Phoenix property is from a 20 year old picture and in the ensuing 20 years the property has been neglected and is now suffering from those 20 years of neglect.

Go there, look at it, kick the tires. Once you get there you might find an entirely different property that will be a much better investment. Serendipity, for those of you interested in words, is when you start out to find something good and you find something better by accident.

Also, you have to bear in mind that if you're investing outside your area, the people who are presenting you with opportunities are only going to show you what they have in their wagon. They're not going to bring the other guy's deal to your attention if they're not going to get a piece of it.

In our view it is always better to buy local where you can do your due diligence locally and deal with a local Realtor. If you live in Toronto and wish to buy in Phoenix, get in touch with a Phoenix Realtor, particularly if someone in Canada tries to sell you a packaged deal elsewhere. The local Realtor has the proper perspective.

Often I like to go to a small town and talk to Realtors, notary publics, lawyers and the real estate board. They often do not see the gems right under their own noses which is another reason to look for the local Realtor when you are not buying in your home town. But when it comes time to sell, by all means sell that Phoenix property in Toronto, you'll get a better price than you would in Phoenix. This is another instance where the prophet is without honor in his own country – the grass is always greener, etc., etc. So buy local, but sell long distance.

Another area where it's important to do things yourself is in the area of making offers. A lot of agents will discourage this because they want to be intermediaries in the process. There's nothing wrong as long as you are controlling the decision-making. The more experienced you get at this the closer you're going to want to be to it. Sometimes a raised eyebrow on the other side of the table can translate into tens of thousands of dollars if you're there to see it.

And when it comes to making offers I want to repeat a theme that I drum on constantly in my newsletter – and that is: If you don't make ten offers for every one property that you buy – and that means *at least* ten offers – which means being turned down nine times – then you are not what I call an investor. You're just someone who owns property that he paid too much for.

I've had investors tell me that their Realtor doesn't like to write low offers. To those investors I only gave one piece of advice: fire your Realtor. Remember that the average commission on a $200,000 condo is $10,000. For $10,000 he should be willing to write offers all day and all night and most professional Realtors will if they know you will stay loyal to them.

One of the most important things that you do yourself is to control the emotional involvement. Objectivity is easier when you are not the owner-user but if you're going to be living there, then the lines start to blur a bit. Still, it's important to ask the right questions.

There's a principle in business that, 'the customer can have anything that he is willing and able to pay for'. When you are the customer, you have to do separate evaluations of the investor factors and the consumer factors. If you simply must have that apple tree, then go ahead and buy but realize that any extra dollars you pay for it are consumer dollars.

What's the difference? The difference is that when the time comes to sell, unless you're fortunate enough to find an apple tree fancier like yourself, you probably won't recover that money. Remember, an investment, by definition, is something you can resell at a profit.

Never lose sight of the fact that there is another investment opportunity coming along every ten minutes. As soon as you become emotionally involved two things happen. One, you start to lose right away because it is just like romance in that whoever cares least has the advantage. And two, you lose your objectivity and you are no longer open and receptive to other, and possibly, better opportunities.

One of the reasons that objectivity is so important is that it maintains a climate for healthy skepticism. If the deal looks extra super-special, this is the time to take out the skepticism magnifying glass. How come I'm so lucky? Why is someone offering an 18% return or selling below market price?

You've got to ask and ask and ask. And now here is one of the most important concepts in this book. This is the distillation of a lifetime of experience and a comprehensive study of the wisdom of the ages. After you've asked the questions, shut up and listen to the answers! You'll be amazed what you can learn from an owner if you ask the right questions. Very often he will tell you much more than he ought to. This is another reason to do this part yourself rather than leaving it to your agent.

Don't be afraid to ask very basic questions, such as, "What are you going to do with this money I'm going to pay you?" If the answer is that he's going to invest it in a mutual fund that invests in mortgages, maybe he'll be willing to carry the mortgage on this very property. That could mean that certain points and brokerage fees could be eliminated and you guys could divide that money. Or, if he's not going to spend the money on something then maybe he'll take a lower down payment – or a deferred down payment, say in six months. Would he give up possession earlier? Will he include the stove and fridge? What about the freezer in the garage? And don't stop there – find out what's going to happen to all the stuff in the house. I know a man who runs a thrift shop for the Wildlife Society who told me how people will call him up to come and get the contents of a house when they are moving out of the country or are downsizing to a condo or an apartment. He has a whole section of his thrift store for gardening tools and lawnmowers that he obtained for nothing. If the purchaser of their property had only asked, he probably could have had all of those chattels included in the deal or at least acquired at a very good price.

If this approach seems outlandish to you, then perhaps you might want to consider modifying your attitudes. If you assume that other people think and act the way you do, you are probably making a mistake. When you don't ask for things then you are making the decision for the owner not to give it to you. That can be an expensive lost potential. I've seen it time and time again, especially with owners who have been transferred out-of-town where they've sold all the furnishings for virtually pennies on the dollar.

Here's another gem. People always want to know why someone is selling a property but almost nobody asks why the seller bought the property in the first place. The reasons he bought will help you define the market of other people who might buy for the same reasons and will help you define the market that you'll be aiming at when the time comes for you to sell.

Finally, expect everything that you do yourself to be hard work. There is no easy ride and there are no free lunches. From the outside perspective it looks like an easy ride but there is a catch – and the catch is that the outside observer doesn't see the cumulative effect of all the trial and error.

Every time you make an offer and are turned down; every time you establish the value of a property – you're going to learn something. And you will adapt and include that information into your personal action plan. If you don't find sellers that fit into your formula, just keep looking. Eventually you will either find the seller to fit your formula or you will adapt your formula to fit the reality. A philosopher once said that the secret of happiness was to strive for excellence but be prepared to lower your standards until they coincide with what's available. Or, if you don't want to lower those standards, if the times aren't right, just stay on the sidelines and watch the game from there until the time is right.

In the final analysis the deal has to make sense to you. You are the only one you have to please and so, selfish as this may seem, you are the only one that matters and that is why you have to do the important stuff yourself.

~

In Essence

Important decisions should be made by the person who is writing the cheque.

Aim not to lose, but if you lose, lose small, and when you win aim to win big.

The more careful an investor you are, the more questions you're going to ask. The greater your risk tolerance, the more careful you should be.

Structure your deal properly before you start.

The money you don't lose is twice as important as the money you win.

When you trust somebody you have to be able to trust their ability as much as their integrity.

Don't take shortcuts – that's real money you're using – or maybe losing.

Chapter 9

THE ART OF THE DEAL

The asking price for a piece of property represents one thing and one thing only: It is the absolute wildest dream of the seller.

This is the chapter that will tell you a lot about the building blocks of the deal and the title, 'The Art Of The Deal', is very descriptive. Structuring the deal is much more an art than a craft – it certainly isn't a science. You can make or save – or lose – a lot of money in how you structure your deal. In fact, the proper structure often will make the difference between being able to buy a property or not.

Early in my career I ran across a real estate book titled, *There Are A Hundred Ways To Buy Real Estate – Cash Is One Of Them*. It's important to bear that in mind. Any dummy can buy a property for the full asking price if he's willing to write a cheque for the full amount. As a matter of fact, if the property is listed and someone is willing to pay full price then nothing more needs to be learned! But if you want to do it some other way than full price for cash, then you're going to be involved in the art of the deal.

Remember the axiom: "In life, you do not get what you deserve, you get what you negotiate." While that applies to all your living transactions, it also applies to your real estate ones.

You don't want to do things backwards. You don't want to select the ideal property and then see how you can tailor the deal. What you want is to have an idea of the deal you want to make and then go shopping for properties that will fit within the parameters of that formula.

The most common formula is to select a property, find out how much of a mortgage you can arrange, put in the difference in cash and then there is your deal. That's how most properties are bought and sold. Let's start by examining some of the components of this equation. And to start with let's talk from the perspective that we are the buyer. Later on we'll switch postures and we'll take the stance of the seller. The main components are:

The Price
The Terms
The Mortgage Amount
The Mortgage Rate
The Mortgage Term
The Source of the Money
Who Will Do What?
Who Will Own What?
What About the Commission?

All of these factors are going to be unravelled in the negotiations. The vendor and the vendor's agent may think that the only deal possible is for full price and all cash. The negotiations are going to create certain modifications of this position and most of these modifications are going to be determined by the motivation of the seller. This motivation is one of the most important factors in the process.

Let's start with *The Price*. As we said at the beginning, the asking price for a piece of property represents one thing and one thing only. It is the absolute wildest dream of the seller. Another way of looking at it is this is the seller's way of telling you the absolute most money that he will accept for his property. This is the way you should approach asking prices. It is a starting point. The same goes for your first offer. The opening offer represents the wildest fantasy of the purchaser. If any vendor ever said yes to any purchasers opening offer, it would create a panic! The purchaser would immediately suspect that he had missed something and would want to reexamine the deal.

The usual scenario is that they are going to meet somewhere in the middle. One of my mentors used to describe the negotiation process as being analogous to two people, starting off from opposite sides of a totally dark room to grope their way towards each other until they meet. The reason we use the analogy of the totally dark room is that one side doesn't know where the limits are for the other side. The vendor doesn't know the maximum of how much the purchaser will pay. And the purchaser doesn't know the minimum of how much the vendor will sell for.

A very important point is that often even the vendor doesn't know the minimum of how low he will go in the sale. Many a vendor has gone into negotiations thinking he is absolutely firm in his price and winds up selling the property for an amount so low that he is astounded. That is why the two parties are groping towards each other in the dark room. When they meet, then and only then, do they find out what the other will do, whether there is a deal or not.

In most cases there is no such thing as a firm price. Oh sure, every once in a while you'll find a vendor who says he wants a certain amount and won't take a penny less and really means it. These are the exceptions rather than the rule. And these properties aren't really for sale. They're on the market but they are not really for sale. Almost all of the time, a firm priced property is an overpriced property. What you often see is that when the market moves up a bit, this kind of vendor moves the price of his property up commensurately so that he is always 'surfing' ahead of the market. The fact of the matter is that when this unmotivated seller acquires some motivation to sell then he will become like all the others. But until that happens he's just someone who is cluttering up the marketplace with his presence.

The reality of the matter is that in any negotiation the two parties are only two dollars apart at any given time. The buyer has an amount that if the cost rises one dollar too high, the deal isn't going to happen. The seller has an amount where if the return drops a dollar below, the deal isn't going to happen. If you're the buyer, success or failure is measured in how close you can get to this amount. If you're the seller, success or failure is measured in how far you can stay away from this amount. But all we're talking about is two dollars.

Now let's talk about *The Terms*. There is a school of thought in real estate dealing that says the price is not relevant. I know this flies in the face of everything that you have been taught to believe is valid. Price is paramount. Price is everything. Not so!

For example, take any small office building. I am willing to buy it for $1,000,000 more than its fair market value. Why?

Because my terms are that I will give you nothing down and I will pay no interest and I will keep ten per cent of the net income and use the other ninety per cent to reduce the mortgage owing. Do I care how long it takes to pay off the mortgage? No! Because eventually the mortgage will be paid off and I will own a building that cost me nothing. In this scenario the price meant nothing and the terms meant everything. Understand that this chapter won't make you an expert negotiator. Only experience will do that. But, if we can just list some of the more important categories it will hopefully assist in pointing you in the right direction.

The terms have to make it as easy for you as possible but it doesn't do you any good if you grind out such a good deal for yourself that the other guy can't live with it and kills the deal. This brings us to the concept of the win/win situation. I'm tempted to say the 'fable of the win/win situation in real estate'.

In reality every real estate deal is a zero-sum game. That means that what one person wins another person has to lose. There's no outside money or outside factors involved. Anything you leave on the table is a donation to the other side. That's not to say that this is either good or bad, it's simply the way it is. If you're in the game to make money, considering you are not going to press a particular advantage, you should know what you're doing and what it's costing you.

The real secret of terms is in the asking. You can't find out where the edges of the envelope are unless you press against them. The people who ask and explore wind up with better terms than the people who don't. Make up a set of rules for yourself and ignore what the other person is asking for. You'll wind up meeting somewhere between the two extremes. But if you don't ask then you're saying no for the other guy instead of having him say no. Ask and ask and ask. You'll be amazed at how often you'll be surprised.

This is a good place to talk about negotiating training. If you haven't had any negotiating training, you should get yourself some. There are all kinds of good books and tapes and courses on negotiating. I'm not going to devote a lot of space to this because I believe that you can only learn it by doing it. But if you're just starting out it would be a good idea to do some reading on the subject.

You'll hear me say a hundred times in a hundred different ways that you make the most money the day you buy the property. And the time that you spend in negotiating is the highest dollar per hour figure that you will ever earn. That being the case it behooves you to learn whatever you can about how to do it.

Here's what I've boiled down into ten simple rules. Of course, it's an oversimplification but all of these kinds of lists are.

Rules of Negotiation:

1. It's okay to ask someone to do something you know they can't do – but don't insist on it.

2. Make sure you're negotiating with the decision-maker. If the guy you're talking to doesn't have 'the pencil', you're wasting your time.

3. You have to know what your 'deal killer' amounts and items are.

4. You need to have an idea of the 'deal killer' amounts and items from the perspective of the other side.

5. You need to know how much time you have in the negotiations. Plus, you try to keep this a secret from the other side.

6. But it's more important to know how much time the other side has for the negotiations. And be patient. Problems get solved one at a time.

7. There is always a hidden agenda. Find out what it is from the other side's perspective. Remember you want to be a risk-assessor not a risk-taker.

8. Any time you make a concession, get something for it. No matter how small, always get something when you give something.

9. The better the deal you make, the more important it is to let the other side 'save face'. Negotiating is a contest and in the process the money is often secondary to the process itself.

10. Negotiate face to face. "If you're not looking in a man's eyes you really don't know what he's going to do" – Lyndon Johnson

11. State your best case and then shut up and listen. The first one who speaks loses.

There you have an extreme oversimplification. I repeat, get yourself some training.

The Mortgage Amount is what's going to be left owing after you've paid whatever cash down that is necessary to do the deal. There are various ways to make this smaller. Sometimes you can pay more down for an amount off the price. Sometimes you can arrange for the owner to carry back some of the mortgage himself. Sometimes you can get a third party to provide some of the purchase price by trading some money for a mortgage.

But you don't always want the amount to be smaller – sometimes you want it to be larger. If you've got a nothing down deal (or close to it), you may see that particular aspect reflected in the price. And that's okay too!

The Mortgage Rate is sometimes just as important as the price. If you are arranging the mortgage through an institution or a bank then, within a certain range, the rates are going to be comparable and competitive. There is a lot of competition for that business and the more you shop around the better deal you're going to make. Even if you know nothing about this at the outset of your first deal, by the time you've gone through the process once, you'll get your education very quickly.

But institutions and banks are just one source. There are all sorts of private players in that game and there the goal posts get moved around a little bit. If you're going to deal with private money, you're going to have to know exactly what you're doing. For this you'll want the services of a good mortgage broker. More about this later.

As we pointed out previously, sometimes the best source of mortgage money is the seller himself. One thing they hardly ever teach in negotiation courses is a technique that I've used for years and that is to ask the seller what he's going to do with the money he's going to get for the property.

I can't count the number of vendors I've encountered who were bound and determined to sell for all cash and that was that. But when I asked what they were going to do with the money they said they were going to invest it in mortgages. Well, you don't have to be a super-salesman to demonstrate to someone that there was hardly anything better for them to invest in than a property that they were intimately familiar with as regards to value.

When you are dealing with the vendor on the mortgage, you can do yourself some serious good because he doesn't have the institution's overhead. You won't be involved with loan fees and brokerage points and he is as anxious to see the sale go through, from his perspective as you are to see it go through from your perspective. Further, there is a genuine win/win here. Vendors that put their money in the bank earn less interest than they can on even a 1% or 2% below market rate mortgage, buyers can save the 1% or 2% negotiated.

Some of the best deals you'll do and some of the most money you will make will be in deals involving vendor take-back mortgages.

The Mortgage Term, or the length of time it takes to pay off a mortgage, is an important factor. The mortgage is not only measured in dollars, it is also measured in time. What you have to decide is what philosophical approach you're going to take to this amount of time. Is it really important to you whether the term is 23 or 25 years?

All of the various factors involved translate into the future value of present money. If you're looking to create cash flow in the present, then you have a much different posture than if you are trying to provide for grandchildren yet unborn. But before you can enumerate the answers you've got to delineate the questions.

A mortgage can be amortized over say, 25 years but with a term of 5 years. That means that your payment is calculated as if you were going to have 25 years to pay it off but in 5 years you have a balloon payment for the total balance owing. Most of us think, that the 5-year term is only an interest rate fixer. While that is true in the majority of residential mortgages, your financial institution has no obligation to renew the mortgage. In 1996 a Singapore owner of a major office tower in Vancouver found out that his $33 million loan would not be renewed, no matter what interest rate he was willing to pay and what equity he had. The loan was eventually taken on by a consortium of different lenders, but not before much worry and grief had come to pass. I am also concerned, that many so called investors will have a scenario where their rents are fixed but speculate short on their term. In my view, fix your mortgage term to the length of the time you plan to keep your investment, or be prepared to not only be a real estate investor but a stock market/interest rate speculator as well.

There is a joke among real estate professionals, that if you want the winter to pass quickly simply arrange for a mortgage with a balloon payment that comes due in the spring.

There is nothing wrong with offering a balloon payment as long as you know what's happening and know what to expect. The uninitiated sometimes are shocked by the ice water splash of reality when they experience it for the first time.

But it is also a technique that allows you to do a deal that would not normally be possible. Some entrepreneurs use this as a means of taking the present problem of not enough money and pushing it into the future on the supposition that when the time comes they will be able to solve the problem then. The seller isn't concerned because the worst thing that will happen to him is that he will get his property back and he'll have it to sell all over again.

The mortgage term can be a tool or it can be a trap. It all depends on how it's used. (Also look at Chapter 14 for the optimum length of term.)

Which brings us to what is usually the most important factor in the equations involved in the purchase of the property and that is *The*

Source Of The Money. In this context we are talking about the source of the equity money, not the source of the debt money. I am reminded of a developer I knew (who shall be anonymous – not to protect the innocent but merely as a courtesy to the guilty) who used to say, "I don't care how big a deal is. I don't care how complex a deal is. I don't care how risky a deal is. There ain't going to be any of *my* money in it!"

I mention this, not to recommend that one be careless in one's dealings but only to illustrate that it is very possible to do deals using OPM – Other People's Money.

You'll find money in all sorts of places. There's your retirement fund, there's other people's retirement funds, there's the cash surrender value of your life insurance, you could pawn your wife's jewelry (it would be my recommendation to get her permission in advance – you have no idea what expensive is until you've tried divorce) or you could get a loan from your father-in-law. The list is really endless.

There is a Zen saying that, "When the disciple is ready, the guru will appear." You can paraphrase that to, "If you've got a good deal you won't have to look too hard for the money, you just have to look in the right place because the money is looking for you."

The main thing to remember when using OPM is not to put too low a price on having the deal. There is a factor, which I call 'The Arrogance of Capital'. People with money think that the money is more important than the deal and therefore should command the lion's share. But the fact of the matter is that there is much more money around that is looking for good deals than there are good deals that could use some money.

The trick is to know how to bring them together – or, if you don't know how, know someone who does know how. We'll talk more about this later.

The next factor we deal with is *Who Will Do What?* There are a variety of players in the deal. There is you, there is the person you are either buying from or selling to, there is the lender, there is the person who is providing the OPM, there are real estate agents on both sides, there is a mortgage broker, there are accountants on both sides, there are lawyers on both sides. Any or all of the foregoing can be present in a deal.

What you have to make sure you do is carefully and clearly outline what each party is going to do and when they are going to do it. This is particularly vital if you have a partner, joint venture or otherwise. Spell out your understanding in writing. It's a good idea to create a *critical path* so you have on paper the various components and the time factors involved. If you do this, you know what you have to do to stay out of trouble and more important, you know when you're in trouble in time to fix it. If the deal has to be done now, tell the other parties, that you will put your understanding in writing, do it when you get back to the office and copy all involved parties. That way, they and you have a record of YOUR understanding of the deal.

What you want to avoid is the situation where everybody assumes that somebody is doing something and everybody knows about it except that somebody. Get it clear and get it in writing and make sure that everyone who needs one has a copy.

Who Will Own What? Here is where we cut up the pie. The very best time to decide this is right at the beginning. People are a lot less greedy at the very beginning of a deal than they are just before the culmination. You have a much better chance of putting a higher price on your participation, if you do it right at the onset. Nothing loses value faster than services already performed.

I have a friend who says, "The only room that people are going to give you at the table is that which you can elbow for yourself." That might be a bit of a jaundiced view of the human condition and it might be a bit cynical but it is often true. And the time to do that 'elbowing' is right at the beginning. This is why negotiating is so important and why the most money is made before you buy the property, not as a result of owning it.

The final factor and the one most often ignored in the negotiating and structuring of the deal is *What About The Commission?* Sometimes the real estate commission is the most amount of cash that goes into a deal.

The percentage figure that makes up the real estate commission is not carved in stone. It is merely a number that somebody wrote on a piece of paper and it takes but the stroke of a pen to cross it off and write a different number in its place. Real estate brokerage is a highly competitive business and all commissions are subject to negotiation.

You will be surprised, once you start asking, what real estate agents will agree to, especially when it's a choice between some cash now as opposed to probably no cash later. The broker has a special place in the equation. He has a time factor attached to his involvement inasmuch as his listing is for a finite period of time. If the property doesn't sell inside that time factor, then he has to renew the listing or lose it.

Also, the commission is an excellent source of equity money. It could be left in for a period of time and then come out at some future date. All you have to do is ask that the broker, who could be a junior partner, leaves his money in the deal. Be creative, be imaginative, and don't be afraid to ask. I have met dozens of Realtors that have taken back a second mortgage to facilitate a deal and actually built a substantial portfolio for themselves and their families.

The first apartment building I ever bought could not have been bought if the vendor and the Realtor hadn't chipped in with imagination and cash. Both won in the end as the vendor was paid out within 3 years and the Realtor within 9 months. Their help made the deal possible.

The real estate agent can see the value of the 'bird in the hand' philosophy as well as the next person.

Remember that we're not building a wall here – these are just numbers on paper and they can be moved around any which way. The important thing to bear in mind is that people can agree to whatever they want to. You will find that people will always do what they perceive to be in their best interests. Your job is to shape and color their perceptions so that what they perceive to be in their best interest coincides with what you want them to do.

But timing here is very important. If you answer an ad for a property and the first words out of your mouth to the agent is, "I'm going to require that you leave your commission in the deal for three years", you're not likely to get much enthusiasm or much agreement. But if you wait until just before the closing when the agent can feel and taste that commission and you say, "I think the only way we can do this is if you leave your commission in for three years otherwise I'm going to have to walk away", you're more likely to get the desired result.

Naturally, this book is going to be read by more real estate agents than any other category of reader. I worked as a real estate agent and I know that I'm not giving away any trade secrets here. This is all just common sense. Everybody has his own axe to grind and that's what the negotiation process is all about – to decide who gets what.

Actually, that is what the art of the deal is all about – deciding who gets what. The more you are aware, the more you learn, the more you apply what you learn – the better off you're going to be.

~

In Essence

You don't get what you deserve, you get what you negotiate.

The asking price is where you start.

In any negotiation the two parties are only two dollars apart – the one dollar below 'too little' and the one dollar above 'too much'.

Every real estate deal is a zero sum game. What one side wins has to be lost by the other side.

Ask and ask and ask. You'll be amazed at how many times you'll be surprised.

Chapter 10

BUYING

Once upon a long time ago, Og the caveman was sitting warm and dry in his cave. Everyone else was standing out in the rain. One of his friends came to him and said, "Og, do you want to sell this cave? I'll give you ten sabre-toothed tiger skins for it."
"You got yourself a deal," said Og – and that was how real estate buying got started.
Moral: Living inside is better than standing out in the rain.
Conclusion: Buying Real Estate is a good way to get richer.

Who should buy real estate? Let's start out by defining our terms. We're not talking here about a place to live. We are speaking in terms of investment real estate. That isn't to say that you can't combine the two factors. You can but when you do you give up flexibility.

So who should buy investment real estate? Anyone who wants to get richer. There are ways to get richer faster; and there are ways to get richer safer. If you go to Las Vegas and put your investment capital on the dice table, you can double it in less than a minute – or reduce it to zero in the same space of time. You could put your money into government bonds and it will double every 15 or 20 years or so. But anyone with any sense of economic history will agree that the best bang for the investment buck is in real estate.

The longer you do it the richer you're going to get, so the ideal time to start is before you're born. The best advice I can give you is retroactive. Retroactive advice is the surest advice you can get because all you have to have is a good memory – unfortunately it's the hardest advice to follow because it always comes too late. But here goes anyway. Choose prudent parents who start a prenatal investment program for you. Better still, as long as we're doing this, choose forward looking grandparents who can amass a fortune in real estate for you so that by the time you come along it will be waiting for you.

Failing that, start as young as you can. The important thing to bear in mind is that it's never too late. Okay, okay – I know that when you get to the point where you don't even want to buy green bananas it might be a little too late but excepting that, the time to start (if you're not already doing it) is now.

I have never had anyone say to me that they had regrets because they started buying investment real estate too soon. Every person I've ever discussed it with expressed the wish that they had started sooner.

So we're agreed. We're going to start now. Next question – what? What shall we buy? It breaks down to two basic categories. Improved real estate and unimproved real estate. You have to ask yourself how busy you want to be. You might want to buy a piece of unimproved real estate and wait for a city to grow up around it or you might want to buy something already improved and rent it to somebody who will pay you for the use of it.

If you rent out something you also have to decide if are you going to manage it yourself or are you going to pay someone to manage it for you. In real estate you can hire people to do absolutely anything. This is one activity where the universal truth is especially true – 'the customer can have anything that he is willing and able to pay for'. However, everything you pay out gets deducted from the net income and eventually if you pay out for enough things you run into that point of diminishing returns.

Having said this let me see if I can give you some advice that will be useful to you. If you're just starting out, buy something that is bite size. Make it sort of a, 'earn while you learn' project. If you're already involved with real estate investing, then you should buy what you can afford. Remember the three ways to lose money in real estate: Greed, Ignorance, and Bad Luck. Don't let the greed get to you. Go a little slower and be a lot safer.

So where are we? We want to be richer so we're going to buy some investment real estate and we're going to do it now so the next question is: where?

If you're buying unimproved real estate you have the whole world to choose from but if you're buying improved real estate, you have to be very cognizant of geography. If you're already involved, you already have your ideas of how far afield you want to venture. So let's talk to the newcomers. You new guys want to buy as close to home as you can, especially if you're going to be doing the management yourself.

Ideally, you should buy the property next door. That way when a pipe breaks on Sunday morning you don't have far to go. The further away your investment is from where you live the more expensive and time consuming it's going to be to manage.

If you think that having a spouse or children is a priority as far as a call on your time is concerned, then owning investment real estate will be a revelation to you. It gives you an entirely new perspective on priorities. You can be at home with your family on a summer's evening with steaks on the barbecue and your tenant phones that something happened – the hot water tank has burst – you've got to deal with it right away. You can be going out the door with those theater tickets in your hand and your tenant phones – the tree in the back yard fell over and punched a hole in the roof – you've got to deal with it.

That's why, especially when you're starting out, being in close proximity to your property is so important. And it is also why, later with many properties in your portfolio and much experience you do not want to be too close anymore. But that is another story.

The next question is when to buy. Not the when of where you are in your life but the when of where the real estate business is in any particular economic cycle. Should one plunge in; should one bide one's time; are there better or worse times to buy and how does one know? The answer is: *Now*.

Every factor in real estate investment translates into a dollar factor in terms of what is the fair market value. Fair market value has no past and no future tense. It only exists in the present tense. We've talked about fair market value in other places in this book but suffice it to say here that if you buy at fair market value the time for you to buy is *now*.

Sure, you can wait and times might get better; but that will be reflected in the price, you'll pay more. Also, times might get worse. Times might get worse and stay that way for a long time – you could wind up waiting forever. If you were around in 1969 you might have said, "Well, I'll wait for times to get better." In 1979 you'd still have been waiting. In the meantime, all through that decade of the 1970s people were buying at fair market value, their tenants paid the rent and they did just fine.

The time to buy is always: *Now!*

There are no good or bad markets, only good and bad deals. One of the reasons that real estate investment is better than other investment mediums is that it's sure. Another of the reasons is that it has a built-in investment discipline. If you've got a mortgage, you have to service that mortgage every month. It's a forced savings plan with the ultimate motivation. If you don't make that payment, the lender will come and take the property away from you.

It's also important to be buying for the right reason. Any investment, by definition, is something that you expect to be able to resell at a profit. You also expect that the money you have invested will perform equally or better than that same amount of money invested with the same risk factors in something else. In other words, if there is something better to do with the money then that's the thing to do with it.

The yield is important. You can't get the optimum yield if you don't buy at fair or below market value. For the umpteenth time we reiterate that you're going to make your most money the day you buy the property. And whatever you do, keep ego out of the equation.

The self-inflicted financial wound perpetrated in the worship of ego can be extremely damaging. Sometimes it's because you want to own the biggest or the best or you can put your name on the building and it becomes the 'John Smith Plaza'. Whatever the reason, save the ego for real estate that's for personal use. Investment should be about dollars.

The same thing goes for tax advantages or tax benefits. The tax benefit should be like the cherry on top of the sundae, 'you get it in addition to ... you do not buy because of... .' Buying into a bad deal for tax benefit reasons is another of the more popular self-inflicted financial wounds. Never, ever look for tax shelters first. The deal must make sense by itself. More money is lost in real estate tax shelters every year, than in any other real estate investment.

Another of the buying decisions that require an answer is how much property to buy. How far should you be stretching? Okay, as we say when playing bridge, let's review the bidding. The more leverage you reach for, the more money you're going to make if you win. There is, of course, a flip side to that. If you lose, that loss is exacerbated by the leverage factor.

If you want to be absolutely safe from the risk involved in leverage, then you have to buy for all cash. For most everybody that means you'll never get into the game. Therefore, let's agree that there is going to be some sort of leverage involved – there is going to be a mortgage.

If you are just starting out, the best advice I can give you is to buy what you can afford. Especially at the beginning, you are better off to err on the side of buying too little rather than buying too much. You would be wise to have a reserve for contingencies. It's even better, if you have room in your other income stream, to take up some of the slack in the event that the tide goes against you for a while in the form of vacancies or other emergencies that can come up from time to time.

When you first go out shopping into the marketplace, you're going to find it a very confusing place. Here is another circumstance where a written action plan is going to serve you in good stead. The entire market is too broad a continuum for anyone to deal with. You have to narrow it down to some specifics.

For optimum results you should let as many people as possible know that you are a buyer. But at the same time that they know you are a buyer they should also know what your parameters are for type, price range, and terms. If you're not specific, you'll wind up wasting a lot of people's time; especially your own.

But don't try to cover the whole spectrum, particularly at the beginning. You will be much further ahead if you specialize. Specialize as to category, like houses or townhouses or condos. Specialize as to price range. Specialize as to geographic locale. (Also review Chapter 21.) The more specific your specialization the sooner you will become an expert in that particular field. Also, this specializing will allow you to deal more effectively with fewer real estate agents.

It won't take more than two or three well placed real estate agents to keep you as busy as you want to be until you find something that fits your formula. If you want to do some grave dancing with financially distressed property owners, you'll want to make contact with some mortgage brokers and loan officers and let them know that you could be a buyer. Any loan officer with a problem loan has a situation that he's going to be anxious to correct.

When you're looking to buy, the last thing you want is to be hiding your light under a bushel. If you ever visit the commodity pits at the Chicago Stock Exchange, you will see those traders who want to buy something yelling and gesticulating to attract as much attention as possible. They only do it because it works. Take a lesson.

There are services you can subscribe to and clubs you can join and yes, my weekly and monthly newsletters are very inexpensive, but when you are starting out you can get also get a lot of information for free.

Tommy Douglas, that good Socialist, was once asked where the money would come from to pay for Canada's Medicare program. His answer was very illuminating. He said, "We'll get it from the only place I know of, we'll get it from those who have it." Same thing with information – get it from those who have it. Your local library is a good place to start. Also look for local – inexpensive – clubs and get to meet others that have done what you wish to do already.

Once you insinuate yourself into the market place, properties are going to start coming your way. Now the question is, 'what should I buy?' If you've got a choice between two or more properties how are you going to go about making up your mind? A good method is to approach the problem from two separate perspectives: 1. Reasons I should buy it. 2. Reasons I should not buy it.

Number 2 is much more important than Number 1. We go back to one of our basic rules: It doesn't matter how many good deals you say no to as long as you don't say yes to something that could wipe out your investment capital. Therefore, don't buy anything that is likely to get you into trouble.

You can get into trouble if you reach for too much leverage; if you buy something too far away for you to manage effectively and if you buy in a category where there is more supply than demand and as a result you wind up with negative cash flow that because it is unexpected you are not able to handle.

Except for raw land, you have to manage whatever it is you buy. Things like single houses or condos, unless you've got a lot of them, do not lend themselves to using professional management. That means you're going to have to do it yourself. When the pipe breaks the tenant is going to call you and you're going to have to do something about it. When the tenant gives notice you're the one who is going to have to look after getting the place rented again. When the rent cheques stop coming in, the buck, or the lack of the buck, is going to stop with you. You will have to attend to the eviction. When the sweet little old lady who you thought would never give you a moment's problem turns out to be the keeper of a menagerie of large ferocious Rottweilers, you are the one who'll have to solve the problems.

I'm not raising these points to discourage anyone; rather I'm just trying to present a balanced picture. Everyone, especially anyone trying to sell you some real estate will extol the benefits of owning that real estate and yet they are understandably silent on any of the drawbacks.

Sure, the benefits are there but all those benefits come at a price and you'll pay that price whether you know about it in advance or not. If you're armed with the information, you can make a more informed decision as to whether you want to pay that price or not. As you grow in financial stature and business acumen you might decide that you want your investment dollar to perform two functions. You'll look at vacation property and decide that maybe you can kill two birds with one stone. What if we buy that ski cabin, use it for a few weeks a year and rent it out the rest of the time. Or, maybe we buy that property on or near the lake and use it for the summer and rent it out for the rest of the year.

My Grandmother used to say that if you've only got one pair of legs it is impossible to dance at two weddings at the same time. (Actually, her version was much earthier but I've cleaned it up a bit because this book is for the whole family.) Nevertheless, the point being made is that you can't make the same dollar perform two functions. The extent to which you use that ski lodge or that cabin at the lake is going to be a direct deduction from the investment performance. That's not to say that it's all bad. It's just one of the realities.

There can be certain tax benefits. After all, everyone knows that if you have a condo on the golf course in Phoenix or Palm Springs you have to go down there for a couple months every year to trim the cactus and tighten all the washers in the taps. Some people are so aggressive with taxes that they consider the plane tickets and all the other expenses as part of the tax deductible management costs.

The problem with any aspect of the buying process is that it's hard to know where to go for advice. Whatever you do, don't go to your lawyer or your accountant or your bank manager. If they knew anything about buying real estate, they wouldn't be in their offices for you to talk to. They'd be out in the field buying real estate. Whatever you do, don't go to your brother-in-law. The person you do go to for advice is someone who is demonstrably a successful buyer of real estate. If your brother-in-law happens to be a lawyer who has made several millions of dollars buying and selling real estate, then you can make an exception in his case.

Here are some thoughts that might help clarify your objectives.
Bankers, Lenders, and Sources of Money:
Don't be blindly loyal to your bank or financial institution. Shop

around. Also, expect to have to pay a slight premium if you're financing an investment property. Lenders are nervous people.

Accountants:

Get advice on the tax ramifications before you buy. Think of this like a runner getting a medical check-up before running a marathon. No point in getting it after, that's called a post-mortem. Particularly as the Tax Act now disallows all deductions on a property you are deemed to have bought that had no "reasonable expectation of profit." Insult to injury. You lose money and they won't let you write it off. More on accountants and on record keeping in Chapter 19.

Record Keeping:

Maintain separate paper streams. Set up different bank accounts for each property. In this day and age when everyone has a computer with an accounting program you might not need this but if you are not quite that technologically advanced, you might want the self-disciplining effect of having separate sets of books with the money in separate pockets. No matter what, no matter how hard it is, how little time you have, record keeping is of vital importance.

Use of Equity:

Once you've used up your borrowing power from your own income stream and starting asset base then link up the equity you have in existing properties. Wrap-around mortgages can get you some of the elasticity you might need to buy that next piece of property. Particularly when your personal timing model shows a return to inflation, leverage coupled with decisive action can make you very rich, very fast. Just be careful, timing is vital. The further you walk out on the leverage plank at the wrong time, the more difficult it is to maintain your balance.

Vendor Take-Back Mortgage:

As we noted before, when you look for a source of money to buy property with, the very best source is the person you're buying the property from. First of all, you don't have to convince him of the value of the property. Secondly, he doesn't have to charge you as much as conventional lenders. That isn't because he's choked up with altruism; it's simply because he doesn't have the conventional lender's overhead. Thirdly, there's hardly anything else he can do with the money that will give him the same return with the same degree of safety.

Line of Credit in Credit Cards:

Another place to look for a source of purchase money is in the line of credit inherent in your credit cards. If you line up all the credit available to you in your credit cards, it's probably an easy $50,000. If you can support the monthly payments you could go out and buy a $250,000 property with that. For the expenditure of a few hundred dollars in annual fees you could easily expand that by another $50,000 of line of credit. Just don't get silly. And – treat this as a very short-term strategy because those interest rates can kill you, if you have to live with them too long.

Abatement:

On most 'no money down' schemes, there is some form of an abatement included as part of the deal. An abatement is just a sum of money the vendor gives back or rebates to the purchaser on closing. You, as the purchaser, could ask for this to cover deferred repairs and maintenance or use it to cover needed renovations. You might want to use this abatement money to cover negative cash flow and put off the needed work until the income from the property will pay for a loan to cover the cost of the work. Often the abatement is simply a way to purchase a property with nothing down. Say the price is $100,000. You get the maximum first 95% mortgage of $95,000. The balance of $5,000 is cash from you. However on closing the vendor gives you a $5,000 abatement. Result, no down payment. When used properly this technique can give you a quantum leap in your investment program.

Deferred payments:

This is another favorite 'no down' strategy. It works well, where the vendor takes back a mortgage. Simplified and using the same example you negotiate the $100,000 sale price with the vendor carrying a $95,000 first your downpayment of $5,000 will be paid in cash 6 months after the closing. At the same time – you negotiate your first payment to start in 6 months from now.

If the property can be rented at $1,000 per month ... well, you get the idea. I have seen combinations of abatements and deferred payments create cash on closing and on rental. This works best where a quality buyer (good credit) meets a well-off vendor in a tough market.

Positive Cash Flow:

Avoid any situations where you don't know where all the money is coming from to cover the cost of operating the building and servicing the mortgage. It all doesn't have to come from the building itself but it does all have to come from somewhere. You have to know where that somewhere is before you buy. That's how you stay out of trouble, particularly when you buy out-of-town or where you operate in a market cycle that is flat or turning down. If your expectation of capital gain is a few years off, you MUST have cashflow. The philosophy of 'The Lord Will Provide' just won't work here.

View and Inspect:
We say it in a hundred places and in a dozen different ways so here it comes again – you make the most money on the day you buy the property. Part of this is in the price you pay and the terms you negotiate. But you can't know what price to pay and what terms to negotiate until you personally view and inspect the property. If you don't know what to look for then spend $200 and take along an expert to tell you what you need to know.

The Staying Power Fund:
"The wise rabbit has three holes for the same den." Nothing in life is predictable. Emergencies arise. You can't make a list of contingencies because a contingency is something that isn't on the list. This might be an excellent use for the abatement monies.

When you're in the buying mode, you are the king. Everybody in the entire real estate industry is working for you. You are the customer and the customer is king. But you are only a buyer as long as you're shopping and you've got those 'buying bucks' in your pocket. Once you've made the transaction you are merely a landlord and a potential seller.

The buying posture is always powerful and you should take full advantage of it. But the same way that you only have one chance to make a first impression you only have a limited time to be a buyer with all the advantages that a buyer has. Any of those advantages that you don't avail yourself of is a waste. It's money thrown away. Make full use of those advantages.

∼

In Essence

The ideal time to start is as soon as possible.

The further away your investment real estate is from where you live the more expensive and time consuming it's going to be to manage.

The further you walk out on the leverage plank the more difficult it is to keep your balance.

Chapter 11

THE REALITY OF THE REALTY MARKETPLACE

Once upon a time a man found a magic lamp and asked the Genie inside to find him a good real estate deal and the Genie did. Moral: If you believe this, you're the person I want to talk to about that swampland in Florida.

This is another one of those chapters that could be a whole book by itself. There is so much to say on the subject but I'll try to hit the high points. One thing about the reality of the marketplace is that it will always obtrude. It doesn't matter what you think it is, and it certainly doesn't matter what you would like it to be – the only thing that matters is what it actually is.

Here it is in a nutshell: The marketplace is a place of hard work where there are no free lunches and lots of competition.

Is it as easy as it looks from the outside? Of course not. What is deceptive about it is that from the outside and to the outsider it does look easy. But what you see from the outside is like the duck swimming through the water. From the top you see the duck gliding along, gracefully moving across the water but underneath those webbed feet are going like blazes. And that's exactly what this business is all about.

So now consider it in these terms. Think of what it took you to learn whatever it is you know about the business you're in. First of all there might have been some schooling. Then there might have been an apprenticeship. Then a sort of journeyman phase. And finally, the rest of the activity, each episode and each instance a learning experience that brought you to where you are now in your job or profession.

Before you leave this idea, consider what it would be if someone came along today who didn't have any of your training or any of your experiences and tried to start doing your job from the word go. What would happen? There would be a lot of mistakes and there would be a lot of learning experiences. Odds and probabilities; just like any business. Don't expect this business to be any different. The reason that you can make so much money in this business is because the mistakes are so expensive. It's like anything in life – it's all a matter of odds and probabilities – you are rewarded according to the risks you take. Like the roulette wheel where you get paid even money if you pick red or black but you get thirty-five to one if you pick the correct number.

Out and out risk taking is what you have to avoid. But in order to know which risks to take and when to take them you have to know how to assess the risks correctly. That is why you want to be a risk assessor first and after that, if you want, you can be a risk taker. There's a whole category of investors who don't want to take any risk at all and yet they find their way into deals where they lose their life's savings. How does this happen?

Keeping to courses of action that are destined to fail is how it happens. It's as simple as that. They didn't assess the risk properly. As this is being written there is a real estate scandal that a prominent firm of chartered accountants is trying to unravel. We refer to this example often because it is such a classic demonstration of what can go wrong when you think the reality is one thing and it turns out to be something else. Well, these accountants are dealing with a situation where there are tens of thousands of investors who invested hundreds of millions of dollars with a company that suddenly turned out to be insolvent. I would be willing to bet that almost every one of those thousands of investors thought that they were making a safe and secure investment. If they had thought otherwise, they wouldn't have put in their money.

What went wrong? Nothing went *wrong. It was wrong from the very start.* From the moment each one of them wrote their cheque it was as if they flushed the money down the toilet. So what was wrong? What was wrong was that virtually all of those people didn't equip themselves with enough knowledge to properly assess the investment and instead chose to take the word of someone, in this case the person selling them the investment, whose interest in the matter was totally in conflict with theirs.

And people selling you three magic beans for your cow come in all kinds of disguises. They come disguised as financial planners and fiscal advisors and economic analysts. Or they may be dressed up as a General Partner at the head of a project in which you are going to be a limited partner. No matter what the title is on their business card it all translates to the same message – your interests are diametrically opposite to theirs.

So, when this happens you can not have a more perfect recipe for total financial destruction and that is why we wind up with all those couples sitting across the breakfast table from each other asking how they managed to lose their life savings.

Warm and safe the world is not. Most of the time the world is cold and cruel and the world doesn't get much colder or much crueler than this.

Reasonable people would expect the government to protect them and look after them and see that they were safe. Whatever you do, don't think that your government is going to protect you in this kind of situation. Sure, there are laws against this sort of thing but they only come into play after the fact. And every time the government makes some new laws the 'sharks' find some new tricks to get to the 'sardines', then there is another scandal, some more new laws and then some even newer tricks. This has been going on since the Phoenicians invented money and it is never going to stop.

If the government knew how, they could have shut this company down the first month they were in business. Or, if the government wanted to they could have shut them down. Those are the only two choices. Either the government doesn't know how to protect you or they don't want to.

The fact of the matter is that if any knowledgeable and empowered person from the government regulators had answered some of the ads, attended some of the seminars, had made some personal appointments and listened to some of the sales pitches, that knowledgeable and empowered person from the government would have been able to conclude in less than a cumulative eight hours of investigation that this particular canoe was headed straight over the waterfall. But please note that in this paragraph the operative phrase is 'knowledgeable and empowered'.

Therefore if the government doesn't want to protect you or doesn't know how to protect you, you better know how to protect yourself.

Each person, unless they were born into a family where real estate is the main business, served some kind of apprenticeship to learn the business that they make their living from. When you were learning your business you made mistakes and you learned from them. The same thing applies here but you've got to be a lot more careful because in real estate, the mistakes, if they are large ones, are so expensive that they can knock you right out of the game.

Now the question to ask is if people are not going to serve the apprenticeship and equip themselves with the knowledge they need then what should they do? The answer is that they shouldn't do anything. They should leave the money in the bank. They should let some bank or trust company manage their portfolio along very conservative guidelines. That way they will probably survive.

But the problem with this approach is that the results are going to mirror the economy.

You don't have to be a Rhodes scholar to conclude that if people are going to play in the game without having the necessary knowledge themselves, then they better learn how to link up with someone who does have the necessary knowledge and who doesn't have interests that don't coincide with theirs. In other words they are going to have to hire the necessary experts or they might as well send all their money to their favorite charity and have done with it.

So now we come to the place where we get all the excuses. I'm too busy, I don't have the time, I'm this, I'm that, I'm the other thing. Sure you are. But there is that law in the marketplace that is as immutable as the law of gravity – "The customer can have anything that he is willing and able to pay for."

Are you willing to lose money? Of course not! But that's what you're describing. And that's one of the reasons that we beat so loudly on the drum of the Written Personal Action Plan. When you actually put your action plan in writing you have a chance to find out if you're too busy to be playing the game. If you are then you should know about it and you should do something about it.

Money is what it is going to cost you if you don't. For some money ranks right up there with oxygen, yet I'd be the first one to agree that money isn't everything. There are lots of things that are more important. But it is also true that in the game we're describing, money is what they use to keep score. You either don't play the game or rearrange your priorities so that you do have the time to learn what must be learned and to do the things that have to be done.

Also, as we said in Chapter 5, you have to decide what kind of a player you are. The first thing you have to do is learn how to assess risk and as soon as you've done that you've got to decide where on the scale of risk taking you fit. This is the kind of thing that is a fluid condition so you have to keep reviewing and repositioning yourself. It's a personal decision.

Let's address ourselves to the fact that as we age we change. The risks you will take at thirty when you're single are different from the risks you'll take at forty-five when you're married with three kids. And also different from the risks you'll take at sixty with most of your working years behind you.

Look at yourself objectively and ask yourself how hard do you want to work? The same set of comparisons apply. Thirty years old, or forty-five years old, or sixty years old – different patience, different stamina, different energy level – different everything.

Many times priorities change as we age – you are constantly going to have to be deciding what's important to you because you're going to have to pay a price for everything you do. It's best to know in advance if you want to pay that price.

Also, bear in mind that nobody exists in a vacuum. If you're married, you have to make these decisions about risks and priorities in concert with your partner. You're both going to benefit or pay so the decisions involved should include both parties.

Another thing that you have to teach yourself in the field of real estate investment is just how unforgiving the world is. The person you're buying the property from doesn't care about you, he only cares about himself. The person you're selling to has no concern for you. You didn't exist in his life before he met you. The minute he cashes your cheque you will cease to exist for him.

And the lender, if there's one involved, is even less concerned. Oh sure, he wishes you well so you will be able to repay his loan without causing him any trouble but at the same time he did not enter into the transaction with the idea of taking any chances. As far as he's concerned your relationship is about money and nothing else.

Just how unforgiving the world is, is something you should be aware of before you start because when you are about to put your pen to paper for that personal guarantee you should know what it really means. (It means that in any default situation you are it!) Also, you should know what happens when foreclosure occurs. Knowing in advance might just possibly make all the difference in the world.

There are all kinds of misconceptions in this business. Misconceptions that come into the public consciousness because some minor miracle might have happened once and because people like to believe in fairy tales that have become part of the business folklore.

One of the misconceptions is that if you just let enough people know that you are in the market for a bargain in real estate, as soon as one comes along, it's going to be presented to you. Not a day goes by where somebody doesn't say to me, "Ozzie, when you see a good deal give me a call and I'll buy it."

Of course I will! Why wouldn't I? After all, I don't know you from a bale of hay but you've just indicated to me that you'd like a good real estate deal at a bargain price so as soon as one comes my way I better alert you as quickly as I can. I certainly wouldn't buy it myself. Or, if I wasn't liquid, I certainly wouldn't give it to one of my children, or an in-law, or a close friend – no, I'm going to give it to you, a total stranger. Come on now!

If you're not out in the marketplace every day then all you are going to get is the leftovers. For one thing, bargains are not all that plentiful. Sure, bargain situations do come along from time to time when someone has a special reason and therefore a special motivation for selling. When this happens those bargains go to the first person that finds them. The trick in panning for gold is just to get rid of the sand, but you've got to be panning all the time. That way when a nugget does come along you have a chance at it.

The formula is a simple one. If you work hard and spend a lot of time in the marketplace, and if you're lucky, then you will get the share of the bargains that that amount of talent and effort and luck warrants. Reduce any of the components of the formula – hard work, time, or luck – and the share you get will be reduced commensurately. Another factor that almost every successful person in this business notices is that the harder you work the luckier you get.

What we are describing here is the pure entrepreneurial function. The fact that you are willing to take the action that will put you into the deal where you will win if you're right and you will lose if you're wrong. That's what the entrepreneur does. But the real key is in being willing to take action.

I have seen innumerable examples where two people are looking at the same piece of property. One person is smarter, richer, works harder to locate deals, and is superior to the other in absolutely every factor except one – the other person is more willing to take action. He decides a day before the first person and moves, winding up with the deal.

It is extremely important for you to keep in sight that in this game you get what you get because you're willing to take action. None of the sifting and comparing and analyzing means anything without the action. That is one of the chief realities.

There is no shortage of people who are willing to work hard. What separates the cream from the milk is that willingness to take action.

And yet, in spite of all the factors and components we have described there is so much competition out there. In all probability most of them, or at least half of them, are going to be smarter than you, work harder than you, outpace you and outpoint you in every category imaginable – how can you possibly hope to succeed? The answer is simple. If you're persistent, you will succeed. You just have to be consistently persistent.

Like any other profession or occupation, as the field grows more complex the various areas separate into various aspects of specialization. It isn't possible to be a Renaissance Man. You can't know it all and do it all. You shouldn't want to. There is simply no way that you can cover the entire spectrum. What you should want to do is specialize in one or two areas. This way you are going to optimize your chance for success.

It might be urban, it might be rural. It might be single family houses; it might be apartment buildings. The only problem with this philosophy of specialization is that the field you specialize in might be attractive at the time you select it – it might be the best thing to do and you might make a whole bunch of money at it. But then a few years go by and things change. All of a sudden, single family homes in one city are a glut on the market. All the money is being made in condos in some other city. Recreational subdivisions with golf courses might be like a license to print money and then after a while you can't give them away. The hot thing is mini-warehousing.

The graph goes up and the graph goes down and I can't count the number of fortunes I've seen made by people who specialized in a certain area but then watched those people give the fortune back because they were just a one-trick pony and that one-trick pony situation turned into a flogging a dead-horse situation because they couldn't let go and move to something else. Of course in a later chapter we discuss what real estate is likely to do well and which isn't.

The Moral? Specialize but stay light on your feet and stay flexible. The reality is that nothing stays the same, nothing is permanent except change. You need to study the trend, the timing of the real estate cycle and the basics of the performance of different real estate investments.

Another reality of the marketplace is that if you try to play in a game where you're not eligible, you will get eaten up. Eligibility is usually measured in financial terms although sometime it is measured in terms of expertise. Most of the time it's financial.

Where most people run into problems in this area is when they use their equity money to get into the deal and they rely on future financing to allow them to continue. And the difficulty here is that they are approaching a three dimensional problem with only two dimensions of awareness. Here is where eligibility comes in. When the people, who are really in a deal bigger than their financial capabilities, go to get their new financing they find that none of the institutions will lend them the money. Yes, they have a healthy debt/equity ratio; yes, the property could cover the new mortgage; but – if something happens to the cash flow of the property, they would not have the financial 'muscle' to service a shortfall and therefore, as far as the lender is concerned, they are not eligible for the loan.

And when this happens it triggers the whole domino effect of having to go to other sources for more expensive money, and/or taking in partners and their position in the deal gets smaller and smaller and the distance between them and the return of their equity gets further and further.

If you want to avoid this particular reality, make sure that you're eligible for the size and the type of deal you go into.

And finally, remember that the face of the reality, of the market place is always changing. Competition is always changing and what's best at any time in the marketplace is always changing. You have to keep up with trends. Yesterday's knowledge and experience is only good if you use it as a base to build on with the new knowledge and new experiences of today.

∼

In Essence

It doesn't matter what you think the reality is and it certainly doesn't matter what you'd like it to be – the only thing that matters is what it actually is.

The reason you can make so much money in this business is because the mistakes are so expensive.

People selling you three magic beans for your cow come in all sorts of disguises.

Every time the government makes new laws the 'sharks' find new ways to get to the 'sardines'.

There is a law of the marketplace that is as immutable as the law of gravity – "The customer can have anything he is willing and able to pay for."

Stay light on your feet and stay flexible. Nothing is permanent except change.

Chapter 12

THE RESALE

Observation: Assets are not money – money is not profit. They only represent potential. Once you sell assets and turn them into cash, then they become money. And then, after you deduct the money that you started with – and spend what's left – that's the profit. But up until then everything is only numbers.

The time to think about the resale of the property is before we buy it. We should have a clear idea of what we want to achieve and how we intend to implement that when the time comes to exit the property. The reason that you make the most money on the day you buy, is because you think about the resale ahead of time.

It's not enough to throw yourself into an investment and then look for a soft spot to land when the time comes to sell. Sure, you can do all right but what we're talking about here is how to optimize and maximize what it is that we're going to get from the investment.

For example, before you buy the property you might want to consider just how you're going to take and hold the title to the property. You might want to sit with your taxman and take into account how much you expect to make and how the title should be held so as to minimize the taxes. Or, you might have some risky business activities in other areas of your business life. You might want the proceeds in the event of a sale to be shielded from possible lawsuit and attachment. So you would consider holding the property either in a corporation or by your wife or your children or some combination or permutation of any or all of these.

All of this would have to be considered, decided, and acted on before you bought the property – because after is too late.

The exit strategy should be composed of time, money, and psychological concerns. We call this the Time/Money/Psychology equation.

First of all, consider the time factor. How long do you intend to keep the property? There are all kinds of investment postures possible here. Some people view their investment portfolios like a black hole in space. Once something goes in it never comes out; it just stays there forever. They buy a property intending that it be passed from father to son and so on forever. These are the 'holders'.

Some people take the other extreme. These are the 'flippers'. They buy a property (maybe with a long closing period or maybe by option) with the objective to resell it before they have to take title to it, hopefully the next day or, better yet, later on the same day.

And then there is everyone in between these two extremes. We'll call them the 'normal investors'. These are the people who want to achieve a certain objective with the investment. They want to hit a particular benchmark and then exit the investment. There is nothing intrinsically good or bad in any of these approaches. It's strictly a matter of 'different strokes for different folks' – what is important is that you know what kind of a player you are and have a clear idea how long you intend to hold the property.

You may not be thinking in terms of time. You may be determining your exit point on the money factor. (Remember, our equation is made up of Time/Money/Psychology.) For example, your investment approach might be to acquire property with a leverage factor of 75/25. You would put down 25% and the rest would be mortgage. Furthermore, you would not ever want to have an equity position of more than 50% in any given property.

Therefore, if you bought a property for $100,000 with $25,000 down, when the value of that property rises to more than $150,000, it would be time for you to sell and take your $75,000 and buy a property for $300,000.

This might take 10 years in a slow market or if the property was rezoned a week after you bought it then you would have reached the dollar benchmark a lot sooner. Again, in themselves, these factors are neither good nor bad. But you have to know in advance what your objectives are so you will know when to act. The time to make these decisions and design the appropriate exit strategy is before you acquire the property.

As we said, a written set of goals helps. You will have all these decisions in place where you will be much more likely to do the right thing at the right time and not be scrambling around and guessing when what you should be making is informed decisions.

The third factor of our Time/Money/Psychology equation is the most subjective and therefore the one with the most variables and the one most difficult to determine.

Each component of the equation has an impact on the other two. So Time and Money, have their impact here and have to be taken into consideration. None of these factors exist in a vacuum. The psychology aspect keeps changing. The greed you had at age 25 is not the greed that you'll have at age 50 or at age 75. The patience you had at 25 is not the same you'll have at 50 and at 75. Your temperament might be patient but you are closer to the end than you are to the beginning. Your risk tolerance is something else that changes as you go along the time line on the graph of life.

You should have the same kind of approach with your real estate that successful stock market investors use. A stock market investor should have a clear perspective on the kinds of stocks he's buying and how they suit his particular requirements, and he should have an exit point delineated (both on the high side and on the low side) as to when he's going to get rid of them.

Selling on a downward trend is something that nobody talks about when they're discussing real estate. Somewhere in our formative years we get inculcated with the idea that real estate will keep going up forever. If it stops going up, we expect it to level off for a while before it starts going up again. Nowhere does anyone even consider the possibility that real estate will go down.

But it always does. The timing of the real estate cycle varies and keeps on ratcheting higher, but prices do reverse. You should have a strategy in place in the event that it happens to you. In the stock market this is called a 'stop loss'. Well, with real estate you should have a stop-loss strategy just in case you might have to use it. Decide ahead of time, that you will hold through tough times, or cut your losses fast.

Of course an exit strategy decision is much simpler and therefore easier to make when all you have to consider is yourself. When you start adding more people to the mix, it starts to get complicated. For example, if you're married then you have to take into consideration the psychology of the spouse.

Once you get outside of the spousal association it gets more complex and much harder to control. If you're in a partnership, then you're into a 'majority rules' situation. You'll find yourself making compromises as a business partner that you wouldn't have to make as an individual.

But before you entered into the partnership you should have done the same evaluation of possible exit strategies that you would have made in the purchase of an individual property. You want to make sure that there are buy/sell agreements in place, and arbitration agreements in case of irreconcilable differences. Plus all the other kinds of 'good fences' that make 'good neighbors'. It is a simple matter of writing down ALL eventualities – partner dies, partner needs money, partner doesn't do his part, partner brings in another partner, whatever – before the joining of hands, minds and money. It's another form of planning the sale before concluding the purchase.

Naturally, if you can't resolve the exit problems, it's going to color your decision to involve yourself in the deal. But that's why we go through this kind of analysis before we buy – so we can make the good deals better and identify the bad deals in time to stay out of them.

The magnitude of the problems you can get into if you don't go through these steps is mind boggling. For example, two families buy a holiday condo with the understanding that they'll 'use it together'. But what does that mean? Who gets Christmas, Easter? Who cuts the grass, does the dishes, beds, and vacuums? What if one family is sloppy and the other isn't? What about pets? What about subleasing to outsiders? Expensive insurance or basic? How do I get out, can I sell my share or does my partner gets it back at the original price? A hundred questions asked beforehand will make for a smooth partnership. I have seen a lot of misery because of the little items that weren't covered.

Are partnerships bad? All partnerships that do not have a clear, clean itemized agreement of all possibilities have a good chance to fail or at least create a lot of unhappiness. All who cover the tough questions ahead of time have a good chance. I once owned a large motor yacht with 3 other partners. Everyone said you couldn't make it work, but we did. But our agreement covered EVERYTHING. We all knew what the expectations, the rewards and the recourse for non-compliance were. Thus, we were able to afford a much larger yacht than had we owned it by ourselves at a much lower price. The same applies to any partnership or joint venture, but particularly a real estate partnership. Things change, so get the eventualities covered.

Many people would have never bought a hotel type condo in partnership with the restaurant owner/ banquet room operator/parking lot owner had they known they were liable for the losses in these areas. Worse, many wouldn't have bought, had they understood that there was no proven secondary market – or at best a very thin one. It's a one way street.

Remember that the definition of an investment is a financial involvement in something that you have a good chance of selling for a profit at some point in the future. If there isn't a 'good chance' of this happening but there is 'some kind of a chance', then we slip from an 'investment' to a 'gamble'. If there is absolutely 'no chance', then I don't know what to call it – maybe we could describe this as 'a tax loss that isn't complicated by the possibility of profit'.

Oh sure, just because a secondary market, or a 'proven' secondary market doesn't exist now doesn't mean that one will not develop in the future. Maybe in the sample of the hotel unit ownership it still will. But that uncertainty has to have a dollar value attributed to it and that dollar amount should be subtracted from the purchase value. But I would doubt if any of the purchasers of these units went through the steps of this kind of analysis.

But let's say that you either did or didn't do everything right and the time has passed and the property went up or down or stayed the same. You are now motivated within the framework of your Greed/Patience/ Risk Tolerance equation to sell the property. Now you have to analyze the methods that you're going to use to do it.

When I get ready to sell a piece of property the first thing I do is look around for a real estate agent to handle the sale for me. Generally speaking, I use different kinds of agents for buying and selling. When I want to buy I want an investment-oriented agent. I want that agent to understand that I am looking for a deal. I want that agent to be a person who will be scanning the market for the kind of seller's motivation that will make the deal I want possible. That agent will be looking for divorces, corporate locations, foreclosures, mortgages in default, an estate turning an inheritance into cash or any other kind of difficulty that would motivate a seller to take less than the current market value.

In short, I – like all buyers – want the best price possible. If someone is going to buy a property for less than current market value, I want that person to be me.

In the olden days the real estate agent represented the seller's interests and his duty was to the seller. Even if he drove you around in the car for three weeks and never met the seller he was still duty-bound to represent him and not you. Now things are a little more sensible and it is possible for an agent to either exclusively represent the buyer or exclusively represent the seller. For that reason alone you want to use two different kinds of agent depending on whether you are buying or selling.

Now when I sell a property the agent has to understand different things. In the buying scenario I want to get within $1 of the minimum that the seller would accept. In the selling scenario I want to get within $1 of the maximum that the purchaser would pay.

This is not as simple as it appears on the surface. Everyone wants as much as possible for his or her property. So do I. But I know from experience that if I overprice that property I am in effect taking it off the market. So it is important to me that my agent for selling is very much attuned to the market because to a degree I am going to use his knowledge to arrive at my price for the property.

I get the agent to prepare a written market evaluation. I get him to tell me the price that he thinks he can get me for the property. I want him to produce what I call 'the three sets of magic beans'. I want three comparables that have sold, three comparables that are currently on the market, and three comparables that have expired. I'll then take a day and look at those nine properties. I want to know whether the agent used the right comparables. I'll do some serious tire kicking and by the end of the day I'll know. I'll be confident that my information is current and accurate and I have a good frame of reference for the competition. Once I'm comfortable with a dollar amount then I'll give him the listing on the basis of that price, but I make sure he understands the rules by which I expect both of us to play this game. I want him to show me the action plan that will be used to market my property. I want to have a yardstick to measure actions by. All agents in your neighbourhood *must* receive the information on your property immediately. You may think your agent will actually sell the property, but 78% of the time an agent from another company will sell it. I want a weekly report even if there is nothing to report. When the property is shown, I want to know the reaction of the people. Price too high, property too small, what? I also list the property no longer than 60 days (minimum time allowed to be on the local board Multiple Listing Service).

I make him understand that he's not supposed to come and try to beat my price down. If you want the agent to convey to the prospective customer that this property is not a good prospect for a low-ball offer, then the first thing you have to do is to convince the agent. He will convey your attitude and position, as he understands it, to every buyer he comes in contact with. So you have to program him.

And you impress on him that you do not want to be snowed under with a blizzard of offers. The two of you have agreed on what the price is going to be and all you're interested in is considering offers that meet your price and terms. Remember his frame of reference. He is trained to bring all offers no matter what they are. You have to help him overcome this conditioning.

There is an added benefit to present this "exterior of firmness" inasmuch as it's going to make him much more effective once he concludes that the price is firm and if he's going to make any money he's going to have to come close to it.

I say 'close to it' because let's face it, when you get down to the short strokes you're going to have to let the buyer get in a few licks. Very few people can find it in their hearts to pay list price for a piece of property. You almost always have to throw them a bone at the end – but it doesn't have to be a big one.

Before you can 'play chicken' with buyers you have to be very much attuned to the market. You have to know, almost to the dollar, what your property is worth as of that particular day. And it will be easy to know when you're wrong. If you're way too low, you'll be swamped with offers; if you're way too high, you'll find out what lonely really is. As we've already said, when you overprice a property you effectively take it off the market. So be accurate.

You have to impress upon the agent that you are as rich as Croesus, as patient as Job, and as skilled a negotiator as Kissinger. Your story is that you don't need the money. The fact of the matter is if you don't get your price, you'll hang on to the property until hell freezes over. If you convince the agent, the agent will convince the buyer.

What explains this? Is this agent mad at you? Are you the focus of an international conspiracy? Nothing so exciting. It's just human nature.

I know from a lifetime of experience that the agent wants there to be a transaction. When I was an agent that was the principal thought that propelled me out of bed in the morning. If there's a transaction, the agent will get a commission. If there is no transaction and if the listing expires, he gets nothing. He's done his work and spent his time to no avail.

Let's look at the numbers. We have a $200,000 listing and the commission is 5%. If the property sells for $200,000 the agent gets $10,000. If the agent persuades me to take $180,000, then he gets $9,000. But he gets it for sure without the danger of the listing expiring. If you were the agent what would you do?

Let me illustrate this with an old fable about the difference between being interested or committed:

Once upon a time a Chicken and a Pig met in the roadway.

The Chicken said, "Let's have breakfast together."

The Pig said, "Good idea. What'll we have?"

The Chicken said, "Let's have ham and eggs".

The Pig said, "I'll get back to you on that."

The Moral: It's important to know what the other guy's priorities are.

What we have here is the difference between interest and commitment. Ham and Eggs is a matter of the chicken having an interest whereas the pig has a serious commitment.

The agent's agenda is not the same as yours. He, of course, is going to serve his intelligent self-interest, as he perceives it. That's why you have to manage the agent very carefully, if you want to maximize your results. He only has an interest while you have a serious commitment.

Because I believe so strongly in the effectiveness of a written action plan that is what I require of any agent that I give a listing to. I want them to tell me in writing exactly what is going to be done for me during the tenure of the listing. In addition to this I require that they check in with me on a regular basis. I will, for example, arrange with the agent that I am to get a call every Wednesday evening at 7:30 PM.

When he calls I expect a report on what advertising was done. If it is print advertising, I want a faxed copy of the ad. If it is electronic media, I want an audio or videotape of the spot. If it's on the internet I want a copy emailed to me so I can see what it looks like.

I want to know how many people called on the ad; how many people saw the property; what was their reaction; and so on. And this is not idle curiosity. I have important reasons for wanting this information. The market might be changing; the agent might be changing or the property might be changing. Whatever it is, the sooner I know about it the sooner I can correct my course. Remember that there were hundreds of miles of open sea on either side of the iceberg that sank the Titanic. If the captain had received the information about the iceberg's location five minutes earlier, he could have avoided it.

I need information if I'm going to make informed decisions. I may want to change something about the deal; I may want to change something about the property; I may want to change the price; I may want to change the agent.

In fact, if the agent lived up to the plan, I renew the listing, if he didn't I will not.

Okay, let's say you're doing everything right and the agent brings you a potential buyer. This is where you get to use all those negotiating skills that you have acquired by dint of hard work and long hours of study. You remember, of course, the first rule of negotiating and that is that whoever is the least emotionally involved has the advantage.

For example, if I convey the idea to the seller that I am a buyer who is prepared to walk away at any time because I know that real estate opportunities are like trolley buses, there will be another one along in 10 minutes, I have a much stronger position. If I convey the idea that I have fallen hopelessly, head over heels in love with the property, I will never draw another contented breath if I am not able to buy it.

You've got to project the image of someone who is totally without anxiety about his involvement with this property. And if you're selling instead of buying you do exactly the same thing. You project the attitude that if you don't get your price then you'll just keep it for three or four generations until some sensible, astute, worldly wise investor is willing to pay what it's worth.

That's not to say that this devil-may-care attitude is the fact of the matter. There may be times when you need to sell this property as badly as you need air to breathe. All I'm saying is that you mustn't convey this to the buyer and therefore you can't convey it to the agent. Human nature being what it is, as soon as there is the tiniest tinge of blood in the water the sharks come swimming over to see what's for lunch.

And 'seller's blood' whips the sharks into a frenzy and the emotions evoked are not of the milk of human kindness sort. On the contrary, the sharks come over to find out just how weak and vulnerable you are. You can be sure that whatever you offer them they are going to bite deeper. Offer the hand and they will tear off the whole arm. Why? Human nature.

Remember, in buying or selling, but particularly in selling the old axiom: "One per cent doubt and you are out!" By sending out the right message about our strengths and keeping all our weaknesses a secret we'll be able to weed out all the real estate investors like ourselves. You're not going to be able to make a deal with someone who plays the game the same way you do. When you do encounter investor types like yourself it will be like playing ping-pong with the mirror. It's interesting but there's no profit in it for anyone.

What you want is to get your share of the good buyers and hopefully some of somebody else's share as well. In order to do this you have to approach the market with the right product at the right price using the right agent. When you do this you will be maximizing your chances to get the optimum results from the sale.

$\sim$

In Essence

The time to think about the resale of the property is before you buy it.

In real estate you should have a 'stop loss' strategy just like in the stock market.

It's important to be in tune with the market because an over priced property isn't really on the market and an under priced property might result in you being hurt in the stampede.

The first rule of negotiating – "Whoever is the least emotionally involved has the advantage."

Send out the signals about your strengths and keep your weaknesses a secret.

Chapter 13

SCAMS & SHAMS

If you give me a dollar I will tell you where the streets are paved with gold. And I'll tell you what you need to know to be smart enough to go and get it. I have that special gift of being able to impart wisdom to people. What's that, you say? If you know where the streets are paved with gold why do you need my dollar? See, it's working just like I said. We've only just met and already you're smarter!

This was one of the toughest chapters to write. Not because there is a shortage of material – no, quite the opposite. There's a mountain of material stretching back to the dawn of history because although the rules of the game change, human nature stays exactly the same. There are thousands of incidents and episodes and anecdotes concerning Shams and Scams to choose from.

If you examined them all, one by one, and after each one you asked the question, "How did this happen? How could people have been taken in by this?". The answer is always the same – Human Nature!

When the first Cro-Magnon said to a couple of his neighbours:

"Look, fellows, you give me ten mastodon skins and I'll sell you those tar pits over there."

"Why would we want them?"

"Because in about a million years someone will figure out a way to extract the oil and then they will be worth a fortune."

They immediatley said: "Where do we sign?"

Today, some glib man in a suit that costs more than you make in a month, wearing a gold Rolex the size of a small cantaloupe, can convince many thousands of people to hand over hundreds of millions of dollars on a premise that is just as far fetched as the tar sands. How come? Human Nature!

There are some almost-universal truths. With the exception of Mother Teresa types and Albert Schweitzer-like altruists, everyone would like to be rich. We are conditioned by our upbringing and by observing the world around us that richer is best. If one is rich, you can buy all sorts of things and do all sorts of things that are denied to those who are not rich. Besides, being rich will prevent you from being poor. Now that part *is* a universal truth.

Another almost-universal truth is that real estate is a good way to get rich. We take this idea in with our mother's milk. By the time we get out of school almost all of us have good feelings about real estate. Sure, there may be some complications here and there but over all, we are conditioned to believe that real estate is good.

So there you have two of the three main components of the Sham/Scam equation. The desire for gain and a frame of reference for real estate. Now we add the third component. That man in the expensive suit with the Rolex who says, "I know how to solve the secrets of the cosmos, subordinate your judgment to mine and I will make you as rich as you want to be!"

And human nature being what it is, people reach for their checkbooks. A sales expert once said to me, "The secret of selling is to find out what people *already* want – and show them how what you've got will help them to get it."

That's why the equation works so well. People already want to be rich. They already believe in real estate. Someone comes along and sings a seductive song and there it is. People simply hand over their money because they believe. And it's this belief that is so easy for the Scam/Sham people to instill. It's an art and it's a mystery to those of us who can't do it, but it's easy for those who can. It is a very simple step for the victims. Instead of making all the individual judgments about the safety and viability of the investment, and these can be dozens or sometimes hundreds of separate value judgments, all the victim has to do is make the judgment that the other person knows what he's doing and is a good person who will take care of them. Once this judgment is in place then this particular universe will unfold the way it inevitably must. The victim will pay over the money and the perpetrator will spend it.

One should note here that there are basically two kinds of these real estate shams. There is the one-on one where a single piece of property is sold to a single investor. These are usually smaller deals. Then there are the development projects where a bunch of investors are brought together to do a development of one kind or another. This latter category rarely involves deals that are one-on-one. They are usually structured as syndications or limited partnerships or some other grouping of lots of people in a single investment or in the same or related series of investments.

For some reason that is difficult to explain, people are more willing to suspend their critical judgment when they are in with a group than when they are by themselves. When it's one-on-one the investor is much more analytical than when a group is involved. Maybe it has something to do with the herd instinct or some atavistic feeling that there is some sort of safety in numbers. Whatever it is, the scam artists take full advantage of this factor.

It is an application of the concept of divide and conquer, but there is a much more important element involved. One real estate philosopher who's name is lost in the mists of time once observed, "Big money has a mind of its own, little money doesn't have any mind at all." As glib as that may sound, pause a moment and examine it.

If you're a big investor and you invest a million dollars in a project, you're going to examine it with a microscope before you go into it. You're going to have your lawyer and your accountant take a look at it. You're going to use whatever expertise you have and bring in whatever experts you may require to examine everything with a fine tooth comb. Because of the size of the investment, you're willing to spend a few thousand dollars to examine it, even if you wind up walking away, if it doesn't fit your formula.

That's at one end of the spectrum. Let's go to the other end of the spectrum where we have someone with a few thousand dollars to invest – maybe ten, twenty or even twenty-five thousand dollars. If you are that person, you are not likely to be as knowledgeable or as sophisticated as the man with the million dollars. And much more relevant is the fact that the size of your investment doesn't have the economy of scale to hire lawyers and accountants to examine it for you.

Besides, if you've ever made a practice of taking deals to lawyers and accountants where you were looking to them for a value judgment you know from experience that they never say yes to anything. Never! If

143

you took them an absolutely perfect deal the lawyer or accountant would say, "I can't see anything wrong with it." That's the best they would say. And it's not their fault; they can't help themselves; it's the way they were trained. If they come to the end of their schooling still capable of saying, "That's a good deal," they don't get the diploma – it's as simple as that.

I never ask a lawyer or an accountant for a value judgment about real estate. I ask the lawyer if the contracts are correct. I ask the accountant if the tax aspects are structured optimally; the value judgments I make myself.

But the small investor is a bit-player in a syndicate and because he doesn't have a big enough investment to warrant spending that kind of money on the investigation he finds it's easier and feels it's cheaper to take everything on faith. It's certainly easier but in the end it turns out to be anything but cheaper. What it almost always turns out to be is a total loss.

For the perpetrator there's another important beneficial aspect of having a bunch of small investors and that is, that as the project goes along no individual feels he has the right to say anything about what's going on. Therefore, there's not going to be anywhere near the ongoing examination or the interference that could come from one single large investor.

This kind of business has a very colorful history. 'Florida swamp-land' is a phrase that has become a part of our language. It is another way of saying, 'worthless, overpriced land that will never have any value'. This is an example of distance making the heart grow fonder. The same way that 'a prophet is without honor in his own country' – it's difficult for a dishonorable con man to profit in his own country. All you have to do is look at those desert tracts in Arizona and California to see what we mean.

Do you think those pioneers of the Scam/Sham milieu sold Florida swamp to Floridians? How many Phoenix residents do you think bought acreage out in the Arizona desert for more money than ground was selling for inside the city limits? Did the people in Beverly Hills pay ten or twenty or a hundred times what arid scrub land was worth just because it was a three hour drive from Los Angeles. Of course not! If it's close enough to go and look at, when you do look at it you know immediately that no one in their right mind should buy it.

But for the perpetrators there's an answer to the problem. Actually, it's easy. You sell the Florida stuff to Californians; the Arizona stuff to Floridians; The California stuff to New Yorkers; and anything you have left over you sell to Canadians.

There just doesn't seem to be any limit to the gullibility of people. They tell the story that in California, land speculators would tie oranges to the Joshua trees (a kind of large cactus) and then sell the land to new arrivals as orange groves.

There's always been this kind of thing going on but it didn't develop into an art form until the late 30s and 40s. It was then that regulatory agencies started getting serious about monitoring the stock market. A lot of sharp operators learned that they could take all the tricks they used selling worthless securities and use them in the area of real estate. Everyone knows that the stock market is risky (look what happened in 1929!) and everyone knows that if you invest in real estate you're as safe as if you're in your mother's arms. The ex-stock market pros became real estate experts, printed up a new batch of business cards and kept on doing business without missing a beat.

The reason it was so easy for them to make the transition was because the principles are exactly the same. It's all just Human Nature – except more so.

You see, the fact of the matter is that you can't cheat an honest man. Go back and re-read that last sentence. It is the key to understanding this chapter. An honest man knows that there is no such thing as something for nothing. If there isn't a spark of larceny in his heart he can't be cheated. So that's the key. You find that spark of larceny and exploit it. Unfortunately, almost everyone has more than a little spark of larceny. And the bigger the spark, the easier the con.

The more larceny in the heart, the easier the access to the pocketbook. It let's greed take over. It blinds people and causes them to ignore their own critical faculties. It suspends the ability to make comparisons and judgments. It's really amazing!

People who have spent a lifetime learning whatever it is that they do for a living, will take all that experience, all that knowledge, all that good judgment (set them aside) and go jump into an area they know nothing about. On an hour's acquaintance they decide to put their trust in someone they've just met and then proceed to hand over their life savings. It is truly amazing!

Almost every time you hear about some project crashing and burning you will hear one of the victims sadly saying, "I thought the government had laws against this sort of thing. How could the authorities allow people to do this to other people?"

That, of course, is one of the main parts of the problem. Because people think that the government is looking after them, so they don't have to look after themselves. It's like the people who step off the curb at a crosswalk as soon as the light turns green for them, virtually under the wheels of oncoming traffic, it's as if the laws of physics have been repealed just because the government says that a car has to stop for a red light. Some investors think the same way. But just because something is against the law doesn't mean anyone is going to do anything until after the fact.

Yes, people think that the government is looking after them, and strangely enough, the government itself thinks that it is looking after people. But people keep losing their money. The government will tell you that they require the people they regulate to make 'full and true disclosure'. It's true, they do. Sit down with any real estate prospectus or offering memorandum and read it from cover to cover. It will say that the project is risky. It will tell you there is an element of danger. It will stress that there is no guarantee. It will say every negative thing just short of having, "Only a damned fool would invest in this!", stamped on every page in red ink. The effect of this bureaucratic overkill is that those few people who do read the offering documents are anesthetized by all the legalese and wind up ignoring the whole thing. "Besides, Martha – did you see the size of the Rolex on that guy's wrist?"

Back in the days of pirate ships in Caribbean various governments were at a loss to control the situation, so they gave 'letters of marque' to freebooters. This was sort of a franchise to go out and catch pirates and any other enemies of the state. They could take their cargo and sink their ships and in various other ways make the world a better place. Well, our government doesn't do a great job of saving us from con-men so maybe they should privatize that particular aspect. Sort of, 'set a thief to catch a thief'. I know a dozen people just off the top of my head who could do a better job all by themselves than all the boards, bureaus and agencies of the government. Just pay a decent commission and you'd be able to stop the scams before they could get started. Someone pinch me, I must be having one of my daydreams!

The main problem is that all the deals start out the same way. You've got three categories of activity and they all look the same at the start. First, you have the out and out Dishonest/Scammer. Then you have the

Honest/Inept person. Thirdly, you have the Honest/Capable person. Everyone looks the same at the start. They all have the same approach. They all make the same claims, the same projections and the investor feels warm and safe with all of them. If any of them don't have the ability to make the investor feel warm and safe, they won't do anyone any harm because they'll never get anyone's money. It's just the convincing ones that we have to worry about.

The Dishonest/Scammer is what he is. If you examine him closely enough you're never going to give him any money. So he is no problem. The Honest/Capable person is no problem because you'll make money with him. The really dangerous person is the Honest/Inept person.

The Honest/Inept person because of his powers of persuasion gathers together millions of dollars and then tries to play with it in an arena where he has no business being anything but a spectator. What usually happens is that he plays in bigger and bigger games with more and more projects. Eventually his need for cash to run his overhead leads him into one nonviable project too many and his canoe goes over the waterfall; and that's the end of it.

Because this scenario looks exactly the same at the end as a Real Premeditated Scam looks at the end, people who were in an Honest/Inept project think they have been cheated. But they're wrong. The fact of the matter is that while the investors only lose what they have in the project, the Honest/Inept person usually winds up totally broke because in an effort to keep the deal afloat he, as the captain, goes down with the sinking ship.

The investor, however, needs to believe that he was cheated. Somehow making an investment that failed because of factors beyond your control or just plain bad luck is your fault, but putting yourself into a situation where you can be cheated is someone else's fault. Therefore if I lost money I must have been cheated – it certainly couldn't be anything I had *any* control over. What explains these thought processes? Human Nature!

We have to remember that although the motivations of the people running the deal are different, the end result is exactly the same. The money is lost. But the steps you should take and the questions you should ask *before* you go into the deal are exactly the same.

What you can't do is you can't insulate yourself from bad luck. If you get into a deal that runs into bad luck, then you're going to lose. As we've already said, the reason you can make so much money in this business is because the factor of the possibility of loss is always present. So how do we filter out the bad deals? You've got to ask the right questions. And if you don't get the right answers you have to walk away. Let's take one example.

I look in the paper and I see an ad that says, "Come to the ABC hotel at the corner of Juice and Spruce on Wednesday evening at 7:30 PM and John Jones is going to tell you how you can get rich and with no risk" or maybe you see the same thing on a television infomercial.

The questions you should ask yourself are:
1. Why are these people doing this?
2. What is their track record?
3. What is the probability for success for a company that markets investment situations this way?

Answer to Question 1: Almost none of the successful real estate developers acquire their investment capital this way. They are doing this because they can't get it from any other sources.

Answer to Question 2: You almost never find that they have a verifiable track record for success in this area of activity.

Answer to Question 3: You will find that more than 90% of the companies that raise money this way wind up going broke and the investors lose all their money.

Okay, let's say that you are a persistent little devil and you get past the first three questions. You decide to attend the seminar. The man with the gold Rolex has the stage and a microphone and he tells you his story. And it sounds so good.

The next questions you should ask him are:
1. Why are you people doing this?
2. What is your track record?
3. What is the probability for success for a company that markets investment situations this way?

His answer to Question 1: We love the little people and because we have all the money we will ever need we are doing this for humanity because all the volunteer positions at the leper colony were taken.

His answer to Question 2: Our methods are so revolutionary that no one on this planet has ever used them. But we have been outstanding successes in practically every other form of human endeavor so don't worry.

His answer to Question 3: Same as his answer to Question 2.

By now any reasonable person would have given up on this situation but if you look in the dictionary under 'persistence' there is a picture of you. So, when this guy phones you in about a week you make an appointment and go to his office. And he shows you the particulars of a specific investment and you ask the same questions again and he gives you the same answers again but now he is stressing how safe and secure and protected you are because your are going to be protected by a *Mortgage!*

And the magic contained in the word 'Mortgage' casts a spell over you. You don't think to examine this closely enough to determine if there is enough value in the property to in fact give you the protection that you need. Just the word 'mortgage' makes you feel all warm and fuzzy.

Besides, if you've gone this far you're probably going to give him your money and eventually you are going to take your place as a casualty in the ongoing battle of the Forces of Evil against the Forces of Good.

The problem isn't with how one regards the answers. The problem is that the person who is going to get stung refuses to ask the questions. It's as simple as that.

Oh, by the way, even after you lose all the money that may not be the end of it. There may have been certain tax deductions that you took that the tax people might not agree with and they'll want that money and they'll want it with interest and even maybe some penalties. Or, the company you invested with might pay you interest for a year or two before they go bankrupt. You'll want to regard that as a partial repayment of your capital but the tax people will regard it as interest earned and they'll treat it as income and want you to pay taxes with interest. Talk about adding insult to injury!

What everyone wishes who has ever experienced one of these deals is that they could turn the clock back to the day they first invested so they could take a different turn in the road. It's no big secret how to not get embroiled in these deals. What you do is don't go looking for them and if you find one presented to you, ask the right questions and then do what any sensible person would do.

Now, let's say that as you are reading this you are in one of these deals right now and it hasn't gone over the cliff yet. Things are still rolling along. What should you do?

What you should do is go and make so much fuss and so much noise and be such a bother that they will buy you out to get rid of you. Get them to pay you off with the next investor's money.

One of three things will happen. Either they will tell you to go jump in the lake and just ignore you, or they will give you your money back. Or you might be the straw that breaks the camel's back and your fuss and complaints will trigger the collapse of the whole deal. But if you don't try to get your money back you're going to lose it anyway, you might as well make the attempt.

How about after the collapse? Here is where people throw good money, time, and energy after bad. One day you pick up the paper and you see where the company can't make its interest payments any more, can't pay its bills, the regulators have issued a cease and desist order, and in general, the fertilizer has hit the fan. Your first knee-jerk reaction is to go see a lawyer. You'll go complaining to the government. You'll join committees made up of other unhappy investors.

If you're looking for therapy, all of this is just as expensive as a psychiatrist and will do the same amount of good as far as getting your money back. Except that with a psychiatrist you might get your medical plan to pay for part of it. Actually, you should have had your head examined *before* you invested, not after.

No, everything you try to do after the fact will probably be a total waste of time. The only practical and realistic thing to do is learn from the experience and get on with your life.

Because as soon as the regulators get involved they are going to get lawyers and accountants involved in trying to put Humpty Dumpty together again. It can't be done. Whatever money is left is going to go for lawyers and accountants fees and the unwinding process will continue until the money is all gone and then that's the end of it. The investors almost never see a single penny. That mortgage that you depended on turns out to have as much substance as a picture painted on a waterfall.

All of this seems so simple. Why is it that every few months we pick up the paper and read about another bunch of people losing their life savings? Don't people ever learn? Sure they learn. But the public has a cyclical memory and it's relatively short. And every year there is a new crop that were in the maternity ward the year before the previous crop. There is a never-ending supply of people who have to learn the hard way. It is the old, old story of the Sardine and the Shark. There is no power on earth that is going to keep them apart – not because of the strengths of the Shark, but because of the weaknesses of the Sardine.

If you know of anyone who is contemplating this kind of investment and you want to do them a favor – give them this chapter to read.

∼

In Essence

The basic component of a scam is one person agreeing to subordinate his judgment to the judgment of another person. Everything after that is just arranging the details.

Big Money has a mind of its own. Little Money doesn't have any mind at all.

Distance makes the heart grow fonder. It is difficult for a dishonorable con man to profit in his own country.

Good deals and bad deals look exactly the same.

Scam or just plain bad deal; it really doesn't matter – the results are exactly the same. Oh yes, there is one difference – in the bad deal you sometimes get some of your money back.

You've got to ask the right questions and if you don't get the right answers you have to walk away.

Chapter 14

FINANCING

Philosopher: "Money is the root of all evil."
Investor: "If money is the route of all evil, someone give me a road map!"

Okay, we've found a piece of real estate that we want to buy and now the next question is, "How do we pay for it?"

The very best way is with no financing at all. Pay cash. That is if you, a) have the cash, and b) don't have anything better to do with that cash. So just write a check and let that be the end of it. That is 100% equity with no financing. This doesn't happen very often. In fact it is so rare that most of us will go a lifetime without ever meeting anyone who has done this. The closest we'll come to it is reading about someone who has done it.

So if we can't or won't do it with our own money then there are two alternatives. We can finance that part of it that is not our own money with equity financing or we can finance it with debt financing. Equity doesn't have to be paid back but someone else owns a piece of the deal. Debt has to be paid back.

If you have the choice, you will usually elect to bring in the equity financing when there is a certain element of risk beyond that which you wish to undergo or, if you're comfortable with the risk, you'll probably elect to use debt financing.

When you use other people's money this is described with the acronym OPM.

A good rule of thumb is – the higher the risk the greater the proportion of the financing should be OPM. If it's the equivalent of wildcatting for oil the OPM should be as close to 100% as you can get it.

If you have the choice, when deciding just how much OPM to use, you have to ask yourself how greedy you are. This leads to the question – how greedy should you be? If you're not greedy enough, you'll be leaving chips on the table for someone else. If you're too greedy, you may do yourself an injury. Everybody has to decide for themselves.

So equity financing could be your money or it could be someone else's money. However, debt financing is always totally OPM unless you are borrowing from your retirement plan or from your spouse at arm's length.

So, we're still at the beginning and we are going to buy a piece of property and we know that we're not going to pay cash so that means we're going to have some equity and some debt. We also know that the equity is either going to be our money or someone else's money or some combination of the two. The rest of the purchase price is going to be debt financing.

Therefore, we have to know what debt/equity ratio we're going to be involved with. If we put 20% down and finance 80%, that gives us an 80/20 debt/equity ratio. This isn't something you will decide. This is something that the lender will decide. Every lender has guidelines for debt/equity ratio and though they will allow you to put in more of your own money, they will not allow you to put in less than the guideline for your particular case.

The leverage factor is very important. This, if things go against you, can cause you more trouble than anything else. Almost everyone who has gone broke in real estate investment will tell you that the major mistake they made was in reaching for too much leverage. They will say that if only they had been more conservative and had aimed to make less money they would have had a better chance of surviving the bad times. But they wanted to maximize the profit so they stretched too far for too much leverage.

Here are the main sources of financing starting with the cheapest and finishing with the most expensive.

First and everybody's favorite is the father-in-law. This is the easiest and best because the price is always right, and if you run into problems you're going to get more leniency here that you'll find anywhere else.

Next is your pension plan or your self-directed retirement plan. If your plan allows you to invest in mortgages on real estate you can sometimes structure things so that you can get at the money in your pension plan. You'll be able to pay yourself the minimum interest the tax people allow (or more, if it suits your purpose) and again, if you run into problems you can be as lenient with yourself as you like.

You can also use your retirement plan as an equity investor. You can grant your own mortgage from your Registered Retirement Savings Plan. The plan must be 'self-directed' and usually it only makes sense if you have a minimum of $50,000 in your plan. Even for business uses there are possibilities. Three people working for a printing plant decided to buy out the owner who is retiring. They persuade eight other employees to join them in an employee buyout. They each had their retirement plans buy $50,000 worth of shares in the company.

The next source is CMHC. This is a good source for investment real estate funding and it is usually a terrific source of financing if you're buying a home to live in. If it's a first home it can be even better. The rates will be the lowest you can find at arms length. CMHC doesn't actually lend you the money but what it does is insure the loans that approved lenders can make to you. If you have the insurance approved, it's a simple matter to shop for the loan. Other than the Vendor Takeback,\ mortgage, this is really the only source where you can get 95% financing. But it costs you. The insurance fee is substantial.

Because the Government is always being pressured to do something about creating reasonable housing you can sometimes look to this source for the money you need, depending on the kind of housing you're involved with and how the tide is running in the money marketplace at that particular time.

If you're investing outside the country, the government of wherever you're investing isn't a very good source. For one thing, you're not a voter, nor a taxpayer, and your other assets (if they want to get at them) are usually in another country – all in all you are neither a very attractive prospect nor are you an attractive target.

Next in line is the Vendor Takeback. This is where the person who is selling you the property agrees to carry the mortgage, or part of it, himself. And why not? If the vendor doesn't need the cash, it's a good investment. Providing there is a sufficient down payment then it's a well secured investment at a better rate than the bank will give on the deposit end. The worst thing that will happen is that a property that the vendor is familiar with will come back into his possession.

But even if you do not have a large downpayment, vendors often provide first or even second mortgages. The Vendor Takeback mortgage is the source of most no downpayment deals, deals that offer abatements and deferred payment structures. It can be the most innovative source of financing.

For you it's good because there are no loan fees, no appraisal fees, no points, it's quicker and it's easier.

Now we have to start going to strangers: Banks and Credit Unions lending their own money – as opposed to CMHC insured money. Now we're talking to people who don't want to run any risks. That's why they grant only 75% maximum first mortgages. They want a big enough cushion so if anything goes wrong they are going to be protected. So the debt/equity requirements and all the terms and conditions are going to be more stringent and the rates are going to be WTTWB – Whatever The Traffic Will Bear.

After the Banks and Credit Unions we come to the Mortgage Companies, Insurance Companies, and Trust Companies. They are just as careful as the Banks and Credit Unions but their rates are going to be a titch higher. If your deal is attractive, you can shop around. If it isn't attractive, you better massage it until it is. For dealing in this arena you are best advised to use the services of a mortgage broker. Your mortgage broker can make sure that your application package is in the form it should be.

Also, the mortgage broker knows his market and knows who's lending in what categories and who isn't. This is one of the areas where you want a professional because the do-it-yourselfer just doesn't fare well. Mortgage brokers can show you the best rate of a number of institutions for comparison.

Next in the line are the private lenders. This is where it starts to get tough. The private lenders take the deals that the banks and the mortgage companies said no to. Their rates are higher. Their fees are higher. They charge higher points. And if you get into trouble you're in a lot more trouble than with a bank or mortgage company.

The last category is what I call the Yellow Pages Lenders. These are the people who advertise a very low rate to bring the customers in but when the deal starts to come together the fees and the points approach stratospheric levels. These are the lenders of last resort. They usually do business in the area of refinancing. Once a borrower has gotten into trouble on an existing loan that borrower will sort of work his way down the financial food chain until he has to go hat in hand to the yellow page lenders.

What usually happens is the borrower is left with just enough financial breath to continue the struggle for a while and a distressing number of these loans wind up going into foreclosure with all the attendant pain and anguish. Naturally, you avoid this category if you possibly can.

Under normal conditions you'll be better off dealing with a lender that is headquartered or that has an autonomous branch office in your area. If you deal with a lender where the person handling your file has to send everything to some other part of the country for approval, you're going to be at a disadvantage. People who are far away don't know the market and they don't know the property and as a result they look at reports written on short memos and make their determinations accordingly. If you have the luxury of choice, you'd be best advised to choose to deal locally for financing.

Refinancing can be easier or harder than the original loan, depending on what has happened with the real estate market and with your property and with the financial markets in the intervening time since you took out the original loan. If you can, you're better off to refinance with your existing lender. But again, it depends. In any case you're going to shop the market and make the best deal you possibly can.

Development financing is a whole separate art form. For this you're definitely going to need the services of a Mortgage Broker unless your name is a household word in the real estate development business. With development financing they care about the security in the real estate but that's just in case you get struck by lightning. What they really care about is the track record of the person doing the development.

Development financing, from the perspective of the lender is not as chancy as it might first appear. That's because of the factor of 'the hold back'. What usually happens is that the lender appoints a Quantity Surveyor whose job it is to measure how much of the development is done and how much it will cost to complete that part that is yet unfinished. The lender, based on the Quantity Surveyor's report will hold back that amount of money from the financing that would be required to finish the project.

That way, if you do get struck by that proverbial bolt of lightning, the only amount of money they will be out of pocket is for the flowers they sent to your funeral. After they have managed to contain their grief, it will be business as usual and they'll get someone else to finish the project so they can get paid.

In any case the lender wants things arranged so that if push comes to shove he can 'fire-sale' the property and come out of it with at least his principle intact. If he feels this is the case the loan will be made, but if not, there is not going to be a loan.

Let's spend a little time on the subject of personal guarantees. There is, of course, the real estate philosophy that says, "A personal guarantor is a jackass with a fountain pen." I think I agree. My overall observation is that if the deal requires a personal guarantee, you shouldn't be in it. I can't count the number of cases I know of where people have been wiped out because they signed a personal guarantee. And I mean really wiped out – not just the business assets, but the house, the cars, the bank accounts – everything gone!

But having said that, there are all sorts of situations where if you want to sit in on the game, you have to sign the personal guarantee. I won't argue with anyone's decision to do that as long as they know in advance what can be involved.

Take for example Christopher Hemmeter. At the age of 58 he had amassed a fortune of $200 million. He got involved in developing a gambling casino in New Orleans and went bankrupt. His bankruptcy statement said he had $720,000 in assets and $87 million in liabilities. The $200 million was all gone. Because he'd signed personal guarantees he lost his homes, his cars, his bank accounts, and – his customized 727 airplane! A reporter asked him in an interview, if knowing what he knows now, would he go into this kind of a deal again. Hemmeter said, "I'm an entrepreneur. An entrepreneur takes chances. Of course, I'd do it again!"

There's a lesson there.

The lesson is that if the game is big enough, you could be betting the whole store. If that's the kind of a player you are, that's all right, you may hit it big. You just don't want to be taken by surprise.

The internet is going to have a large effect on how mortgage business will be done in the future. Today you can go to www.jurock.com, get qualified at a number of different lenders, get the mortgage amount quoted in 64 currencies and best of all find out the very best interest rate for every term.

Every bank, every trust company is on the net. More importantly, mortgage brokers that compare the best rates are on the net.

The old ways of the mortgage dinosaurs are going to be displaced by the new ways of electronic technology. This will be especially true in the area of single homes.

Right now, considering the technology available, it's kind of silly that the entire home buying process has to grind to a halt and everyone stands around and twiddles their thumbs for anywhere from three days to two weeks while the mortgage process limps along with copies of paperwork being physically transported from point to point. The internet is going to change all that.

The first part of the equation is already in place. The borrower has the ability to communicate electronically with a lender or a group of lenders who are anxious to do business. Borrowers have immediate and secure access to these lenders.

The second part of the equation will be a 'scoring' system where the credit checking will be done electronically and actual documents will only be required 'for the file'. Preliminary approvals will be given where merited and final approvals will be given subject to the full-scale document review process.

So get yourself all set for this modern era. No matter which part of the game you play – be it buyer, seller, Realtor, lawyer or lender, you're going to have to know the new ways of doing business. It also is a lot simpler. Before you go to your friendly bank, you can be armed with the best rate and speak with confidence on why you should get it.

Here's some 'how to' pointers. Some ways of saving money in the area of mortgages.

1. *Try not to take the mortgage as a total package just the way it comes off the shelf.* Mortgage concessions are negotiated in exactly the same manner as any other kind of business dealing. The lender is going to present his standard package which is really just his wish list. If you want special treatment, you're going to have to ask for it and you better be prepared to sell the lender on why you deserve special treatment. You better have some arguments ready on why your application is different from the dozen others that he has on his desk. For example, the length of time you've been dealing with the institution, the fact that you have your RRSP and your business and other accounts there. All this will help to negotiate the best rate.

2. *The better you look the better deal you're going to get from the lender.* There is almost always a three-quarter to one-and-a-half per cent discretionary leeway from the posted rates. The operative word here is 'discretionary'. It's up to you to make the lender want to use that discretion. Most of the time all you have to do is ask. The rule of thumb is

that you can knock off three-quarter of a per cent off any mortgage up to a three-year term and a full one per cent for a mortgage over that. And yes, bigger discounts are available at times. If the lender perceives that you are a shopper and if you've given the impression that you know what you're doing then the lender will give you what you want just to keep you from going somewhere else. If you're a 'heavyweight' borrower, you should be able to squeeze out another quarter or half a per cent just because you've got some muscle. One thing is for sure; you won't get any of it if you don't ask.

3. Ask for a longer grace period. We advise our subscribers to always be pre-approved – in writing. Most people take the verbal commitment seriously. I don't. In a fast changing interest rate environment – particularly when rates rise fast – your verbal agreement isn't worth beans. Even if your bank manager is your brother, get your pre-approval in writing. Once you have it you can then make low no subject offers on the real estate you buy. On a pre-approved mortgage, ask the lender to extend the standard 60-day grace period to 90 days. This extra time will help you in your negotiations.

4. Make the lender feel that you will direct more business his way. When you are asking for reductions and concessions and allowances you are asking the lender to take less money. You can sugar-coat this pill by making the lender feel that you are a steady customer who is going to give them more business. If you're dealing with a bank, you could shift your other checking and savings and retirement accounts over to them. This can sometimes make the difference between a yes and a no.

5. Be prepared to put on paper all the factors that point out your strengths. Lenders rarely rely on 'charisma' and other such intangibles when making their decisions. Okay, the Reichmann brothers were an exception – but look what happened there. The more your strengths are delineated and reinforced on paper, the better the chance you will have of getting the loan and some, if not all, of the concessions you're asking for.

6. The person you see at the institution may not be the person who decides, so give your contact person the tools needed to get you what you want. The person you see and charm at the lender's place of business may just be an information taker. There are three principle factors that are going to be considered.

a) Equity You have to know in advance what debt/equity ratios the lender requires for the type of loan that you require and you have to make sure that you have enough equity to qualify.

b) Stability Have you had a presence in the business community for some time? If you're employed or in a business of your own, does your work history extend for enough time to make you look good. If not, be ready to explain why. Erratic behavior and erratic work histories make lenders nervous.

c) Cash Flow Is the lender going to be satisfied that, after allowing for emergencies, there is going to be enough money to service the loan?

7. Give as much security as you can in order to get a more favorable debt/equity ratio. By placing a mortgage on any other property you have, or by offering it as a co-guarantee, or by cross collateralizing, you can dramatically increase the amount that will be advanced. But do it only if you need it for a larger or better loan.

8. Make as large a down payment as you can if it will make a difference in determining the rate. Remember that you're going to be paying this for 25 years and those little fractions of a per cent can translate themselves into tens of thousands of dollars of extra payment. Take a minute and work out your deal. Often, people take out CMHC insurance even if they have 20% down (banks will lend only 75%). Yet, they would be better off taking a 75% conventional loan from the bank, get a small 5% second from either the vendor or another lender and save the (large) CMHC fee. CMHC fees run into several thousand dollars. Only use the CMHC insurance if you take out the full 95% loan.

9. If your 'stability' looks lessened because you've changed jobs recently, do something to make yourself look more reliable. Maybe you can do this by emphasizing a long and uninterrupted period prior to the move. Or, a concise explanation of the reasons for the move that can accompany all the other documentation.

Also, before submitting any loan application, always check with the credit bureau to see what they're saying about you. If there is something amiss in your file that is incorrect, then send in the appropriate documentation and get it corrected. Also, you can enter a narrative into your file to explain extenuating circumstances behind any credit difficulties.

10. If you're self-employed, get your accountant to help you with the numbers part of your application. Lenders have a little more trouble with self-employed people than they do with wage earners. Wage earners are simple to evaluate as far as measuring their ability to repay. Self-employed people are complex to evaluate. If your numbers come from an accountant, it will carry more weight with the lender.

11. If you're dealing with a bank and you're uncertain of your standing and your 'clout', make your initial run at the bank manager rather than the mortgage officer. The manager can make an immediate call on amounts and rates and rate-reductions. The mortgage officer almost always has to get permission.

12. Take advantage of the 'new customer' factor. In the markets where lenders are slugging it out for new customers, you can often score brownie points just by walking through the front door. But if the marketplace is crowded with borrowers you'll do better where they know you. This is particularly important at renewal time. Do NOT automatically renew your mortgage with the existing bank. For some inexplicable reason, banks treat their new customers better than their old ones. You can always get a better deal if you switch!

13. Save tens of thousands of dollars by shortening the amortization period. Don't get locked into the mindset that the 25-year loan is a concept carved in stone. My own favorite term is 17 years. This maximizes benefits without unduly increasing the mortgage payment. The amount you save is astounding! For example: $100,000 over 25 years with a payment of $861, if carried over 17 years at the same rate will require a payment of $978 or an extra $117. That extra $4 a day (if you smoke and stop right now, there's your $4) will save you $82,656 in interest. If $117 a month is too much – do it for half and save $41,328.

14. Check rates to the last minute. Even if you are pre-approved and are closing in a week or so call your mortgage broker to check. Financial institutions like to match their funds. Sometimes, for fast closings and particular terms, institutions give a very favorable rate. Check it out.

15. Try to match your renewal dates to the election years of the U.S. In the autumn of election years – 2000, 2004, 2008 etc. – interest rates are traditionally the lowest. A more cynical person than I am might suspect that the politicians in power do this in order to cheer up the voters. Is this possible? Naaah!

16. Frills and thrills Many times mortgage companies give you the 'thrill' of a toaster, a carwash, airline points, first month payment and other goodies. These are NEVER better than getting your mortgage rate reduced. Think about it. On a $200,000 mortgage a 1% reduction in rate comes to $2,000. That's just in the first year! Now think about the term and multiply. Forget the frills, get the rate cut.

Negotiating financing can be simple or it can be complex. Before you approach a lender it's wise to contact them and get a handle on whatever the policies are for calculating and evaluating things like cash flows and payment abilities. If you're too weak in this area you might need a co-signer.

Everything we said about a guarantor being a jackass with a fountain pen goes double for co-signers. My advice to you is never be a co-signer unless you are getting paid exactly what you'd be paid if you were investing the amount of cash that you are co-signing for. But if you need a co-signer you better just hope that person hasn't read this book. (Also, a benevolent parent or a father-in-law comes in very handy in these situations.)

Equity, stability, and cash flow: Different lenders put different weight on each of these three elements at varying times. A particular ratio that might fly with one lender might flop with another. You need to know in advance what each individual lender requires in this area so you can tailor your application accordingly.

If you're refused by one institution, don't be discouraged. Find out why, do what you can to rectify the problem, then try again. If they say no again, then go on to the next lender. This is where the mortgage broker comes in real handy. But if you're going to use a mortgage broker, use him from the beginning. If you've shopped your deal all over town and everyone has seen it and said no to it, there isn't very much a mortgage broker will be able to do for you.

Don't lose sight of the fact that 'attitude' counts. Lending has a very human element to it. If you're organized, courteous and make a small effort to assist the loans officer, you'll often discover that he will bend over backward to accommodate you – if he can.

A lot of mortgages are turned down just because of poor communication between borrower and lender or when the borrower makes a bad first impression. So, comb your hair, dress like a business person, have your paperwork in a tidy and comprehensive form – in other words, try to make it easy for the loans officer to give you what you need.

Remember that you're going to live with that loan for a long time – bargain hard. You only get one kick at this particular can.

Happy hunting.

~

In Essence

*A personal guarantor is a jackass with a fountain pen.
If you want special treatment you have to ask for it.*

*Time your mortgage renewal dates to coincide with the U.S. presidential
elections.*

*Never be a co-signer unless you are getting paid exactly what you'd be
paid if you were investing the amount of cash that you are co-signing for.*

*Do whatever you can to make it easier for the lender to give you what
you're asking for.*

Chapter 15

VALUE

A cynic is a person who knows the price of everything and the value of nothing. What you want is to be able to tell the difference between price and value – that's the only way you'll ever know if you're really buying wholesale.

In real estate there are four common principle methods of determining market value. In life there is one other overriding principle of value. We'll talk about all of them.

Method 1 is the Replacement Cost Method. This is where all you have to do is calculate what it would cost you to replace it tomorrow in the event that a tornado blew it away. This is a bricks and mortar approach where you separate the building from the land. The bare land is worth whatever it is worth – that you arrive at by the comparable method. Then you figure out what it would cost to replace the building with another building of the same size and quality. Then you make an allowance for the age of your original building plus any wear and tear, and you arrive at the value of the property.

Lenders and insurance companies like to use this method. It is important for them to know what it would cost to replace the property in the event that it burned down tomorrow. Especially when, in tough times, there are so many borrowers who would like to see it burn down.

But again, you have to be equipped with all the information. Let's take for example a property that I've been watching for several years. This property was occupied by a dry cleaning plant for several decades. The property was eventually rezoned for high-rise residential development and was purchased for that use.

The purchaser, because he was buying with the intention of tearing down the building, was only concerned with the value of the land and the demolition costs. What he didn't know was that for about 30 years this dry cleaning plant had been dumping their chemicals into the ground their building sat on. The ground was so polluted that the new owner couldn't get a building permit until he found some way to solve the pollution problem. It took him about three years to solve the problem and get the building permit.

That purchaser thought he was comparing his property to similar properties in the neighborhood that had the same zoning – but he was wrong. The cost in time and money of solving the pollution problem would have had to be taken into account before he was dealing with a true comparable, so in this particular case the replacement method without that information got him into serious trouble.

Another example of one of our very basic precepts – 'Ignorance is not bliss'.

Another place where you can get into trouble with the replacement cost method is if you overbuild an area. If you are in a neighborhood with $200,000 homes and you build a $500,000 home you can use the replacement cost method to tell you the *cost* of the improvement but it won't tell you the value. The only way it will have that value is if you find someone as crazy as you are to sell it to. We've said this before but it bears repeating – all the normal people who can afford to live in a $500,000 home will want to live in a better neighborhood. They will want their $500,000 home to be with all the other $500,000 homes. The replacement cost method is very unreliable. Replacement costs have very little to do with the value a buyer will place on a property. In fact, he doesn't care what it costs. In all markets that experience downturns, the cost of the building doesn't interest the buyer, only the best price. If the price is half of what it costs, so much the better. Conversely in a fast rising market the vendor wants cost plus normal profit plus whatever the market will bear.

Method 2 is the Return On Investment Method. You don't use this for single family residential but you do use it for income producing property. Income producing property is a business or an apartment building, (yes, an apartment building is a business) and businesses sell on the basis of how much money you can make on the money you have invested in relation to the risks you have to run.

Let's take any apartment building. You can separate the land and evaluate that by the comparable method, and you can evaluate the building by the replacement cost method, but the real value is going to be determined by how much money can be made from the investment of running that apartment building.

And that evaluation has to be done as of a certain moment frozen in time. You can't say, "Well, we are in an inflationary economy and every year the value is going to go up X number of dollars so that will add to the return and so my price is going to be calculated with that increase factored into it." Nice try, but that won't work. You can't charge people tomorrow's price today. If you want tomorrow's price, you'll have to keep the property until tomorrow.

The value of any income producing property can only be based on what it will yield. If you try to charge more, people will take their money somewhere else. If you offer it for less, you'll be trampled in the stampede.

Method 3 is the Comparable Method. This is where you compare a piece of real estate to comparable real estate. This is the most widely used method. The accepted wisdom is that comparable pieces of real estate have the same value. The key words that appraisers use are 'recent' and 'similar.'

For instance, you have a three bedroom, two bathroom home with a full basement sitting on a 50 foot by 120 foot lot in a residential neighborhood. One block over there is another one just like it and a block from that there is another one just like the first two. Maybe they were all built from the same set of plans and maybe even built by the same builder.

One could say that if the second and third house each sold last week for $100,000 dollars, that the value of the third house was the same. That would cover the basic concepts of 'recent' and ' similar'. And that's all right as long as we are talking comparables. There is a basic precept in logic that, 'things equal to the same thing are equal to each other'.

But supposing house number one is right beside the city dump and the others are not. That's going to mean that they are not really comparable. The word 'similar' was not properly satisfied. Comparables were similar in look and size but not similar in lot location. So every plus and negative factor has to have a dollar amount attributed to it and that amount has to either be added to or subtracted from the value.

In a fast rising market 'recent' can mean comparable sales from last week, in a slow one it may mean comparables from 6 months ago. The same could apply to out-of-the way odd-ball properties that rarely sell. An acceptable ' recent' comparable sale may be relevant as far back as a year ago in that case. Generally 'recent' means the freshest possible sales are used to compare the property.

You've already read about how important we feel it is to shop the market yourself and examine every property yourself so you will have an accurate frame of reference regarding value. The reason we bring this up is we want to stress the point that in evaluating comparables you can't tell by looking at statistics on paper and you can't even tell by going and looking at property from the outside. You've got to get inside. You have to know the whole story if you're going to draw an accurate comparison.

For example, I know of a house that was used as a comparable in an evaluation. This was an unusual situation because the owner had a very unusual hobby, he raised foxes. Yes, he had dozens and dozens of foxes that lived in that house in cages and the stench that had permanently permeated that structure was unimaginable. You couldn't be in that house for more than a few seconds before your eyes started tearing and your stomach started to do flip-flops. Naturally, this house, which was on the market, was priced about $30,000 less than it would have been if it weren't for the foxes and yet that house and that price was being used as a comparable for houses in that neighborhood.

You have to make sure that you are comparing apples to apples. Otherwise, you're going to have an incorrect picture.

Method 4 is the Cardiac Method. This is the least popular of all the methods. With the cardiac method you stand in front of the property and put one hand over your heart and you say, "This property is worth X number of dollars – I can feel it here – right here, in my heart!" It is, of course, the least accurate of the methods but it never ceases to amaze me how many people actually use this method.

The real point is that you shouldn't allow emotion to enter into your thinking when you are determining value. If you encounter someone on the other side of a transaction who is using emotion and the numbers are in your favor, then by all means let it work to your advantage – just never let it work against you.

We alluded to the four methods and an overriding principle.

The principle is this: Value does not exist in any physical permanent way. Values change and move based on perceptions by buyers and sellers in any given marketplace ... be it real estate or the stock market.

Thus, value can be a very nebulous thing. To some extent value depends on where everybody is bidding and on what! In an earlier chapter we pointed out that it is a fallacy to believe that interest rates drive market values … If you and I believe we can make 30% on an investment, we do not care that we pay a 15% interest rate.

We also discussed that you are not safe with your "location principle." Rather it is the perceptions of the greatest number of buyers bidding for the same commodity that drive values higher (we all want it) or lower (where is the door?).

Thus, remember that no one can forecast a market from emotion. You see a market rise you say: "there it goes I missed it"; if it goes down, "oh shoot, I should have sold." The biggest enemy is always yourself. But the market – any market – is the only analyst that is never wrong.

Your biggest challenge is to overcome emotions and take a reasoned fundamental approach. You have your plan of action, you understand your clear cut objectives and you govern yourself accordingly. Emotions will be kept to a minimum.

When people talk value they sometimes refer to a 'buyer's market' or a 'seller's market'. The seller's market is a myth. The buyer's market is the only kind of a market there is. There is no such thing as a seller's market. The buyer always sets the price. Always. The only thing the seller can determine is if there's going to be a transaction or not.

If there ever was a situation where the seller could name the price then that price would go through the roof. The fact of the matter is that any time the seller moves his price to a point where it is more than buyers will pay then that property for all intents and purposes has been taken off the market.

So please forget about sellers' markets. You've never seen one and you never will. And it's important that you have the right perspective because when you're buying you have to know what your strengths are and when you're selling it is even more important to know what your weaknesses are.

All real estate values have to be calculated on the basis of what they are today. You want to frame your deal on what the values are today. If you have an opinion of what is going to happen in the future that's well and good. But the property you buy today has to be evaluated on the basis of what it's worth today.

The 'opinion' part of the process is a different hat. Your opinion of what is going to happen with trends and prices is your commodities trader's hat. But that's a separate thing. The value of the property on which you're basing the price at which you will either buy or sell is the value that exists right now in the present.

Now just because we say that your opinion is not a part of the present value doesn't mean that it isn't a very important component of the investment process. Real estate is a commodity and as such you can make a lot of money with practically no risk if you do it right. If you have an opinion about what's going to happen in the future, and if you buy at the right price today and that opinion that something is going to happen to make it worth more is correct, you put yourself in a position for an extra win.

If your prediction is accurate, then you win. If what you predict doesn't happen, then you still have a viable investment because you bought at the right price in today's market. For this kind of activity it helps if you have a crystal ball. That crystal ball can be research or it can be knowledge of the market. Whichever it is, your success will be determined by how much information you have and how well you interpret that information.

The dangerous thing about research is that in real estate a lot of the research is history and history is like moose tracks in the snow. The moose tracks in the snow will tell you where the moose has been but they will not necessarily tell you where the moose is going. Only the moose knows that. The history will tell you the trends but trends only continue in one direction until they stop and go in another direction.

Remember that entrepreneur who when asked if he believed in miracles said, "Yes, I do believe in them but I do not rely on them." You should be the same way with trends – believe in them but don't rely on them.

Still, history does have a way of repeating itself – especially the bad parts. And it's especially true with real estate that, 'he who does not learn the lessons of history is doomed to repeat them'.

We should know from either personal experience or from what we read that trends really do not go on forever. Growth in a positive direction is not necessarily a given. People don't keep coming into an area indefinitely. Inflation can't be depended upon like we depend on the sun to come up every morning.

So never pay good money for the future benefit of a trend and never let it be the reason for your buying decision. Future benefit should be like icing on a cake, you get it in addition to, you never buy because of.

Value is also very much a matter of perspective. The most important is the perspective of the buyer. The reason his perspective is the most important, as we've already said is because the buyer is going to set the price. The other two players in the equation are the seller and the end-user. If there ever is a difference of opinion in value between the buyer and the seller, the main player is always the buyer.

His perception of value will determine what he will pay for the property. No matter how strongly the seller feels will only, as we've already said, determine whether there is going to be a transaction or not.

The end user is really another kind of buyer. His perception of value will determine what he will pay for the use of the property and this payment for use will tell the buyer what the property should be worth to him. Like we said, it's always a buyers market – always.

Value, of course, is not a static thing. It changes with the ebb and flow of the demand for the use of the property and changes as property depreciates with age or appreciates from inflation. However, there are things we can do to increase the value of real estate.

We can do physical things of a purely cosmetic nature. Cleaning up and making the place look better can add to its value. We can make physical changes that are a little more serious – we can paint and remodel (good). Or, we can get really serious and start moving walls around and putting on additions (bad). Or, we can get really, really serious and knock the building down and put up something new in its place (it depends).

All of this adds to the value of the property – up to a point. That is the point of diminishing returns. Once you reach the point of diminishing returns you are not adding to the value, you're merely adding to the cost.

So, you have to be careful that you don't put a dollar in, if you are not confident that you're going to be able to get more than a dollar out. And the extra amount you get out has to be worth the time, effort, energy, and risk that you undergo. It's the old story – if there is something better that you could do with the money then that's what you should do with it.

There are other ways to add to the value of property without making physical changes. You can alter the terms so that you make it easier for someone to own. If you do that, it can be said that you are merely adding to the value of your money invested in the property rather than adding to the value of the property but who cares? It all adds to the bottom line.

Sometimes just by taking different factors and marrying them allows you to create value. Take the case of a business that rents premises. You buy the business from the owner and buy the premises from the landlord. Now you're in a position to marry the good-will of the business, which is an intangible, to the real estate. You create a new whole that is greater than the sum of the parts.

Sometime you can attach amenities to the property that didn't exist before. They tell the story of an investor who bought a condo project that was in dire straits. The developer had built a nice product but he got caught in a shift in the market and went broke because he couldn't sell the units and the lender wouldn't give him any more time. Then the lender tried to sell the units but didn't have any more luck than the developer. The investor optioned the property under very favorable terms and then put a very creative plan into action.

He owned an athletic club a half a block away from the condo project. He attached a membership in the athletic club to each condo. If you bought a condo you got a two year membership in the athletic club for free. In a very short time he sold out the entire project and made a pile of money.

What we have here is another facet of the 'empty seat factor'. In the travel business when a plane takes off or a cruise ship leaves the dock with empty seats the owner has lost that money forever, it will never come back. Well that's the same way with the space in the health club. If the health club is not occupied to capacity then every day an exercise machine is idle or a steam room is empty is lost potential. So this investor was adding value to one piece of real estate by attaching an amenity to it that was costing him nothing.

This is just one example. Maybe you could grant an easement, or cut down trees to open a view – the list goes on endlessly.

Speaking of trees, there's all sorts of things you can do with them to add to value. You can cut them and sell the timber. You can cut them and open up views or create extra parking. You can plant them to provide shade and privacy. Think of trees like great big blades of grass and you can 'mow the lawn' every fifteen years or so.

Just watch out for the ecologists and the 'tree-huggers'. Take an axe or a chain saw to a tree as a real estate investor trying to earn a dollar and you will never be lonely again. You will have enough nature lovers around you to provide you with company for a lifetime.

Sometimes there are hidden factors concerning the property that will allow you to add to the value. Or you might see a use for something the current owner doesn't see.

Things like encroachments, easements and zoning limitations can all be contributing factors. For example: I know of a property that abutted a large tract of undeveloped land. Because of a misinterpretation of boundaries the owner of this property had built a very expensive swimming pool and cabana on the tract of land, not on his own property. A new purchaser for the tract, when researching his prospective purchase, noticed this encroachment.

He bought the tract and then told the pool owner he could either buy an easement or remove his pool and cabana. The pool owner paid an amount that was just a few dollars less than what it would have cost him to remove the pool and cabana and rebuild them on his own property. He came out of the whole experience, sadder, poorer, and wiser.

This was a case where someone knew something that someone else didn't know, saw how it could be used to create value and then acted on it. Another example: There was a large abandoned vineyard on the edge of the high desert in California. For decades the land was vacant because no one could figure out a use for it since the vineyard owner had gone broke trying to make wine that no one wanted to drink. Everyone had forgotten that there were four abandoned wells, each one of them about 600 feet deep. In fact there was an unlimited amount of water available from these wells because the property sat on a huge underground lake.

One sagacious investor found out about this underground lake and the four wells by reviewing old county water records. He bought the property for practically nothing, drew up a plan to plant eucalyptus trees and sell the wood for firewood. His rationale was based on the fact that eucalyptus trees grow 15 feet a year, especially if they have all the water they need. He then turned around and resold the property with that plan in place.

When he bought the property the water wells weren't even mentioned. He used the presence of these wells and a use for them to practically double the price of the land. Thus demonstrating that the 'demand for use' is the most important factor in what makes up value.

You have to stay light on your mental feet. Nothing ever stays the same. So look for changes and look out for changes because sometimes things change for the better and sometimes for the worse. Whoever gets the information first and interprets it correctly is going to have the advantage.

And, because nothing stays the same there is no such thing as security. General Douglas MacArthur said, "There is no security. There is only opportunity." This is doubly true with real estate investment.

So the question comes up – when we talk about opportunity where is the line between Investing and Gambling? Hard question. I suppose that if you're interpreting data and 'moose tracks in the snow' and acting accordingly, then you're investing. If you're using a crystal ball and depending on luck, then you're gambling.

Gambling about future changes is very chancy. It depends what kind of a player you are. This is part of the 'knowing thyself' process.

One thing is for sure. If you are going to gamble on changes, you do it for the long term and not for the short term. If you try to do it for the short term, you have a better chance with lottery tickets.

Everyone knows the old saying attributed to Will Rogers, "You better buy some land, they're not making any more of it." Well, that isn't exactly true. Whenever land changes from unusable in some context to usable, or from low density to high density, in that regard it is the same as if some new land has been created. But for this you need the courage and the conviction. The conviction is part of the crystal ball process, the courage is in taking the action.

All kinds of changes can happen. Highways get built, land comes out of the agricultural freeze, ferries move or get established, land that is recreational becomes urban, zoning gets changed; but all of this moves with glacial slowness. If you play this game you don't use a stopwatch, you use a calendar.

Different skills when combined with a specific piece of real estate can add value to that real estate. A sheer cliff face may be of no value to almost everyone, but if you are a bungee jumping teacher or a hang gliding instructor this could be the perfect place for you to open your school. Ideally you, as an entrepreneur, would buy this cliff face from someone who was ignorant as to this possible use and sell it to someone who had the necessary expertise. The equation here is buy ignorance/sell expertise.

Last but not least is the factor of finding that person who will either buy or sell for an amount that will put money in your pocket just because of their subjective opinion of the property. Either they want it or don't want it for a reason that is particularly theirs and has nothing to do with comparables. There are as many examples of this as there are people on the face of the earth. Just remember that value, like beauty, is more often in the eye of the beholder.

∾

In Essence

Basic Logic: Things equal to the same thing are equal to each other.

In real estate you have to attribute a dollar value to every positive and negative factor.

You must not let emotion enter into your thinking when you are determining value.

Value does not exist in any physical permanent way.

There is no such thing as a seller's market. The buyer always determines the selling price.

Value changes with the ebb and flow of the demand for the use of the property.

Chapter 16

SHARKS & FLIPPERS

Anytime there's a real estate transaction somebody is probably making a mistake. When a Shark or a Flipper makes a transaction somebody is making a BIG mistake!

This chapter is going to be about Sharks, the predators who swim through the real estate waters looking for an opportunity to feed. They look for the weak and the unwary. When they find one they gobble him up. They are not bad people. They are simply opportunists who take advantage of other people's misfortune. They don't make the people weak and they don't deceive the people into being unwary. They simply avail themselves of the opportunities when they arise.

We are also going to talk about the Flippers, those real estate investors who look for short-term opportunities to buy and resell very quickly. Very often the function of sharking and flipping is found in the same transaction.

In either case we are talking about real estate practitioners who are constantly sifting through the inventory that is available in the market place until they find someone who is either ignorant or in trouble or both.

As we've observed before there are certain elements of real estate transactions that make it a zero sum game. A zero sum game is where what one person wins, another person loses. For example: your Thursday night poker game is a zero sum game.

Well, in short term real estate transactions one person's win is the other person's loss. If the potential is there for a quick resale at a higher price, then that difference that is a gain to the buyer could be said to be a loss to the seller. Sure, if he had the knowledge or the staying power then he would have sold for fair market value. The difference between that and what he actually sold for is his loss and the other person's gain. In real estate every transaction can be said to be a zero sum game. There is no magic by which value can be created just because property changes hands. The value is always there and what we're measuring is the awareness of that value and/or the ability to hang on to it. This is the milieu of the Shark and the Flipper.

You will hear people say, "Oh, you only can be a Shark when times are very bad," or, "You can only be a Flipper when times are very good and there's an active market with a high inflationary factor." As with so many things in life, this is so and not so – both at the same time. True, bad times make it easier for the Shark and good times with lots of inflation make it easier for the Flipper, but both of them can ply their trades in all kinds of markets and all kinds of conditions.

Good markets and bad markets are relative conditions. Take a duck swimming across the pond. The pond could be twenty feet deep but it only comes up a couple of inches on the duck. That's the way it is with markets. The market is only a template. You could be in the best market in the world but if you have a mortgage you can't pay, that market becomes a very secondary condition. Besides, the quality of the market simply tells us how many various transactions make up the averages. However, the Shark and the Flipper don't deal in averages – they deal in the *exceptions!*

Exceptions happen in all kinds of markets. The trick is in finding them, recognizing them, and taking action before someone else does. The opportunities are always there but you've got to be out there in that marketplace taking advantage of those opportunities or someone else will.

It sounds brutal to say that the Shark is out there looking to do some grave dancing to prosper from someone else's misery. It also sounds cruel to describe the Flipper as an opportunist who will take advantage of someone else's ignorance to deprive them of potential profit. You have to ask yourself where you draw the line between morals and business. Everyone has to decide that for himself or herself.

If you're an idealist, I suppose you might come across someone a day away from being foreclosed on and you might say, "No, I cannot bring myself to profit from the misfortune of one of my fellows. I will go on to something else where I can pay fair market value but at least I will be able to face the person in the mirror." Or, if you have philanthropic tendencies you might find someone who has his property on the market for less than fair market value and you might say, "Hold on a minute, you are way too low under the market. I insist that you let me pay you fair market value so I will be able to sleep with a clear conscience."

Or, to balance the picture we could consider the Jewish boy who was sent to a Catholic parochial school by his parents because he would get a better education there. One day one of the teachers said, "I'm going to ask each of you to tell me who was the greatest person who ever lived and there is a shiny silver dollar as the prize for whoever gives the best answer." One little girl said, "Mother Teresa." Another said, "The Pope". The Jewish boy said, "Jesus Christ is the greatest person who ever lived." And was awarded the prize. As he accepted the silver dollar he said to the teacher, "Just between the two of us, we both know the greatest person who ever lived was Moses, but business is business."

I hold no argument with either view and I'm not recommending any particular philosophy, all I'm saying is that if you play in this game these are where the goal posts are. That's all.

The Shark will always be able to find customers whether it be good times or bad times. All the various categories for grave dancing apply. Illnesses, deaths, divorces, job transfers, business reversals, job losses, bankruptcies, people who got too greedy, too sleepy, or too stupid are all grist for Shark's mill. Bad times simply make the soup a little thicker, but it's always there.

The Flipper has his advantage on the other side of the scale. For him the good times with a rising market and rapidly rising inflation give him the most opportunities. But even in a flat market with no inflation he can find deals, he just has to work a little harder and wait a little longer for them, but they're there. What the Flipper has to watch out for is that 'bigger fool theory' we were talking about in Chapter 8.

There is a tendency in a rising, inflationary market to jump on the conveyor belt at any price because a bigger fool will come along and take you out at a profit. This is fine as long as you are not the last fool in line. Here is where you take advantage of options and subject clauses to give you a way out in case the music stops before you're sitting in your musical chair.

Often you will find an investor who is both a shark and a flipper depending on which way the wind is blowing in the market place. The common characteristics they have to have are the ability to recognize the signs, interpret them correctly, and then to act quickly and without hesitation. Those three characteristics are the toughest things to learn about this business.

When I think about this aspect of the business I picture an old time miner standing at a sluice box, shoveling sand and gravel in and letting the water wash out everything but the nuggets. The more sand and gravel he processes, the more nuggets he's going to wind up with.

We are the miners and the problem is to get the most amount of sand and gravel into the sluice box in the most efficient manner. Okay, what's the answer?

Back in the Roaring Twenties there was a famous bank robber named Willie Sutton. During one of the rare times he was arrested he was asked why he robbed banks. His answer was very illuminating. He said, "Because that's where they keep the money."

In this case our sand and gravel is information. Our job is to process as much information as possible and to interpret it correctly. So where do they keep the information? The information is in the databases and the multiple listings of all the Realtors. The solution is easy. Find yourself an unbiased, independent real estate advisory service or find yourself a professional Realtor. For instance, our weekly *Jurock's Facts by Fax* service features 5-10 deals each week. These are sent to us by banks (foreclosures), owners (that want to get out) and Realtors (looking for quick sales). Since we have a very large subscriber/investor base and we charge NO commissions this is becoming very popular. Call 1-800-691-1183 for a *free* 1-month sample fax subscription. Or find yourself a Realtor (or a handful of Realtors) and let them provide you with the information you need.

I read about one Shark/Flipper who had an interesting modus operandi. He'd developed a technique that allowed him to go up the downstaircase. Rather than try to associate himself with the most successful agent in a company he would walk into an office and talk to whomever had the 'floor duty' for that shift. His theory was that the really big producers had their hands full and probably already had a set of pet clients that were going to get first look at any of the good opportunities that came along. But the newer agents or those who were less busy had all the time in the world to provide him with the information he needed and to do the research that he wanted done.

You certainly don't have to be shy. If you identify yourself as someone who is in the market and who will act decisively when you see something that fits your formula, then you will have no shortage of agents who will want to work for you. But you have to make sure that they understand the important elements that make up your formula.

Almost all the trouble that ever arises between clients and real estate agents comes from a breakdown in communication. It is always the fault of the client because he hasn't communicated the parameters of his formula to the agent in a form that he understands and believes. Remember, it is not enough for the agent to understand when you say you will only buy houses with red roofs – he has to believe you or both of you will waste a lot of time looking at other colors.

The supply of cooperative agents is practically limitless. This is especially true when there is a down turn in the real estate market. Anytime you pick up the paper and see that real estate offices are closing because of a drop in the volume of business or that the sales statistics are down by even a small percentage, you know that there are hundreds of agents who will do almost anything to be able to take a buyer in tow.

I've seen situations where in a slow market an agent has shown a fussy buyer over 50 properties, simply because this was the only buyer he had on the string.

Once you've actually done a deal with an agent you will own that agent for life.

Having said this, from the client's perspective, let me direct my remarks to any agents who might be reading this.

As an old branch manager, I spent a lot of time teaching salespeople this principle:

Work with anyone you think is a buyer – but if he gives you a set of parameters and you bring a property that fits those parameters and he doesn't buy, then something is wrong. If you've misinterpreted his parameters then you have to recalibrate, but if he still doesn't take action than you better cut him loose.

What you've got is a time waster and your time is the most valuable commodity you have as your stock in trade. Knowing what to do and who to do it with are parts of the equation. The next question is where? Where is the best place to find these opportunities? The quick answer is – everywhere! The Shark and the Flipper find their deals everywhere because they are looking for anomalies. Situations where the owners, for one reason or another, are out of sync. But a slower, more considered answer is to go where the competition might not be quite so prevalent.

This will not be so much a geographical designation as it will be an economic one. You will find the least competition in deals that are a little too big for the small investor but not large enough to be of interest to the big investor. This is also where you will be able to make the best use of the real estate agent because he will have fewer people to show this size of deal to.

Those are the waters that you want to fish in. You want to fish where there is going to be the most opportunity in relation to the amount of competition. But being in the right place in the market is only a part of the equation. The factor of acting decisively is the single most important element that separates the winners from the also-rans.

You've heard the expression; "Cash is King". It is one of the universal truths. The only exception would be that rare situation where one of the parties to the transaction is in a tax continuum where taking cash will not be the best thing for him to do. But that is so rare that it isn't really a relevant factor. Everything else being equal – cash is indeed king.

You will make your best deals where and when you can buy for cash and sell for paper. You'll get your lowest prices and best terms and move to the head of the line when you're buying for cash – particularly in a down market. And you will get your highest prices and best terms and be the first choice of purchasers when you are selling for paper.

We know lots of people who make a business of this. They buy for cash and sell for paper and then when they have amassed a little portfolio of paper they sell that paper and turn it back into cash – or, they hypothecate it and borrow cash to do it all over again.

If you're Sharking or Flipping these techniques are going to make you as effective as it's possible to be. This, of course, is only possible if you actually have the cash. If you don't, you have it do the best you can.

Sometimes you'll be better off to partner up with someone who does have the cash. If you have a good deal you should have no trouble finding someone with cash to be your partner. Two of our subscribers, a young couple, went to Edmonton in the summer of 1997 and in 9 months assembled a portfolio of $1.9 million in real estate. All of it comprised of single family homes (best for capital gain), all of them with a basement suite (best return for low down payment properties) and none of them were bought with their own money! They found willing investors in BC who wanted the play but no work; they put up between $5,000 and $20,000 per property and the couple and the investor bought the property together. The couple did the work, found the deal, the tenants and now manages the properties. Cash flows run over 15% and in three pre-determined years (remember the good joint venture agreements spell everything out beforehand) they will sell and split the profits. Of course, here is where good timing really helps.

Robert Allan, the author of *Nothing Down*, used to boast that you could take away all his money and his credit cards, take him to any city in the U.S., give him $100 for expenses and in 72 hours he would have bought at least one piece of property.

If you have a good deal that needs cash, you could make up a sign that says, "I have a good real estate deal but it needs cash and I will split the profits with whoever puts it up." You could then put on your best suit and go stand on a downtown street beside that scruffy person who has a sign that says, "I will work for food". Just stand there holding your sign and before the day is over someone will be willing to talk to you about your deal.

Speaking of Robert Allan, let's talk about the real estate gurus that want to teach you how to get rich in real estate. This is always a seductive song for would-be Sharks and Flippers. It seems so simple. Just take their course for X number of hundreds of dollars and then just go out and do it and you'll live happily ever after.

The information that is taught in those courses is readily available in any number of books on the subject that are on the shelves of the public library. All you need to have to get a library card is a pulse.

The information is readily available for free so I am not a big fan of any of those courses. Mind you, they can't hurt – the information comes to you in neat little bundles that sound just terrific when you first hear them. They just aren't the be-all and the end-all that they purport to be. Most people who take those courses go home afterwards and put all the material up on the bookshelf and they move onto 'Someday Isle'. They say, *"Someday, I'll do something about this."*

Getting out in the field and taking action is still the most important part of the equation. When you do go out in the field the question is always, 'How far afield do I go?' In geographical terms, how far in miles or how far in travel time should you be prepared to go?

It all depends on what's happening in your own area. If times are good and the opportunities are available, you can do business in your own back yard. If times are tough and all the action is somewhere else, then you might have to cast a wider net. The successful Sharks and

Flippers I've known have done their most and their best business fairly close to home.

Although it helps to be a contrarian, too. Our lead story in January 1996 was "Not A Cow In Sight," and we talked about Calgary. This city in our opinion was no Cow Town, it was the second largest head office city in Canada, vacancy rates were falling, and inward migration was strong. But the crowd was still playing in Vancouver. The time to buy in Calgary was then. In 1999, while everybody was playing in Calgary, we were telling our subscribers to look at the troubled situations in BC.

I know one very successful person who has as a rule of thumb that he won't go more than three hours driving time from his home. That way he can, at the very worst, go there and back in a single day. But it depends on a lot of factors. It depends on the size of the deals you're doing and how much money you can make. Hey, if the price is right, you'd go to the dark side of the moon. If the price isn't right, you wouldn't go across the street.

Another question to consider is when to keep and when to flip. This question is a toughie. You run across it in all the areas of business, especially, for example, in the stock market. When to stay and when to go – what's the answer?

Let me use an analogy to shine some light here. I have a friend who in his younger days was a taxi driver. And he was the best taxi driver in his city. He consistently made more money than any other taxi driver did. His secret was a simple one. Taxi calls are dispatched from various zones that the city is divided into. They go on a first-come-first-served basis to the cabs that are booked into those zones. He knew from experience where the active zones were at various times of the day and as he explained it to me this way – "The zones of the city are like the squares on a chessboard. I know where the other cabs are and I know where the calls are likely to originate. I never let my cab stand still if there was a chance to improve my position; and I never moved my cab if I was in the best possible place to be."

If there is something better to do with the money, then get rid of the property. If there isn't something better to do with the money then stay where you are. However, you have to be examining your position all the time because the market is always changing. Nothing ever stays the same. It's like that old movie where Lilian Gish is running across the ice floes – if it's time to jump, you'd better jump!

One of the things that you've got to watch out for when you're looking to play the flipping game is to make sure that you're not trying to do it with another pro on the other side of the net. You will find that this is usually an exercise in futility. Sort of like taking in each other's laundry. Unless, of course, the market is running up like a rocket and everyone is playing the 'bigger fool game'. But with that sole exception, you don't want to be dealing with another pro.

One of the things you look for is how long the property has been on the market and how long the current owner has had title. If the property has only been owned by the current owner for a short time, or if it is still in the name of the previous owner, then this is a great big red flag that says, 'Flip in progress'.

There is only so much room for profit and sooner or later the property has to be sold to someone who is either going to keep it or use it, operate it for cash flow or keep it for the normal effect of inflation. As with everything in the jungle, 'there are only so many bites on the carcass'.

Another category of seller that you want to avoid, is the developer who is selling off a project that he has just developed. There's no room to flip here because you're up against the marketing budget and the marketing personnel of the project. The only exception to this is a project that is so wildly successful that you are able to get one of the last units. The only problem here is that the last units sold out of a project are usually the dregs. There are rare exceptions to this rule but they are so rare that if you discounted the possibility, you wouldn't be far wrong.

One of the most powerful tools that Sharks and Flippers can use is the long closing. A long closing is like a free option. If you have 60 or 90 days to find a new buyer and effect your resale, it will be like the money fell from the sky. If you are fortunate enough to be able to write in some subject clauses that will allow you to get out of the deal without a loss, it's even better.

The powerful thing about subject clauses is that after 60 or 90 days you can go to the vendor and say, "Look, I can't consummate this deal because my subject clause hasn't been satisfied but if you give me a 60 or 90 day extension I'm sure I can put this together." Then the vendor has to choose between the devil he knows, which is you, or going back on the open market where he has to start all over again. You'd be surprised how often and how easily those 60 and 90 day extensions are forthcoming. After all the dust settles, you wind up having the equivalent of a six-month option for free.

We've spoken about cash being king. One of the places where cash is really king is at real estate auctions. To play the real estate action game you need to have certain qualities to avoid getting killed. You need:

• Market Knowledge
• Discipline
• Patience

Without all three they will hand you your head. You have to be able to go to an auction and sit there all night, bidding only up to your limit and no further and then be able to go home empty handed. You've got to be able to do that time after time until you get what you want.

Auctions have been around for centuries. In Canada, auctions are relatively new. In Australia almost all real estate is sold by auction. *There are two kinds of auctions.* One is driven by the developer wanting to find a new way to market units. This one you want to avoid. Few deals here. Generally, these are reserved auctions (if the developer does not get his 'reserved' price he doesn't sell). The other auction is the one driven by the financial institutions. They want to clear out the development to get the most cash back as soon as possible. This is where you want to be. Generally, all of the units or at least a good portion have 'no reserve' (any price will get the unit).

Things to remember about auctions:
1. *Auctions are never haphazard.* They are carefully coordinated and timed to create the maximum level of buying urgency. The idea isn't to give you a deal. The idea is to get the maximum possible return to the vendor/developer.
2. *Watch out for shills.* While no reputable auction house would do such a thing, the un-reputable one might employ a shill to bid against a legitimate bidder to boost the final price.
3. *Do your due diligence beforehand.* Look at the units. Identify one or two you will bid on and don't bid on anything else.
4. *Position yourself in the auctioneer's sight.* If bids are made at the same time, tradition says the bidder closest to the auctioneer takes the deal.
5. *Auctions are a psychological game.* Do a head count when you come in. If there are lots of noses and not too much product, come in bold and strong right off the bat. If voice bids are allowed, don't wait for the

auctioneer to chide the bids along but jump in with a strongish bid. This will overawe the other bidders (there is so much time left after all) and allow you to scoop up a place. A good auctioneer with a full room will actually encourage a 'good buy' up front to get the crowd's appetite heated up. But as the night goes on and the remaining bidders fight for dwindling product, bidders actually end up buying at over market prices.

6. *If it is a cold and miserable night – maybe the sale wasn't well advertised – and the auction room is half empty, the opposite might be the best strategy.* Rather than roaring in, wait for the true buyers to spend their budgets and then make your move.

7. *Never go in without your finances primed and ready.* As in a large enough deposit to hold your suite and a pre-approved mortgage to allow for a fast close.

8. *Make your bid in smaller than asked for increments.* Once the bidding slows and the auctioneer has bounced along in $10,000 increments, offer a much smaller increment. Say you are slowing around $120,000, to his question "who will give me $130,000" offer $121,000. Often that will become the final bid.

Never forget that both a bank auction and a developer's auction have only one objective: sell the units. If the unit you pre-inspected didn't sell and/or your bid wasn't accepted, consider going back to the auctioneer immediately after the auction and offer to buy the unit if the price is right. The auctioneer eats only what he kills. He will go to the developer to check and maybe you will still get it at your price. I have seen this work very well, if the bank or the developer needs to have some sales and the auction was a disappointment. The frustrated developer might decide to wash his hands of the whole thing and let you have your unit for cheap.

When it comes to auctions, you never know when you're going to get lucky. People get tired, people get bored, people get impatient and all of the sudden it's towards the end of the auction and you're the only customer in the place and you're there with the knowledge and the cash and no competition and you can do yourself some serious good.

An auction is a great way to buy low and flip high. An auction really appeals to the flipper. Quick in, quick out.

Generally speaking, I have seen a lot better deals made at auctions (sometimes even with reserved opening bids) than at foreclosures.

While foreclosures appeal to the shark, in most parts of Canada (unlike the United States) you have to be a very patient shark – which is in itself an oxymoron. The foreclosure dance is carefully choreographed to benefit the homeowner as much as possible. Banks and lenders have a tough long drawn-out process ahead.

If you are trying to find a foreclosure property, be very patient and don't expect anything to be easy. The only successful sharks fishing the foreclosure waters are found in those sharks that deal with the owner during the 'order nisi' period directly and consummate a deal with the owner before it gets to court.

Be aware that you have to be sensitive. Rather than pounding on the door, chortling in the owner's face and demanding a deal, always be aware of leaving owners with face. Give them a call, drop them a note or even make that 'gentle' tap on the door and tell them their property just caught your eye and you are wondering whether they ever considered selling.

Negotiating with the owner is different than doing the dance with the bank. Stresses are fewer, particularly if the deal can be consummated leaving the owner with some cash in the transaction. With all the write-ups in the regular press to the contrary, we see very, very few investors in this particular area that are consistently successful. The same goes for the much touted late night TV 'tax sales'. Usually they refer to U.S. situations where foreclosure and repossession laws are much tougher on sellers. Rarely, unless you are dealing with vacant land in the boonies, does a property sell for taxes owing in Canada.

Another good area for flipping is land assemblies. If there are several parcels involved, you can step in and get long options and advantageous subject clauses at prices above what the fair market value would be for the individual parcels. When you've got it all together, you're in the position where the new whole is much greater than the sum of the previous parts. After all, if you were one of the parcel owners and someone comes along and wants to pay you more than your property is worth wouldn't you give consideration to such an offer? These kinds of assemblies are particularly effective where zoning has just changed or is about to change.

So whether you are going to be a Shark or a Flipper, or both, your success is going to depend on accurate, up to date information that is properly interpreted and then acted upon expeditiously. If you say it quickly it sounds easy, but it is as much an art form as a business. Start small and build to where you want to be.

~

In Essence

Sharks and Flippers can both ply their trades in all kinds of markets and in all kinds of conditions.

The Shark and the Flipper don't deal in averages – they deal in the exceptions.

You will find the least competition in deals that are too big for the small investor but not large enough to be of interest to the big investor.

You will make your best deals where you buy for cash and sell for paper.

There is only so much room for profit and eventually the property has to be sold to someone who will keep it.

Chapter 17

REITs, HOTEL CONDOS & LIMITED PARTNERSHIPS

*Once upon a time there were three brothers. One of them invested
in Real Estate Investment Trusts (REITS) and Syndications,
another invested in Limited Partnerships and the third became a
bull rider in the rodeo. The first two always considered the third
one to be the sissy of the family.*

In this chapter we're going to talk about REITS, limited partnerships and
condos operated as hotels. In short, we're going to deal with a lot of
ways that you can go into business with strangers where you have
virtually no control over what's going to happen to you.

Actually, this chapter should be in a book about the stock market
because these activities have much more to do with securities than
they have to do with real estate but we're going to deal with it here
because these investments involve the use of real estate and they are
sold as if they were real estate.

Before you deal with the matter of how you evaluate and rate these
kinds of investments you have to deal with something that is much
more basic and that is the question, "Should I or shouldn't I be a player
in this game?" After you finish reading this chapter you should come
back to this paragraph and ask yourself that question. If the answer is
no, then there is no need to reread the chapter.

Any time you are a minority shareholder or participant in a venture
then you are in effect handing over your money to someone and saying,
"Here you are, take this money and do the best you can with it." Therefore, the only thing that counts in the evaluation process is track record.
That, of course, is not the only thing that counts but it outweighs the

other factors by so much that it might as well be the only thing that counts.

As we said in Chapter 13, you have to ask: "Where and when did the guy who's going to be running this show do this kind of thing before where the investors were satisfied with the outcome?" That seems simple enough doesn't it? You would think so, but the fact of the matter is that almost no one ever asks that question.

And that's too bad because the answer, if it isn't the right one, can save you all kinds of money. Mind you, it can only save you money if you turn on your heel and walk away.

You'll hear all kinds of sales pitches. You'll hear: "Well, this guy hasn't actually done this exact kind of project before but he's done things similar to this and he's really a marketing genius!" Or they'll tell you: "This is new, this is unique, this has never been done this way before and this has some new twists and besides market conditions like this have never existed before."

But, if you're wise, you will require a satisfactory answer to the question: "Where and when did the guy who's going to be running this show do this kind of thing before where the investors were satisfied with the outcome?"

The odds are that if you make an investment without getting a satisfactory answer to that question you're going to be sorry. The sad fact of the matter is that most people allow themselves to be distracted from the question or don't even ask it to begin with.

Okay, having put in the necessary preamble, let's examine what it is we're talking about.

The Limited Partnership and Syndication

Unfortunately, most of the scams and shams, many of the investor losses, are found in the limited partnership area. That is not to say that there are no good ones and that there will be no good ones in the future. Just that many of the 'fringe operators' fish in the limited partnership waters. It sounds so sexy: 'Limited Partnership'. My losses are limited, right? True but so are your rights. Let's take a quick look at the bewildering array of partnerships and joint ventures – limited or otherwise.

In the end it all comes back to Chapter 7. What is your business plan? What do you want to achieve?

Like all deals that go sour there remains that investors did not have a clear understanding of what they were buying. They didn't think through the potential downside and the implications of what and how they are going to be able to deal with it.

In a small partnership, the staying power of the other party is vital. Will he or she have the nerve to hang on, or decide to bail out, if the market gets volatile? All too often one person goes in with one set of expectations; the other goes in with another. While they've spent hours crunching the hard data, they've often not spent the heart-to-heart time analyzing the deal from their mutual point of view.

Joint ventures encompass a broad range of relationships and structures and can mean vastly different things to different people.

1. A single-purpose corporation that is owned jointly

This is the simplest way. A one time company is formed with each participant a shareholder. Here there is limited liability for the participants (if the deal explodes, at least you do not lose your shirt in a lawsuit). This entity doesn't permit any flow-through of income or expense.

2. A co-tenancy relationship where each party has an undivided co-ownership interest in the real estate

Here the liability is separated; the parties aren't jointly and severally liable for the actions of the other. Income and expenses can be lifted out for tax purposes at the individual level rather than at the joint-venture level. The benefit comes directly to you. Co-tenancies have no communal ownership and the intention is to share gross returns and not net income. They're often used for a situation where there's a passive and an active participant. They're often effective where one party provides land and/or financing and the other puts in the management or development expertise.

3. A partnership formed for a single project

Here a joint contribution of money, property, assets, knowledge, expertise or other contributions come together for a specific project. There may be a right to a joint property interest in the subject matter, a right of mutual control or management and a right to participate in profits.

There are two kinds of partnership. A general partnership is where all parties have unlimited joint and several liability. In a limited partnership, the liability of passive participants can be limited to the amount they've contributed or agreed to contribute to the venture.

There are more subtleties and other types of co-ventures. There are limited partnerships that have the lender participate; there are others where partners in property are secured by mortgage bonds ... the list goes on. All varieties come with different tax structures, benefits and pitfalls.

Before entering into any partnership you should know:
1. Who owns what and what precisely is the percentage everybody has.
2. How much everybody put in and if they are putting in know-how instead of cash, how is the non-monetary contribution measured?
3. Really understand the financing of the deal. Recourse or non-recourse? Collateral security? Guarantees?
4. If something unexpected pops up, how will it be met?
5. What fees or compensations will be paid to the parties? Particularly if the deal is marketed through the financial planning community. I have seen dozens of limited real estate partnerships that paid the financial planner 10% up front, the financial planners 'house' – the company a further 3% – 5% and some 'front-end loads' in deals sold between 1993 and 1999 were as high as 27%!
6. When and how will the cash flow be distributed? This is really important. In some there is no expectation of return for 10 years and it says so right in the 'offering memorandum' - that of course no one reads.
7. How do I get out? At what point can I sell? When is the partnership wound down?
8. What happens, if? What are the remedies in event of default? Will my interest be diluted? Can I be forced out and if so, will it be at a discount? Can the other party make a default loan and at what rate?
10. If everything refuses to break apart cleanly, what (shot) guns can be brought to bear to remove the impasse or dispute? Is there a right of first refusal?

You have to know. In order to know you must ask. Don't be shy. Ask direct questions and make your own inquiries. Ask for financial statements and the names of prior business partners. Check them out. The biggest deal killers aren't the scammers. Usually it is either a lack of 'additional financing' that can't be raised or shifting real estate markets (the timing is off by a year) and again interest costs kill the deal.

Often we are asked to get into limited partnerships for tax reasons. The reason is simple. In a corporation, tax is calculated and payable at the joint-venture level. On the downside, losses can be 'trapped' and rendered useless or it becomes difficult or impossible to use other business losses to shelter income. In a partnership the income is calculated at the partnership level but then can be attributed to the partners. This means the income or loss can be 'flowed through' to the individual participant. But never lose sight of the fact that the investment must stand on its own feet. Tax considerations are important but should never override the question: "Does the deal make sense if there was no tax consideration?" Again, I have seen dozens of limited partnership participants in real estate not only lose all of their investment monies in a sour deal only to face recapture by the tax authorities as well. Clearly if there are 5 friends, one a lawyer, one a general contractor, one a builder, one a developer, one Mr. Moneybags and the timing in the real estate cycle is right as well as that they all know what they are doing ... limited partnerships can work well. All others ... caveat emptor.

The Real Estate Investment Trust (REIT)
Without going into tedious detail, REITs are sort of like a mutual fund pivoting solely around real-estate investments. You put your money into a common pool; properties are acquired, sold and moved around. The assumption: the clever folks overseeing the REIT will make money from the hither and yon. And, of course, you will get a proportional piece of it as – it's assumed – your share value appreciates. The popularity of REITs throughout North America in the nineties is astounding. The fast rising stock market has seen huge pools of cash move into these income producing real estate plays.

Just look at the numbers. In 1991 these kinds of trusts owned 50,000 condo units in the U.S. Just six years later, in 1996, the *Wall Street Journal* reported that they held 600,000 condo units. There are projections showing REITs owning over 900,000 units in 1999.

Now, although the investment medium is the same, there is a big difference in investing in a real estate limited partnership and investing in a REIT. When you invest in a limited partnership you are almost always locked in until the property is disposed of. You're in and you can't get out. If circumstances change for the worse, you're in there for the duration. But a REIT is traded on the stock exchange and you have liquidity.

REITS usually have strict limits and a specific mandate as to what they can do. If they invest in income producing property, there are regulations on how they distribute the dividends. Again, this is an element that you don't find in the average limited partnership.

These vehicles have not always been successful but generally they perform better than limited partnerships that contain provisions for investor redemption. The reason they perform better is because they don't have to sell real estate to meet these redemptions. They simply take less and less share value out of their sales. But never lose sight of the fact that with all investments of this type you are buying the management.

Should they be your investment of choice? Well, first, the caution. Like most real estate oriented mutual funds or the equivalent, REITS have already had a very checkered history. Colour it painful.

In the mid-1980s, REITS in the United States and Canada experienced huge losses when business properties in certain cities got pranged. While some REITS saw solid gains in the 1993 to 1997 period it's all relative. Most are again off in value.

Be aware of the essential difference between a REIT and a real estate mutual fund. Real estate mutuals are 'open-ended' in that the client/customer could ask to redeem the value of the shares – and redeem whether or not the fund had the ready money or not. Result: when markets cool slightly and investors want out, many funds find themselves carrying a heavy redemption load. Forced to sell into an already depressed market, the end result is a sort of dreadful snowball. Sell to meet your obligations, watch the fund value fall as a result, watch while more panicked investors rush in waving their unwanted paper. No fun for anyone. Of course, there's fun, and there's fear.

While REITS also rise and fall with real estate values, they are 'close-ended': X number of units are issued and traded on the stock exchange. The value of the limited number of units is dependent upon the perceptions of the stock-market investors. If it's beloved, it's worth 'lots' of bucks. If it's not, it's not.

REITS do give the investor a proportionate piece of the assets held by the trust. Real estate assets. Often and primarily this means commercial properties. There are implied risks:

1. The buildings owned by the trust may not generate enough cashflow to carry them. Result: a drop in income.

2. If the stock market slips in general, REITS slide down in tandem whether or not that individual REIT has great assets.

3. To control the maximum for the minimum, REITS usually invest in highly leveraged properties. Translation: high risk and the potential to lose a lot.

Still, it's not all bad news. Courtesy the capital-cost allowance, REIT income is somewhat sheltered from the ravages of income tax.

If you think to invest in REITS, look at the specific REIT and really look closely at that REIT and the management and/or principals' previous performance. (Many of today's REITS are yesterday's real estate mutual funds. Although they're dressed in new clothes, they have a pretty threadbare history of terrible performance.) Check out the asset-mix (actual properties, not 'potential' buys) owned by the fund. You want to see the actual meat and not be fobbed off with a bunch of magic has-beens. It's all a matter of perception. And that is the key to all such investment. We investigated a number of REITS in 1998 and concluded that – in our opinion they paid too much for properties and would be underperforming in terms of expected income ... and yet investor bid up the stocks. Thus, primarily you have a stock market play here, not a real estate one.

The Condo Hotel

In January 1997 the headline in our newsletter read: "How to take a $220 per sq. foot apartment and sell it for $480 per foot? Just call it something else."

It used to be so easy. In the beginning there was the fee simple, the clear title, guaranteed by the Torrens System of Land Registration assuring your ownership against any and all. Then there came the Strata Title and to some all was lost. Even in the enlightened seventies there were those who foresaw trouble in the hallways, debates about "my wall goes exactly to the center of your wall" and fist fights around the communal garbage container.

We have come a long way since the original strata suites were on top of each other or side by side strata townhouses. Now we have two level strata townhouses on top of a suite, suites on top of townhouses, a mix and match of design – a veritable hodgepodge of variations of the theme: residential home ownership with shared common areas. But hold it ... only residential? We also have strata warehouses, strata mini storage, strata retail space, strata office space ... again all designed for a single purpose: to provide space for living, working, storing individual owners who share some common purpose of use.

While in some cities the concept didn't really catch on (Edmonton has fewer than 16% of its housing stock available as strata units), Vancouver's condo buyers are grabbing more than 50% of all real estate units sold; 72% of buyers on Vancouver's Westside buy condos.

Is it a function of lifestyle? A new acceptance? Perhaps it is a little of both with a healthy dose of 'lower price' added. Many people can simply afford nothing else in high priced cities.

But as earth shaking as the strata title introduction was, now we have something as new, as revolutionary. The 'hotel' strata unit has gained new popularity. After spurts and starts for some 18 years (with some cases of huge losses for the investors), strata hotel units are popular once again.

We experienced buyer line-ups at Whistler hotel units, weekend hotel blowouts and downtown slam-dunks. What is happening, what is the attraction, why the sudden excitement? It sure isn't the investment performance of past hotel deals that makes investors rush in. Clearly, while some of these previous investor-created hotels are today fine operating hotels, investors took a long cold (hotel) bath.

It all started at Whistler, when measured against the traditional sales performance of real estate, new hotel type units sold like the proverbial hot cakes. Statistics indicate that single family homes and lots appreciated in value much faster, that 'phase I' units rose in value somewhat less and 'phase II' units rose in value *a lot less*. Yet, people couldn't wait to jump in. (A 'phase I' unit carries an implied moral obligation to rent, a 'phase II' has a legal obligation to be rented out with limited personal use), Because of the successes, a bewildering array of 'differing use' options were produced in the later 'phase II' units in 94/98 and culminated in the new hotel type units. (Also see Chapter 21.)

Who can argue with one-day 'blow-out' successes? With line-ups? With this or that resort's grand future?

Well, I do. We have seen many units sold with a projected occupancy rate of 60% - 65% in markets that operate at between 35% - 55% occupancy rates. (Many resorts have high occupancy in the winter, low in the summer.) Also many resorts (remember our chapter on Timing) did well for a while – attracting tons of new capital with the result that new hotels are added to the point that competition for visitors intensifies and the occupancy pie shrinks for everyone.

More worrying than occupancy rates is the fact that not all hotels units are alike. The payoff to investors lies in the management contract. How well did the developer negotiate? How much does it cost to operate? What guarantees does the management company hold? What ability exists to honour the guarantees? What performance bonuses will be paid? Are the projected net profits achievable? Who earns what first? If the hotel loses money, is the investor liable to get additional cash calls?

In fact, some investors have in the past and will continue to *face cash calls* at some hotel properties. I wonder how many really knew that they might be asked to step to the plate above and beyond their original equity and mortgage liability.

Add to this the financial strength of the developer, the experience of the operator and it becomes ever more important to get the answers.

Remember also, that the pioneers often get killed by the Indians, and then the next wave of settlers reaps the harvest. Often commercial real estate users that buy first feel they are being scalped as developments start later, construction keeps customers outside while their spare cash erodes. Clearly it is better to be a 'settler'.

Of course the success at Whistler, where strata apartments sold at $250 odd dollars per foot and hotel units at up to $600 plus per foot, raised the eyebrows and lust of Vancouver developers and a blizzard of hotel type deals hit the Vancouver and other Canadian markets from 1993 till now.

I use the term 'hotel type deals' purposely, because, there are a lot of different racehorses in the stable, some dead before they start, some doped before every race and few thoroughbreds.

Complicated as it is, suffer through the explanation you must. Simply put, there is:

1. *The traditional condominium* – you own your four walls to the center of them and have common area joys and obligations with others. Inside you decorate to your delight; and cleaning is a privilege you enjoy doing yourself.

2. *The furnished condominium* – as above, but you get furniture as well and pay for it.

3. *The furnished and serviced condominium (executive suite)* is bought by a purchaser committing to both a residential and a furniture package offered by the developer with the option of placing his/her unit into a rental pool. Units are rented on a 'minimum monthly stay' basis, rooms

are cleaned, there is maid service and in some cases room service.
4. *The Flagship hotel operating as a hotel with true daily bookings.*
Several have come to market in the last year. As investors we must be aware of the key features and differences in these. To what extent is the 'flag' or chain affiliation applicable, who really manages the property and to what extend is the unit defined as a 'security' and hence subject to possibly severe restrictions in terms of liquidity and thus, resale.

In the latter two you have further distinctions of personal use of one week or one month or no such personal use, a rental pool with all others, a possible rental guarantee agreement and a host of variations – such as 8-12% return on gross rents promised, guarantees offered through letters of credit and the like.

The whole thing became even more exciting when developers analyzed some highly successful sales of 'hotel like units' in the city. Buildings in some areas that offered 600-900 square foot apartment units at approximately $250 per square foot (unfurnished) were left sitting, outsold by buildings nearby selling units of 400-500 square feet at approximately $350 per square foot as a 'Hotel like investment'.

Units were sold local and offshore. In fact, ads in Singapore read "Guaranteed 50% rental return within 5 years" for a building that "...operates like a hotel with all the hotel services, 24 hour concierge/ security services."

The perception was created by some buildings that they are to op-erate like a daily hotel, yet their buildings carry residential zoning (only monthly rental allowed). Advertisements made promises unmatched by statements in the operating budget. (In one case, concierge services and 24 hour security was promised, but were nowhere to be found in the budget!) Well, you get the message. Additionally, some offshore investors were promised better deals than local investors (through additional guarantees) … add it all up and you would wonder what the outcome will be.

Well, I was and am still wondering. Investors were not, they just kept snapping up the goodies. Regardless of vacancy rates and regardless of past history. Regardless of guarantees whose amount was insufficient, could not be verified and kept in numbered companies. When you're hot you're hot.

Of course not all hotel units are alike. Not every building is the same and some were marketed without such excess promises. Some offered no guarantee. Said one notable developer: "We don't give a guarantee.

There is no magic, no smoke and mirrors at our hotel. If you believe in our flag, if you believe in Vancouver's growth, if you believe in the superb management contract we negotiated, we want you. A guarantee contract simply adds cost." Almost refreshing.

So first of all, if interested, make sure you are buying a hotel and not an apartment 'looking like a hotel.' But even if you buy a 'flag' hotel you must understand that you are in the hotel business, with all that implies. A business implies that the contract that the business operates under is favorable to it and its investors. In the hotel business where 'flags' are bought for the reservation systems and stature, but the hotel is operated by someone else, you better study that operating agreement. (Almost every new hotel sold to investors 'rents' the 'flag', but a local/minor player operates the hotel.)

The reality is that the way these kind of units are sold is by stressing the benefits, being silent on any drawbacks and stressing the association with the hotel company that will be operating the hotel. People get the idea that they are investing in Hyatt or Hilton or Marriott but if you examine the fine print, you find that this simply isn't the case.

Hilton or Marriott will 'lease' their name but have nothing to do with the operation of the hotel. The lessee gets the benefit of the world wide reservation system, pays for the name, and that's it.

In the end we as investors have to appreciate that a serviced apartment offered with 'guaranteed' revenue is only as meaningful as the combined ability of the project to generate the revenue forecast and the financial strength available to support the guarantee.

If a two-year old suite in downtown anywhere can sell for between $200 and $300 per square foot, think long and hard before you pay $450 to $600 per foot for a hotel unit. In addition and in the words of one major marketer, whose company currently does not market any hotel units: "Until we are sure that there is a secondary market (someone to sell the original units to), we will not be in the strata hotel business." Well said.

The risk to income stream in a regular apartment is found in the general vacancy rate of the city the apartment is located in. At worst, you can cut your rent or move in yourself. The risk in a hotel type unit is far more dramatic. In a hotel type situation you are buying a business and a strata unit. A poor operational management agreement could sink the finest property for the investors; projected incomes could be lower, in fact easily negative.

Major Points:

1. Understand the difference in what you are buying: a straight apartment unit, a furnished one, a serviced furnished one, a monthly rental hotel, or a daily fully operating hotel.

2. Understand, that if there is a guarantee with a mandated rental pool it is a security and not classic real estate.

3. Understand that if you are buying a security, you could have a possible problem with the re-sale. In fact there is no proven secondary market for these units.

4. Understand the management contract that a hotel on behalf of its investors negotiates with the Hotel manger/operating Company.

Ask yourself these questions:

a) How strong is the operator?

b) Who is the actual operator of the hotel? (No, the 'flag' operator may have nothing to do with the day to day operations.)

c) What is the operator's experience?

d) How much of the performance is guaranteed?

e) What is the fixed annual fee and will that fee be paid regardless of operator's performance and hotel bottom line or does the operator suffer penalties for lower performance?

f) Does the promoter of the Hotel understand the Hotel business? Has he negotiated a great hotel management deal on behalf of his investors?

5. Is the performance guarantee offered secured by a realistic amount of money accessible to you in case it is needed?

6. Are you liable for your mortgage only? Or are you expected to step up to the plate for a cash call, should the hotel operate in the red?

7. Are you responsible for the performance of the restaurant, the parking lots, the banquet facilities, and the commercial lease space? (No, it is not an added benefit to you, it is a way for the hotel to insure income for itself. Your duty is only to pay, if objectives are not met.)

If your head is swimming, your eyes are glazed over – good. Better now, than after you bought.

Let me finish up by saying that the average person just doesn't have the financial, business, time and real estate experience to do an adequate analysis of these kinds of investments. There are too many ways to lose and only a couple of ways to win. For the average investor there are just too many other, simpler, and better ways to invest the money in conventional real estate.

The question really comes down to: "What do you need it for?" I say this being very much aware that the salesman who brings you his deal will have all the reasons why his deal shouldn't be measured by my yardstick. All you have to do is re-read this chapter, ask the right questions – and let your common sense keep you safe.

~

In Essence

Anytime you are a minority participant in a venture then you are in effect handing your money to someone and saying, "Here you are, take this money and do the best you can with it."

If you're wise, you'll require a satisfactory answer to the question, "Where and when did the guy who's going to be running this show do this kind of thing where the investors were satisfied with the outcome?"

You can make a pro-forma say whatever you want it to say as long as you've got a pencil that writes at one end and erases at the other.

The less regulation in a jurisdiction the more likely that the sales methods are going to be aggressive.

Powerful marketing techniques and superior sales skills can always corral the unwary.

Chapter 18

CONSTRUCTION & DEVELOPMENT

Once upon a time a real estate investor decided to do some development. At the bankruptcy somebody asked him why. "Well," he answered, "it's like the drunken cowboy who danced naked in the cactus – at the time it seemed like a good idea."

This is going to be a very short chapter. The title of the chapter is Construction and Development. The advice is – don't.

I should stop right here but I'll elaborate a little. If you have a burning desire to have a career in construction and development, then go out and learn how to do it. No other area of business has a higher casualty rate. And no other area of business has so high a fatality rate when there is a casualty. But this book is about real estate investing and from our perspective the returns for real estate investors should be commensurate to the risks. When the returns are not commensurate to the risks then that situation should be avoided.

The learning curve for construction and development is very long and very steep. Until you learn what you need to know you're going to be playing someone else's game. We all know what that means.

Historically and statistically it's a bad bet. In real estate investment there are simply too many other things to do with the money that are much more suitable to the average person's investment objectives. However, if part of your investment objective is to have that same rush of adrenaline and the same sinking feeling in your stomach that one gets when riding a roller coaster, then construction and development should be ideal for you. Otherwise, you might want to give it a wide berth.

Having said this, let's narrow things down a bit by defining our terms.

What do we mean by construction and development? Let's first talk a bit about what it is not. When you buy a lot and build a house on it you are constructing and developing a single house but that's not what we're talking about here. Sure, you can learn how to do this. It's like anything else. But that's not what we're talking about when we speak of construction and development.

It's one thing to build a single home or maybe even a single duplex. It's another to build a multi-home subdivision or a multi-unit apartment or condo project. If you build a single home and it doesn't appeal to a buyer, you can move into it yourself or give it to the bank or lower the price until someone will buy it. You might get financially bent but you won't be broken. You will be a bit grumpy and the Realtor will lose out on the commission but the damage is contained. With a multi-unit project if you miss the target market, you are going to be in the glue. Here the difference between joy and misery may be missing the cycle by a few months. With many larger projects operating on margins of 15% annual profits, it doesn't take too long a period of no sales to wipe out profits. The carrying costs go on, even if sales do not.

Even so, it's a seductive area of activity; especially if you look at the winners. You can pick up your newspaper and read accounts of how a mega-project sold out in a matter of a few days and you think to yourself, "I'd like to have some of that." In the same paper there could be an account of projects that have been on the market for years and they're still not sold out yet. What makes the difference?

The difference is that the developer of the successful project was a better judge of what and where and at what price the public was going to give a suitable response to. The successful developer has that unmeasurable, unquantifiable element called 'talent'. He can put himself into the psyche of the consumer and know instinctively what will work and what won't work.

Is there any place to go to learn how to do this? Don't be silly! But if you don't have the talent, don't sail away from the dock. The most dangerous situation of all is to think you have the talent when you don't. But the most dissatisfying situation is when you've given your money to someone who thinks he has the talent when in fact he doesn't. It's always less dissatisfying to make your own mistakes than to have someone else making them for you.

There's another important, hard to explain phenomenon and that is that even the talented and experienced developers have failures. Why?

As one developer friend of mine said: "I have an engineering degree and a degree in architecture. I can put up a very fine building, high quality, good amenities and lose my shirt simply because I come to the market at the wrong time. Yet, I have seen shoddy buildings, slapped together with no regard for functionality sell in a weekend only because the marketplace perceived that it was a great time to buy and the developer spent a fortune to create a pre-selling circus. It is a frustrating business." Indeed.

Here is a very important lesson: It doesn't matter from the perspective of the investor why a project either succeeds or fails. The only thing that is important is, "Is the return commensurate with the risks and does the investment fit the investment objectives of the investor." Everything else is just commentary.

In the case of the multi-unit development, if it doesn't sell, the damage is extensive indeed. And once the loss is recognized as being irremediable everyone wants to know what caused it. There will be as many reasons as there are failed projects. The thing to focus on is the successful projects and, much more important, what it took those developers to get to the point where they could do a project successfully. (Just remember that past success doesn't guarantee future success – the only constant in the equation is the danger.)

If that's what you want to do, then by all means go and do it but know in advance what you're going to be involved in. If you already have the know-how, you're not going to learn anything reading this, and if you don't already know how, you're not going to learn anything here except that it's not a good idea to try.

It takes about the same amount of learning to become a successful developer as it takes to be any other kind of a professional. The big difference is that with any of the professions, such as law or accounting or medicine, when you make a mistake you send your client a bill for your services and the next client with the same problem gets the benefit of that experience. In development when you make a mistake you wind up in the bankruptcy court.

Suffice it to say that you only find developers in two places: You find them cavorting around with all the rich people or you find them in the poorhouse. There doesn't seem to be any middle ground.

"All right," you say, "I know just what to do. I'll find a developer who knows all about what to do and I'll partner up with him and we'll all go to the sea-shore."

Apart from the fact that a successful developer doesn't need you, it is not a good idea. At this point you're not being a developer. You're being a mooch. You'll wind up somewhere between being a lender with no security and a buyer of securities where you're going to be the last guy on the list to be paid. There are a whole lot of better uses for the money.

~

In Essence

If part of your investment objectives is to have the same rush of adrenaline that you get from riding a roller coaster, then real estate development should be ideal for you.

Even talented and experienced developers have failures.

The most important factor is whether the return is commensurate with the risks and does the investment fit the investment objectives of the investor.

Past success doesn't guarantee future success – the only constant in the equation is danger.

In professions such as law, accounting, or medicine when you make a mistake you send the client a bill for your services and the next client with the same problem gets the benefit of that experience. In development when you make a mistake you wind up in the bankruptcy court.

Chapter 19

SELECTING YOUR EXPERTS & ADVISORS

You're going to pay for expertise whether you buy it or not. You're going to pay for it whether you use it or not. You're going to pay for it whether it works or not. But if you buy it and use it you'll wind up paying less.

This is one of the most important chapters in the book. The reason it's important is there is an almost universal confusion on the subject. Experts are those persons who have specific knowledge and who can show you what hoops to jump through and how to perform those jumps most efficiently and therefore most effectively. Advisors are those persons who have had the necessary life experiences that make their value judgments valuable and therefore make their advice worth taking.

The problem most people have is they confuse the two functions and either use an expert for advice or use an advisor for expertise. Or, even worse, they use either for both functions. Except in very rare instances this is a recipe for anything ranging from slight inconvenience to total disaster.

Another area where people make a sometimes serious mistake is when they assume that the person who has expertise in one field also has expertise in a related field. Because most of these experts charge by the hour, unless all their hours are spoken for, they are not likely to turn you down when you want to buy some of those hours even though they know in their heart of hearts that they are not the best people for the job. They sometimes mistakenly think they know or even if they know that they don't know they are not averse to a little on-the-job training

– especially at your expense.

I am not sure where this is from, but here is some philosophy:

There are those who know not and know that they know not. They are Children – Teach them.
There are those who know and know not that they know. They are Lost – Lead them.
There are those who know and know that they know. They are Wise – Follow them.
There are those who know not and know not that they know not. They are Fools – Shun them.

That's what makes this area of value judgment so dangerous and therefore so important. We go to experts for the special knowledge that they have and that we don't have. We, by definition, being laymen in their field, are not in a position to make a value judgment in their area of expertise. The only person who can evaluate a good doctor, lawyer, or indian chief is another good doctor, lawyer or Indian chief. That being the case, we would be much further ahead using an advisor to select an expert rather than looking in the Yellow Pages.

Some experts are easy to evaluate. Barbers, for instance, are easy. You could stop a stranger on the street and say, "Hey Mister, I like the way your hair looks. Who's your barber?" or you might be in a restaurant and say to the waiter, "This is terrific bread. Who's your baker?" Unfortunately the real estate investment business is more complex and the task of matching the right expert to the right application is therefore much more complicated.

It's interesting that in real estate investment there seems to be a correlation between the amount of money involved and the amount of danger that's inherent. I suppose it's because when the mistakes are more expensive, the danger quotient, and therefore the importance, rises proportionately.

In an attempt to make our thinking on this subject more linear, let's take for example – a lawyer. You have all kinds of lawyers out there. Let me preface my remarks by saying that some of my best friends are lawyers. Lawyers break down into two basic categories, Barristers and Solicitors. Solicitors do paperwork. Barristers appear before the bar of justice. And after these two major divisions you have all sorts of sub categories of all kinds of specialties and focuses. Real Estate, Securities and Tax are the three main categories that you as a real estate investor are likely to come in contact with.

Let's say I want to buy a house and rent it out to a tenant. Any lawyer who can hear thunder and see lightning should be able to accommodate me in this matter. But suppose it's a little more complicated than this. As this is being written there is a case in the newspapers about a co-op housing project where a lot of the people thought they were buying into a condominium project instead of a co-op.

The difference is that in a condominium you own your own unit and everyone owns the common areas in concert. In a co-op the co-op owns the units and everything else and the co-op participant owns his share of the co-op. But where the difference becomes huge is that in a condo when you stop making your mortgage payments the holder of the mortgage will foreclose and resell the property, if he can, and that's the end of the story. In a co-op when one person defaults on the mortgage the other members of the co-op are all responsible for it.

In this particular instance the building had some construction deficiencies and the place leaked like a sieve. Some of the people with very small down payments just walked away because the cost of repairs was almost more than what they owed on their mortgage. This left the people who had made sizable down payments and the people who had paid cash holding the furry end of the stick. Every time someone decided to walk away, the burden for repairs and defaulted mortgages became more and more onerous.

It sort of reminds you of the Titanic. As one compartment filled with water it then spilled over into the next compartment and eventually the boat sank. The same thing happens to real estate projects such as we've just described.

Okay, what has this got to do with lawyers and the subject of experts and advisors? Well, we have to look at this from two perspectives. First, the developers of this co-op made a value judgment when they selected the lawyer who did the paperwork for the development. His job was to make sure that they were coloring between the lines, as we used to say in kindergarten. Secondly, the people who bought units in the co-op made the value judgment as to whether they were going to be advised in this matter and if so by whom.

Because these two perspectives were filled with undotted I's and uncrossed T's all kinds of people have their tails in the wringer. The developers of the project want to blame the lawyer because he didn't provide them with the safeguards that, in retrospect, they so desperately want. We have to bear in mind that these safeguards; meaning a brutally frank explanation of the reality of what could happen if things went wrong, if explained to prospective purchasers in realistic terms would have made the units difficult to sell. The reason for this is that every time you set up a hurdle of unpalatable fact for the customer to jump over you create a negative impact on the sales volume.

The lawyer wants to blame the developers because instead of rubbing their potential customers noses in all the potential dangers they chose to gloss over some of the stickier issues such as how quickly the people who stay have to start carrying the can for those who flee.

And everyone who bought a unit had the opportunity to take the paperwork to their own expert before they bought and say, "Read this and tell me what it says." If they had done that, some of them might not have bought and would not find themselves trapped in the untenable position that they find themselves in. Who knows how many prospective buyers did just that and decided not to buy. No one will ever know.

In the case of the people who did buy, they probably all got advice based on expertise of one kind or another from one source or another. It might have been their brother-in-law who was a plumber or their cousin who was a brain surgeon. Maybe it was an uncle who made a fortune selling encyclopedias door to door – who knows? It really doesn't matter. A wrong choice is a wrong choice and the reason for it doesn't matter.

Your job, if you don't want to make these kinds of mistakes, is to match up the right expert to the right job and match up the right advisor to the right job. The toughest words to wring out of anyone are, "I don't know."

We are all of us in this business of real estate investment because we want to make money. I don't know anyone who does it just for the love of it. Oh sure, there is the thrill of the chase and the adventure of the unknown and money is just the way of keeping score. Yeah, sure! Take the money out of the equation and see how soon it is that the arena would be empty of participants. Having said this as a preamble let me get to my next point.

Your professionals – that is – your lawyers, your accountants, your real estate agents cannot make you any money. Gasp! What kind of heresy is this? I put this concept nearer to the back of the book because I didn't want you to get discouraged too early in the game.

Your professionals can't make you any money because they don't know how. The very fact that a lawyer or an accountant or a real estate agent goes to the office every morning and hangs out a sign that says that they will perform their services for money tells you by definition that they don't know how to perform the real estate investment function for you better than you know how to do it for yourself. Because if they knew how they would be doing it for themselves and would not be available to do it for you.

You don't believe this? When was the last time any one of these people called you up and said, do I have a deal for you? I mean, when it really turned out to be a deal and not something they wanted to sell you. Oh sure, miracles happen but the probability is so slim that it's a non-factor.

Lawyers are for dotting I's and crossing T's so that you stay out of jail and you keep your property. Accountants are for keeping track of money and paying as little as possible to the government in the way of taxes. Real estate agents arrange deals that you find or that they find for you and that you recognize. That's it! Their function is not to make you money. Your function is to make you money.

If you use them as experts for anything else, sooner or later you're going to wind up being sorry. If you use them as advisors, you will also be sorry.

If you want advice, you have to go to someone who has been down the road that you want to travel and you have to somehow motivate that person to give you their advice. No, let me rephrase that – you have to get that person to *sell* you their advice. That is usually not an impossible task. For example, I consider myself knowledgeable in the area of real estate investment and my advice is for sale. You can find it in my monthly newsletter, my weekly fax service, you can listen to my tapes or attend my various lectures. There are many advisors out there that will sell you advice. The key questions for you to ask: "Is the advice unbiased and independent? Is the advisor selling anything else? Does he or she benefit by steering me into this or that direction?"

Unbiased and independent advice!
I continue to be amazed at people's laziness to investigate and their strong desire to have someone else make key decisions for them. Take many financial planners for instance – although there are many excellent ones – some have not much education, some very little qualifica-

tion. Many work for investment houses and all work for commission. The hard working couple shudders at the thought of paying a lawyer $200 an hour for independent, unbiased advise or would not think of buying a financial newsletter for a couple of hundred dollars per year, but they will plunk down their life savings and have a financial planner make decisions and hope for the best.

But that is somehow allright ... the advice after all is free. Well it isn't free. It can actually be very expensive.

A financial planner has a multitude of choices to place your money: Mutual funds, stock funds, money market funds, real estate funds, limited partnerships, mortgage funds ... all bearing different commission rates. It is human nature for him or her to recommend a 'balanced portfolio' of 10% and 2% commissions.

Please, I am not knocking the profession. As we get older we need more and more advice. I use a financial planner from time to time. But I also know exactly what I am invested in (quick: "what exactly are the shares *you* hold in *your* Mutual Fund?") and what the advice I am getting is worth.

Remember the advice we are talking about here must be 'independent and unbiased', otherwise learn to make your own decisions.

If you don't have any money, read books. Hundreds of books have been written on the subject. This very book you are reading is another example.

The point being made is that most experts are for hire in one way or another. The very important job *you* have is to match up the right answerer to the right question. The question is how do *you* go about picking the right person for the right job?

What you want to avoid is asking your professional to do something that he doesn't *already* know how to do. Oh, he'll do it all right, but he'll either research it on your nickel or he'll do it by trial and error with you paying for the error part.

You want to get it right the first time. You do this by first delineating the problem and then getting the right advice on which professional you should use to solve it.

For the simple stuff a good real estate lawyer is all you need. If you start getting fancy and put together a group of people, you're going to need a securities lawyer. Depending on how much money you make you might find that you need a tax lawyer. If you get into financial trouble or if you're involved with people who get into financial trouble, you may find yourself in need of a bankruptcy lawyer. It could be that the strain of all this is too much for your marriage and you will find yourself in the need of a divorce lawyer. (I've always found it interesting that these particular practitioners all refer to themselves as 'matrimonial' lawyers. Seems to me there is precious little matrimony going on and a whole lot of divorce.) God forbid, but you could even find yourself in circumstances where you need a criminal lawyer! If things get really extreme, you could even find yourself looking for an immigration lawyer!

In each of these instances you want someone who already knows the specialty. Although I wrote the previous paragraph somewhat with tongue in cheek it is not really all that farfetched. I could name countless individuals who have lived out that scenario of needing just those lawyers in that exact sequence except for the criminal and immigration lawyer part. For those I could only name a handful of people.

In every case, their degree of success in surviving each individual trouble was in direct relationship to the quality of the lawyer they selected and how appropriate the lawyer was to the task that needed performing. Of course, it should go without saying that a really top professional in any area would not take on a client for a task where he didn't have the expertise, but would instead refer that client to someone who was appropriate for them. But in this imperfect world we sometimes find that there are more horses rear ends than there are horses and that is especially true in this particular arena.

Let's leave the lawyers for a while and turn our attention to the accountants in our lives. They say that a person who acts as his own lawyer has a fool for a client. Most people don't do this because they sense that it might not be such a good idea. But when it comes to the accounting side of the picture, most people feel a little more confident so more of them are willing to dabble at it themselves. Most of the time this is all right except when we get to the area of income tax.

I suppose what we should really do is separate in our minds the concepts of bookkeeping and tax planning. I suppose anyone who can add two and two and get four most of the time can do bookkeeping. But tax planning gets to be more complicated because the operative word is 'planning'. One thing the government will almost never let you do is to do your tax planning retroactively. Most of the time it has to be done in advance and any aspect of it that isn't right is going to cost you.

The entire message of this chapter (or for that matter, the entire book) could be – learn from someone else's mistakes. There is no need to go out and reinvent the wheel. The only task you're faced with is selecting the professional that you are going to use. Most of the time you can do this by asking someone in a related field for a referral. Ideally, if you are a real estate investor, you would ask some successful real estate investor who he would recommend for such and such a task. But if you don't know such a person you can ask a person in a related field because most of the time a good tax lawyer will know who the good securities lawyers are. The lawyers know the lawyer specialists and they also know the accounting specialists and vice versa.

But you can't get any answer at all if you don't ask the question. The most important step is to ask the question. That way you can build cumulatively on the experience and the expertise of those who have walked the road ahead of you.

Up to this point we have talked only about the necessity of having these experts and advisors and how to select them. For most people that's the entire process. The common attitude is that once you select a professional and hire them for whatever it is that they are going to do for you that there is where all your decision making ends. From that point forward these gods that walk the earth in three piece suits tell you what to do and you do it and at the end of the month they send you a bill for their fee and you pay it.

That's a continuum that you don't want to be a part of. If there is only one lawyer with the specialty you want in the whole city or if there is only one accountant of the certain type that you need for a hundred miles in any direction, then maybe it would be a different story. However, the reality is that the yellow pages are filled with the names of all sorts of people who are in competition for the guy you want. It's important for you to know this and it's even more important for the professional to know that you know it.

On your first meeting with a prospective professional, after you have established the frame of reference for what you want done, you have to ask him in plain language to describe his fee structure. You want to know how much he charges and how the charges are computed and what kind of reporting you can expect. The answers he gives are nowhere nearly as important as just the fact that you've asked the questions. The very fact that he knows you're watching and the awareness he has that you have a frame of reference for what is going on in his marketplace is going to save you money. He's got all kinds of clients who don't have that awareness who he can charge whatever he feels like. You want to be one of the ones who he knows is watching.

Let me illustrate with a little story. An optometrist was teaching his son the business and after he had taught him everything that he needed to know about optometry he sat his son down and said, "Son, I am now going to teach you how to charge for your goods and services. When you are sitting in front of the patient and you are fitting on the glasses you say to him, 'The glasses are $100.' When you do that you watch his face very carefully and if he doesn't flinch, you say, 'That's for the frames. The lenses are another $100.' You continue to watch his face. And if he doesn't flinch – you say, 'Each!' "

The point here is that no matter what the professional names as his fee structure or as his hourly rate, you have to flinch. He has to know you're flinching so that he just may keep some kind of a rein on his charges. Remember, what is being decided here is who is going to take the money home to spend. Anything you pay him is deducted from your net.

Don't be ashamed to haggle. Try to make him take his fee out of downstream profits. Try to make him take a share of the profits. In 99% of the cases the answer is going to be no. But the main benefit is in the asking. When he makes up those bills at the end of the month, perhaps he will not press that pen quite as hard.

Once you've got the money question temporarily settled, I say temporarily because you have to keep people on their toes or they get complacent – it's just human nature, you have to keep monitoring the performance. It is important for you to know what it is that you want your professionals to accomplish for you so that when you are reviewing you will know if the benchmarks are being met. If they are not then you've got to find out who's responsible. If it's you or someone on your side of the fence, then it has to be fixed immediately. If it's him or someone on his side of the fence, it has to be fixed much sooner than that.

The important thing is that you have to be measuring all the time so that if something goes wrong you find out about it as soon as possible. The least expensive mistakes are the ones you find out about the soonest. Therefore, you have to know what everyone is doing so that you can determine as soon as possible when it isn't being done right.

The single biggest mistake that people make in dealing with their professionals is that they buy into the mystique that there is something wonderful about these people just because they practice some arcane craft that is a mystery to us lesser mortals. You shouldn't feel any different about them than you feel about anyone else you hire to do work for you. Feel exactly the same about them as you do about a plumber when you have a plugged toilet. Except with the plumber it's easier to tell when the job is being done correctly.

That's another reason why I am such a big advocate of the written plan. When you have your plan in writing you have concrete benchmarks that you can measure by. If your progress doesn't meet your benchmarks, either your expectations are unrealistic or someone isn't doing their job. If that someone is you, then you have to change your behavior or change your expectations. However, if that someone is someone in your organization (and this includes your professionals), then you've got to have changes. Again, either in your expectations or in their performance. You have to be watching and measuring all the time or else you won't know when to reward good performance or, much more importantly, you won't know when to take steps to effect changes to correct poor performance.

Now we come to a sticky subject. Every once in a while it becomes necessary to fire a professional. It's rarely easy and it's never pleasant. Sometimes it's because they're not doing a good job, sometimes you've found someone you think you'll like better, whatever the reason, you're not satisfied and you are ready for a change. Remember that the kindest way to cut off a dog's tail is not one inch at a time. The best way to handle it is to be forthright and frank. Sit down with your professional, state your complaints and tell him you're making other arrangements.

You'll practically never get any kind of an argument. Just remember one very important factor – you better be prepared to pay his bill if you want your records delivered to you. This presumes you're not in disagreement on the bill. Also, it is best to have your new arrangements lined up before you terminate your old ones.

Real estate agents are a category of professional that can make you a lot of money, if you handle them right. Some people might take issue with the real estate agents being classified in there with the lawyers and accountants. I can tell you from the basis of considerable experience that the good real estate agents are every bit as professional as their colleagues are in the legal and accounting professions. The key word here is professional. You want a Realtor that practices his or her profession, not one that practices on you.

When I buy, I like a Realtor who doesn't argue with me when I want to write a low offer. I am always amazed how many Realtors do not want to write a low offer. Yet, time and again, they are surprised by how low this or that property sold for. Well, someone made the low offer. I also am a proverbial tire kicker. High flying Realtors don't like tire kickers. And that is alright, they have a business to run. I may kick tires, but I buy. One Realtor whose grey hair is probably entirely due to me has shown me properties beyond the proverbial line of duty, but he also sold me seven homes over a 10-year period. So, I like a Realtor that is on my side when I buy. I also don't haggle for the amount of the commission to be reduced, but at times ask for commissions to be deferred as we discussed in an earlier chapter. Commissions don't worry me, I want a professional, and if he or she is one I gladly pay a professional fee. I also find that usually – not always – I like a different Realtor when I sell.

I also like a Realtor that I can deal with personally and not one that fobs me off on a half a dozen assistants. Seventy per cent of the time, properties are sold by another salesperson than the one you have hired to sell. That is alright, as long as your professional understands this and leaves no stone unturned to wheel the maximum amount of potential buyers into my property. But all this is personal; the important thing is that the Realtor – buying or selling – gets the job done.

Although it is possible to build relationships that continue over the years and I have many in a dozen different areas, most of your involvement with them will be on a piecework basis. You have to be especially sensitive to what kind of a job they are doing for you. This is especially true when you have a property listed for sale. You have to keep a careful finger on the pulse of what's happening because you have to know, almost on a day to day basis, if your interests are being served.

You want that delicate balance of an agent that is busy enough to be successful but not so successful that he's too busy to give you the attention you require.

Just so you'll know that I'm entitled to an opinion on Realtors, I have sold real estate as a salesperson, served as a branch manager for 5 years as well as a general manager and finally had the privilege to lead some 7,000 Realtors as president of Royal Lepage (Residential). During my last year their gross commissions came to over $500,000,000. That's not volume of sales. That's cash commissions in the door.

The important thing to remember about your professionals is that they are going to make the difference between your real estate investment activities producing average results and producing excellent results. If you select them, manage them, and use them effectively, you can get optimum results. It's a three-step process. First you have to know what questions to ask, then you have to ask the questions and then you have to act on the advice you get.

∼

In Essence

Real estate investment is complex and so it should come as no surprise that matching the right expert to the right application is extremely complex.

The toughest words to wring out of anyone are – "I don't know."

Your professionals can not make you any money – they don't know how. Your job is to match up the right answer to the right question.

It's important to avoid asking your professional to do something that he doesn't already know how to do.

Chapter 20

TECHNOLOGY: ENEMY OR FRIEND TO REAL ESTATE?

*In the future there will be only two ways that you can earn an
income with information:
You will be the only one who has it – the originator
Or you will interpret it.*

Not a minute goes by where we're not peppered with information
about the New Age, the internet, email and the shift from a have/have
not society to a know/know not global community. Today, talk of technology permeates everything.

But why?

One word: information. But only a certain type of information: ready,
accessible, and useful. Instantly ready. Instantly accessible. Instantly
interactive.

The availability of this information, when coupled with a new no-
nonsense "tell-me-how-much" consumer has changed the world. It
can easily be argued that it was the free-flow of information, which
quietly corroded the Iron Curtain and finally toppled the communistic
world. Today, that same flow of information is utterly transforming our
own.

From the collapse and painful transformation of an ideology, to
supplying consumers, the world is fragmenting and solidifying into
niches and mega-niches.

Thanks to the information explosion, we can compare before we
commit. Service, warranty, quality, it's all laid out before us in those
niches. Rather than being loyal to one supplier, retailer, government or
even ideology, we can now compare and either embrace – or discard –

the various bits. Truly, the sum of the parts is now much greater than the whole.

The information explosion has driven down prices, raised quality and killed non-aligned competitors by the thousands. It still is. It's also killing off the unwary or those unable or unwilling to change.

Bad or good, it's also quite likely affected your own life, Gentle Reader. Buzzwords and buzz saws, the concepts of 'down-sizing' and 'right-sizing', 'down-shifting' and 'up-marketing' are all driven by the new consumer – you and I. Finicky, fed-up and armed with new information, we're doing it to ourselves.

Okay, you ask. What do the internet and Boris Yeltsin's woes have to do with real estate?

Lots and lots (pun intended).

The next five years will see a huge shift in how real estate is being appraised, assessed, marketed, sold, distributed and registered. And all because of readily available new information distributed to the same consumer over ever-faster highways, received by ever more knowledgeable, ever more demanding consumers on ever cheaper and ever faster computers. The comparative information, which drove the cost of a stock transaction to fractions of a percentage, is now shaking up the real estate and related industries top to bottom.

When the 'founding fathers' of Vancouver's real estate companies – Henry and Arthur Block – ran Block Bros. in the 1970s, they owned the market. For several years in a row, Block Bros. outperformed its 10 biggest competitors collectively. It was a giant looming above the vertically challenged.

Was Block Bros. that good? Did it have better salespeople, a better vision? To a point, yes. But its biggest weapon was information. Jealously guarded information bundled up in a comprehensive catalogue accessible to its own people and only them. Right throughout the 1970s, Block Bros. did not list its properties on the MLS of the Board. When it did co-operate with the competition, it did so only on its own terms.

And then along came 1980. The competition and the real estate boards created its own MLS real-estate catalogues. At the same time, fortress Block Bros. caved in to the continued intense pressure from within, and allowed its own salespeople to pick up some extra commission and list MLS as well.

The wall was breached, the competition rejoiced.

But while all the other biggish guys were happily shifting information – real inventory – to the real estate boards' multiple listing services, they didn't realize that they were actually shifting their real power – control of the crucial information – into the hands of the real estate boards.

The real estate salesperson became more and more independent as he/she owned the information through their boards' multiple listing services. Real estate companies changed and changed to try and accommodate the ever increasing demands by its sales forces ... but alas, the big weapon, exclusive access to information was no longer owned by them.

Rather like the invention of the crossbow, it put real killing power into the hands of the foot soldiers and a real shock – literally – into the hearts of what had been, up to then, invulnerable armored knights, nobles and kings. The democracy of the battlefield prevailed.

Until the early 1990s, the slug fest raged on. Big real estate firms were collapsing everywhere, bled dry by salespeople who played off their 'employers' one against the other. Armed with full access to information, demanding and getting all of the commission, loyal only to themselves, essentially freelancers despite the banner under which they rode, the salespeople controlled the field. Hence the joke: I know why you're a real estate broker; you're going broke.

Of course, I am making no value judgments here. Just laying the foundation for my argument about real estate selling in the future.

Events unfolded as they should and as they had to, given the unstoppable flow of information and the evolution of the well prepared, fickle, well-educated salesperson.

However, the same pressures that put the key information into the hands of the salesperson are now putting it into the hands of the consumer via the internet.

Thus, in the New World of tomorrow, if you wish to earn money as a disseminator of information, you can only have a future if you are either:

a) The ORIGINATOR of the information – no one else has it or;

b) The INTERPRETER of information – no one else sees it quite like you. Your unique interpretation. Or your unique know-how applied.

Simply having and hoarding readily available information will be less and less worthwhile.

For example, the whole question of easily comparing the costs of a transaction – from legal fees, home inspection costs, MLS and appraisal fees, to mortgage costs – will force the industry to be more efficient and more cost sensitive. Mortgage lending is already dramatically affected by the new telecommunications now that the more resourceful lenders let you originate loans through the internet.

As more and more consumers take more personal responsibility for their investment decisions generally, expect the world to change even more. The most astounding change (particularly to internet naysayers) has to be the explosion of online stock purchases. In 1996 no one bought stocks via the internet, a year later over 1 million and in early 1999 some 5 million customers are buying stocks direct from financial institutions, forcing big brokers to offer the same services.

All driven by a consumer in a continued quest for lower and lower costs, fewer and fewer middlemen ... spell broker. Companies like Dell Computers sell $10 million worth of computers a day from their web site and fully expect to have 50% of their multi-billion dollar sales marketed via the net by 2001. At the same time www.AMAZON.COM sells 60,000 books per day through its site and even yours truly sells many thousand dollars worth of books, tapes, business plans through www.JUROCK.COM. Okay, okay we're not a Dell yet, but all orders come from places that we never dreamt to sell to in the past.

Information always had power in the hands of the few. Today, information distributed to millions in a nanosecond adds power to all. Real power. If we accept the premise that control of information is everything and accept the fact this information is now uncontrollable and will become more and more accessible to all, then clearly the real estate industry will be undergoing a huge shift, a huge transformation.

The 1970s belonged to the big real estate companies. The 1980s and 1990s belonged to the real estate salesperson. The 2000s will belong to the consumer.

It's all rather like the 1980s when all the hungry big firms and their leaders pushed their agents aboard the MLS system. And with possibly the same results. Only this time, it's the agents' turn. It's their power – the access to the product and the ability to see, touch, evaluate, rate and decide commissions – which will be handed off onto the consumer.

But not quite yet. There is some breathing room, a window for smart real-estate firms and agents to adjust, to shift, and to benefit from the coming change. Many real estate boards are sniffing the wind and are leaping aboard the internet bandwagon in a mad bid just to 'be there'.

In fact all real estate boards in Canada are online in 1999, when not one was on in the fall of 1995. Mega sites like www.REALTOR.COM in the United States and www.MLS.CA in Canada are representing organized real estate, but there are hundreds of other players each with several hundred thousand listings. Microsoft's entry (www.HOMEADVISOR.COM) is a huge resource site and will allow even Joe Public to place their properties there directly creating what I called in my newsletter the "Gunfight at the Internet Corral" among the giants. Smaller players, like our own www.JUROCK.COM site, have seen a huge increase in traffic in the last three years, going from 10,000 hits per month in 1995 to over 3 million hits per month in early 1999. More importantly the over 600 clients at *Jurock New Media* report more and more hard results: spelled – sales. As more and more customers get more used to buying on the net this trend will increase.

Many big companies are using technology to boot out the middleman. Many industries will come under enormous pressure – particularly the real estate related service industry. For example, CMHC's E.M.I.L.Y. computer program with its four-level market evaluation (local area stats, provincial stats, economic outlook, and lender criteria) will eliminate 95% of ALL residential appraisals for CMHC-insured properties by the middle of 1999. Talk about pressure on the appraisal industry.

But don't despair. Instead, prepare your ground.

Sure, although the information is indeed more and more readily available and becoming more and more detailed the consumer is not totally ready yet, the sky is not falling.

Millions of people are still getting lost, tangled up weeping in the web. The internet is still disjointed, it is still frustrating. There is still a bewildering array of sites without much information, and there is another group of sites with too much information without clarity or direction. Some are overly elaborate; others have been extremely expensive to build but then are not monitored.

But any mine requires a lot of surface work first. While frustrating now, within the next five years the net will clarify, purify, and amalgamate itself into a cohesive new consumer-driven information system.

Clearly, the internet is a great research tool for those having the stomach to do the digging. As a professional real estate investor, it's vital for you to get in there with your shovel.

A tremendous ocean of change has swept the industry already. Since 1986 some 21,000 real estate offices in the U.S. have shut down. 2,400 offices in Canada fell by the wayside. The Realtor population in the United States shrank from 1,050,000 in 1989 to 640,000 in 1999. In Canada, Realtors numbered 95,000 in 1989, in 1999 that number is down to 64,000.

There has been a relentless thinning of the ranks throughout North America. Change is upon the industry with a vengeance. Technological change. Working from home change. Transactions are fewer. Baby boomers are staying in homes longer (kids are still with us, you know). We have a more mature market.

Relocations have shrunk by over 70% in the last 10 years. Why? Because you and I are undergoing the greatest personal transformation ever. We don't move just because our company says so and when we move we look for lifestyle, quality and possibly self-employment.

More access to information, means more informed decision making, means lower prices for information. The power of the past was the "thou shalt not read the MLS catalogue." The power of the future – all the information is on the internet.

What's in store for Realtors? Fewer, more independent salespeople doing more deals for less commission. The commission payment may shift more and more to the selling side from the listing side. Less commissions for listing a property, bonuses (coming from the listing side) for the actual selling agent.

What for investors? Easier, faster access to deals. Buyer's agents will become more prevalent as consumers understand their function better and insist on personal representations.

And for everybody else? Everything will become more performance based as today's fickle consumer demands more service for less payment.

However, for the 'add value' Realtor, the new fresh company that interprets information, the savvy investor, the New World will also have new rewards. The internet – and real estate displayed on it - will take on an ever-increasing role of importance.

Predictions (keeping in mind that forecasting is never easy, particularly when it is about the future!):

The internet and its new technology hasn't just arrived, it is continuing to arrive. It is not a destination but a new always-ongoing fascinating journey. We have barely seen the beginning of this fascinating journey. This journey to the moon has barely left the station. The implications of the changes ahead for the real estate industry are bigger than the introduction of the MLS catalogue or the fax machine was. They will be as frightening and full of new promise as the change the farmer experienced as he was drawn into the industrial age.

1. *While changes are ahead for all industries,* the real estate industry in particular is in the throes of a major transformation. The new power of selecting properties, real estate companies and representatives will rest in the consumer. In fact, *the whole home buying and selling process* will originate in the buyer's and seller's home computer in the future.

2. *Buyers will have extensive, detailed information at their fingertips.*

a) 'How to' preparation – real basics

b) Total courses on 'how to negotiate', 'how to close', on-line, FREE.

c) Sophisticated market evaluations

3. *Neighbourhood information* You will be able to:

a) Order a crime statistics report by neighbourhood

b) Order a School match report – matching your family's and kids criteria

c) School statistics, where located, what levels taught, private vs. public schools, etc.

d) Trend information – population growth, job growth

4. *Easy to understand explanations of the legal differences of types of ownership:* Strata condo, single family, mixed use; detailed explanations and evaluations; comparison of the differences by actual building.

5. *Demographic mix report:* Neighbourhood make-up, likelihood of race, age group, income, religious compatibility. There are some huge implications here!

6. *Mortgage information* Comparison of ALL financial institutions nationwide and their best rates as opposed to their stated rates. Detailed information on exact products offered.

7. *Live mortgages will be shopped for from home.* After rates are compared, applications filled approvals can be received in your own home and all in a few minutes. (Unless you just had your TV repossessed ... and yes, they will know!)

8. *Any kind of mortgage calculation can be accomplished on-line.* Length, size of payments, a thousand options to play with. Already our mortgage calculator at www.JUROCK.COM not only allows for a multiple variation of down payment options and payment schedules but also

calculates every mortgage in 64 languages in seconds (this is a real benefit to the overseas visitor).

9. Comparison of legal conveyancing rates by individual quote and law firm

10. Comparison of appraisal rates by appraisal group, by individual quote and appraisal firm

11. As a buyer: Home searches by area, by neighbourhood, by property type. Home searches by matching the criteria of all of the above against your family's personal criteria.

12. As a seller: Full comparable searches of recent and similar listings; full on-line independent market evaluations.

13. Buyer or seller: Pushed information. Here you list your personal criteria based on your wants and needs. Such as entering: "Wanted, 3 bedroom home, high school within 2 blocks, price no more than $100,000, family area," just once and then receive emails fitting your criteria of every new home coming to market – every week until you say stop.

14. Get a credit report on yourself.

Okay, you say how far off is all this? How many years to wait before this is reality? Well, all this is available today in 75% of the U.S. and 60% of Canada!

But there are also some things we will be able to do in the not too distant future:

1. There will be huge increases in download speeds. As download speeds intensify (Rogers Cable is already 15 times faster than your standard 28.8 modem), pictures will become 360-degree virtual reality – the camera takes 13 shots in a 360-degree circle and a computer program will merge them seamlessly into one picture – offering a full 360-degree view. You are able to zoom in and out to see every detail.

2. The same will go for video clips. Today, most video clips still need to be downloaded. By 2001, we will have real time, real online video. You can watch a 1-5 minute video on any property in the privacy of your own home. It will change how we buy real estate forever.

3. As we said above, you are already able to enter your housing requirements, log them on a site and get email once a week when houses with your criteria become available. In the future every real estate company will offer this as a minimum.

4. You will be able to use map based systems. From a satellite photo down to your town, down to the street and down to the top of the house, find out all the information about the property. How often was it sold in its history, when built, what did it sell for each time, etc?

5. Map based systems will drive the New World. Already some systems allow map based detailed viewing of property. In the future this will explode. Angle views, multiple pictures and hard information available at the push of a button. You will be able to put your cursor on the corner of a picture of a home and it will calculate the square footage. The shadow of a home can determine the height of a property within a 3 CM error range.

6. The assessment authorities will go into competition with real estate boards as far as providing sales information to the public in a careful, predetermined way. In fact, the assessment authorities have more information on houses than you can begin to even imagine. The pressure of extra income will drive them to market.

7. MLS turf wars will increase. In addition to the scrape between Microsoft's WWW.HOMEADVISOR.COM and Realtor.com in the United States the turf war for MLS listings throughout the U.S. and Canada will heat up. In 1998 a Bergen County superior court judge temporarily ended a turf war between MLS Boards, ordering Garden State MLS to continue sharing listings with New Jersey MLS until another hearing could be held. Garden State MLS – which is owned by Weichert Realtors, Coldwell Banker, Prudential and Burgdorff/ERA – had instructed brokers to stop placing their listings in the rival NJMLS, which is jointly operated by two Bergen County boards. As well, CyberHomes asked competitor HomeScout to discontinue 'scraping' the CyberHomes site for property ads – a decision that will affect about 350,000 of HomeScout's estimated 1 million advertisements. Microsoft is accusing Realtor.com of offering special deals to its companies; while at the same time it makes deals with brokers for FREE lifetime listings.

8. Mega players will interfere with the operation of real estate companies and will blur the distinction of who can distribute real estate information. For instance in late 1998, more than 500 Re/Max brokers in 40 states signed agreements to place their listings on the Microsoft HomeAdvisor site, just weeks after Re/Max International headquarters in Denver announced it was embracing HomeAdvisor's chief rival, Realtor.com, as its web service vendor. Clearly the battle between Microsoft (all listings including 'by owner') and the 'Realtor only' oriented sites will intensify.

9. Affinity programs will flourish cutting into real estate commissions.
Costco Wholesale, MonEnet Money Malls, Paralyzed Veterans of America
and the National Vets Archives and others have banded together with
AmeriNet and are getting kickbacks from a variety of real estate companies as well as giving some of it back to the consumer. AmeriNet
Financial Systems reports it did $50 million in business in one month in
1999, the strongest month in the history of the loan brokerage. It cred-
ited the results to widespread acceptance of its Consumer Advantage
Real Estate Services (CARES) program, which offers customers rebates
on real estate commissions. The CARES Program is currently active in
Washington, Oregon, California, Colorado, Arizona, Maryland, Virginia
and the District of Columbia. AmeriNet expects to offer the program
nationwide by mid-1999.

10. But this is nothing as compared with what lies ahead. According to
an ActivMedia study, real estate is the most likely industry to lead
explosive e-commerce revenue growth over the next few years. Private
MLS services will continue to grow from original internet services. Some
senior real estate executives see a time where 'big companies' will walk
from MLS systems and try to wrestle back control over the information.
Already big players like Royal LePage and the Prudential are experiencing a renaissance. In our view it all won't matter. The relentless
onslaught of the information-rich consumer will continue to cut into
commissions, dramatically change services provided and kill off unwary real estate companies caught between the old and the new world.
At the December, 1998 San Francisco 'Real Estate Connect 98' confer-
ence it was made clear by the organizers that: "While you can still buy
a home, lease an office or purchase a building without signing a stack of
paper 4 inches deep, the day is rapidly coming when e-commerce and
the real estate transaction will be a seamless experience – an automated real estate process that is fricton free and liberated from unnecessary fees." I presume that 'unnecessary fees' include appraisal fees,
legal fees, placement fees, mortgage fees, and commissions.

There aren't just changes for the real estate industry ahead. Tremendous advances in computer technology will continue for all sectors.

Applications include: real-time translation; voice recognition; image processing; real-time control of distant experiments; holographic
imaging; decision modelling; and surgery at a distance.

Four powerful forces will alter the telecommunications landscape and revolutionize how we acquire, transform, and communicate information with one another: regulatory reform; cross-border alliances; emerging infrastructure; and technological advances.

Several ambitious satellite systems will become operational by 2002 and provide new global telecommunications infrastructures. Data transfer will vastly eclipse voice communications. Phone calls will be transmitted on the internet. By 2005 they will effectively be free.

A New World indeed, but not a world without great new opportunities. Dozens of new jobs will spring up.

New Computer/Internet Jobs

Basic html programming: Do not let the word 'programming' scare you ... basic html is like typing (huge amount of jobs increases ahead).

Industry News writer: Most real estate companies on the net do not have the resources to write their own news.

Know-how writers: Here, intranets will be a playground for know-how, offering content for internal members. Business plans, how to offer writing, cold calling scenarios, etc.

Internet 'Manual writers': Ever tried to follow instructions to put together your 'easy to assemble' babycrib? This refers to the talent of writing a manual for the company's internet site (huge opportunity).

Intranet news and writing: Internal rewrite of policy manuals, updating information, company newsletter, frequent Q & As, etc.

New creation of Map based systems: City maps with superimposed house information need creating. Statistical and historical information matches need doers.

360 degree virtual reality: Become a camera man/woman for virtual reality photos.

Real Estate Consultants: There are a 1000 questions in an uncertain world. This will be a huge growth industry. Both on the commercial and residential side (how to increase the value in my office tower by adding a coffeshop, gym, etc.) The key here is to be independent and give unbiased advice.

Interpreters: The new jobs will be in the interpretation of information.

Real estate marketing will become more niche oriented, more specialized. The new interpreter of information Realtor will charge for information that he or she gained through hard work. There will be negotiation specialists, joint venture specialists, money raiser specialists, property management specialists, resort management specialists, home inspector specialists, building envelope specialists all merging out of the new drive to find new ways to get paid as commissions overall shrink.

The consumer of real estate in the future – once used to the wealth of information and knowing where to find it – will have a much simpler world. He can already listen to his favourite music program and *only* his favourite music programs without commercials and he will watch only the news he wants – be it sports or business. Radio stations and TV stations will push only requested info to him daily.

For the real estate end of things, the transaction process will increasingly be streamlined. While he listens to his favorite music, the new consumer will identify the kind of neighbourhood he wants to be in, even the type of income he wants his new neighbours to have, and he'll check the crime stats. Then after posting his needs, he leisurely looks daily over the email (matching homes newly available to his criteria) which will be sent to him automatically from a variety of competing companies. He will download the 360-degree pictures he likes and only then look for the negotiator. And he will select him from the image that negotiator will represent through his web page. He is a good buyer, having been pre-approved at the very best rate possible and he is sophisticated.

A better world? A more exciting world? Who knows the final version that will develop, but clearly a New World of real estate buying and selling is already here.

∾

In Essence

He who owns the information will own the future.

Electronic commerce will soar in the next 5 years.

Mega-internet sites will out-muscle traditional real estate brokerage.

The consumer will be king.

Shopping for real estate companies, Realtors, and homes will change dramatically.

Chapter 21

BUYING OUT-OF-TOWN

The grass is always greener on the other side of the fence. What you've got to make sure of is that it's the grass that's green and not you.

The senior executive of today reads in his local paper that his company is 'lean and mean' and he knows why. He just laid off ten people and he is wondering whether he is next. Also, all these people that were laid off did something, now he is doing all their work too. He starts earlier and stays longer and at night he doodles and thinks, what if?

What if I packed up my kids, grab a satellite dish, my laptop and moved out-of-town? What if I sold the house in the city and really did it? Or he wonders: what if I bought a recreational property now and had a place to hide for the weekend. And he is not alone. People throughout North America are on the move. Population growth in smaller towns is exploding. Californians move to Oregon and Arizona, New Yorkers joke at the rain but move to Washington. The ski resorts and lakes are teeming with 'former' city slickers clutching cash and the hope for the elusive 'better quality of life'.

In Ontario, it always was the 'cottage' on the lake, in BC the 'cabin' in the mountains and the roads into the promised land are a hot sweaty affair Friday (out) and Sunday nights (back). Proving further our preoccupation with 'getting away'.

What is new is that now families actually uproot and move 'kid and caboodle' into the new out-of-town and bring their jobs with them. Some commute to the city, some live in both places, and most generate their know-how into a new enterprise.

Canada's population growth rate from 1991 to 1996 averaged 1.21% per annum or 6.05% for the period and BC's overall growth rate clocked in at double that. Yet, places like Kelowna grew by 22%, Gibsons on the Sunshine Coast by 23%, Courtenay on Vancouver Island by a whopping 48% and Whistler was king at 53%.

Many went, saw and bought. Others simply fell in love with the rolling hills, with the mountains. Some older yuppies bought without regard to amenities such as transportation, closeness to hospital or non-compatibility with locals. And some came back – reality destroying the dream.

Like all investments, but particular out-of-town type investments you must start by investing time for questions to yourself. What type of person are you? You dream of roughing it, but could you really? You dream about living on an island, but could your small children?

You want to make money on timber, on large acreages, but are you prepared to plunk down 50% cash.

Long before it became popular to talk about 'demographics' *Jurock Real Estate Investor* talked about the trend to 'out-of-town' in 1993. Our subscribers made money on timber and invested in rental properties in small towns long before it became everybody's fad.

But there are some principles we urge you to study. Trends are fine and you want to know where they are going but there are things to watch out for. Particularly, where the herd is involved.

Nowhere do you find the herd instinct harder at work than in the real estate investment world. When times are good everyone wants to buy in that locale. They rush in like the bulls of Pamplona rush into the streets toward the bullring. When times turn bad then they all rush to sell just like the people who run in front of the bulls in Pamplona. In both cases there's no shortage of competition. And just as good a chance of getting gored.

It is just as important, if not more so, to do your due diligence when the property is out-of-town. The reason for this is that you will be on unfamiliar ground as far as the people you would normally go to in the process of your due diligence and so you have to be even more careful.

Also, every time you go into a new area you are competing with the people that live there who have the advantage of local knowledge. Some times that works against you and sometimes it works in your favor. I have no way of explaining why, but sometimes there are investment treasures right under the noses of the locals and they just don't see them. Someone can come in from out-of-town, with a fresh perspective, and snap something up. But – and this is an important 'but' – you *must* always ask yourself the question, "Why am I so smart and so lucky that this plum of an investment opportunity is just waiting to drop into my lap?"

The answer might very well be that you are indeed smart and lucky – or – maybe the locals know something that you don't know. That's why the due diligence is so important. You need to check and double check to make sure that your basic premises are valid.

Only after you've done that is it time to act.

Every piece of recreational land has a use. That swamp might be just the thing for monied moose or duck hunters, that wind-buffeted cliff just right for a hang-glider enthusiast with a death wish. With that said, however, there are some truisms when it comes to selecting recreational property, property from which you can realize a profit.

The first hurdle: selecting the right land for your pocketbook and investment goals and timeline.

According to those who know, the right setting is often more important than the per-acre price. A small but lovely piece on a knoll or next to a fishy creek will be often worth more and show better appreciation than that really big chunk of dull. Whenever possible, think quality, either present or latent.

To help you clarify your thinking, here are the types of investors that get into the 'out-of-town' dance:
1. The Recreational Land Buyer
2. The Major Resort Buyer
3. The Profit Seeking Vacant Land Buyer
4. The Stressed-Out Seeker of Escape
5. The Offshore Escapee
6. The Kookhead
7. The Opportunist

The Recreational Land Buyer

The recreational land buyer is not primarily an investor. He's buying the property for a lot of reasons and 'investment' is quite a way down on the list. Oh sure, if the property goes up in value and if he should happen to sell it at a profit, he will take the money, but that isn't his primary purpose for buying the property.

This guy is an owner-user. He wants to boat, water-ski, hunt, fish, or maybe he just wants to sit on the property and contemplate his navel. But what he wants is to do this from his own property. He wants privacy, he wants control, he wants pride of ownership and these things only come when you own that property yourself.

The recreation person also might want proximity to other recreation such as ski hills, marinas, golf courses, hiking trails and stuff like that. If that's what he wants then he's going to have to pay extra for it.

As a general rule there is an inverse ratio between time and distance from an urban area and the price or value of the property. By this we mean that as the distance or travel time from the urban area increase, the price of the property decreases. The farther out you go, the cheaper the land. But this buyer generally wants to get to his property fast. A maximum 2-4 hour travel time is what he is looking for.

Even if your main interest is personal use, you still want to keep an eye on the investment aspect of your property. You have to take into consideration amenities nearby such as rivers, lakes, ski hills, golf courses and all the other factors that people will value when they are spending their recreation dollar. Waterfront, river, lake, ocean within 4 hours driving time is best. Next best is 'close to waterfront'.

The Major Resort Buyer

It is winter, you just came back from a day on the mountain and have that warm glow of the second bottle of wine and you say to yourself: "I should really buy here and kill two birds with one stone. I will have income *and* I will also have personal use." Well, I have news for you; you are not the first person to think of this.

We cautioned about this before. It's not possible to estimate where on the scale of financial mistakes this rates but it must be very close to the top. Anytime you confuse your investment objectives you'll be making some kind of a mistake. In my experience almost nobody ever meets the two objectives of personal use and investment in a single recreational property. And yes, one reason is the fact that the time you want to go skiing, everybody else does too and you end up needing the 'large income nights' and stay with a friend anyhow. But more importantly, you may find that buying property at a resort is not like buying regular real estate.

First, a ski resort has real 'quality of construction issues', it has real location issues (here location 'ski in, ski-out' does matter) and it has investment class issues.

You must understand what the investment implications are, particularly on the latter one.

Resorts, and particularly ski resorts, need careful studying of all of the details.

First, if your resort consists of just a parking lot and a lift the potential for capital appreciation is minimal. It may be a great place to have a winter home and ski, but then you are really a recreation-only buyer.

Major resorts have huge cash invested, the latest quad chairs and restaurants and stores a' plenty. Here – if your timing is right – you can have a real cash appreciation play. But even if your timing is right understand that a resort plays by different rules. Apart from properties located in National Parks that do not grant ownership, places like Whistler have a variety of restrictive covenants.

The resort association knows – particularly at the beginning – that most people buy for holiday purposes only. Since visits rise tenfold in the winter, they restrict the personal use of units in a variety of ways.

The reason is simple, they want to have 'warm beds,' but this is their reason not your reason. You don't want to have your use restricted. Our statistics show that this kind of restriction comes with a double insult: greater taxes and lower capital appreciation. Let's look at the kind of properties with or without covenants in place at Whistler in 1999 (they are all more or less the same at other resorts):

A. Single family homes and single family building lots

Unrestricted use. This has been and will continue the best possible investment class at a resort for price appreciation. We have seen well located building lots rise 400% in value in a 24-month period, something you never see in the other classes. Remember to try and buy the best you can afford. View, mountain, lake, golf course.

B. Single family condos with a 'phase I covenant'

You can have personal use year round. This covenant implies a 'moral obligation' to rent out your unit, but you can use it yourself at any time, you can have it managed by whomever. It is like a regular strata unit in town. This is the only kind of condo ownership I would want at a resort from a capital gain perspective and safety in a market downturn perspective. You can always mitigate your loss. You can move in yourself, take a lower rent, you have options in both A and B.

C. Single family condos with a 'phase II covenant'

Personal use is restricted to approximately 56 days a year. You are also usually part of a management pool. You must pre-book your own use, in some cases pay for the time you use the unit. In any case, any revenue collected from your unit belongs to everybody as does theirs to you.. In a downturn you cannot move in to help your cashflow. Even if you find your own tenant when the operator can't, the revenue is accredited into the pool and not to you. To add insult to injury these units carry 1.8 times the property taxes of 'phase 1' type units. I can hear the cries of the council and other interested parties already: "They are not all the same, covenants vary, some are not pooled," and they would be right. There are a myriad of differences. But this book is concerned with giving the best advice I can to investors. We have seen phase II type units rise in value, but not nearly as much as phase Is and in a downturn – see above.

D. Hotel Condo Units

They are similar to a phase II covenant with personal use restrictions. They also vary in restrictions and additions and penalties to very large degrees (look again at Chapter 17). There are some earlier ones where all you are liable for are your mortgage and common area costs. Most of the newer ones reverted back to the dark days of the early eighties were buyers can be responsible for the performance of restaurants, commercial and parking spaces, etc. and could be liable for any shortfalls. The Delta Mountain Resort at Whistler for instance was sold to some 260-odd investors in 1982. Almost immediately there were disputes between investors and Management Company. Many investors lost it all, the eighty or so that stayed in fought a legal battle for some 9 years and finally won control over their own units in 1998 after very little return for a very long time. Oh, by the way, this is one of the few hotel units sold where investors actually got some money back!

E. The time-share unit

Usually a small investor is away on holiday somewhere and it's a bright sunny day and to kill some time he finds himself walking into a time-share building and by some mysterious chemistry he finds himself having this vision of owning the suite that is being shown. That investor should at that point run for the hills as fast as he can.

Time-share units bought on holidays are not an investment. They are almost always a self-inflicted financial wound. To begin with they are not real estate. You own that investment with 51 other investors and you have to ask yourself this question. "What happens if I own the week of July 1-7 and I want to show it to a prospective purchaser in

December?" It's going to be very difficult for you to do this when someone else owns that time segment.

The resale market is very difficult. The secondary market operates
usually at less than 50% of original value paid; carrying costs can be
substantial, often more than renting a holiday suite. The 'mix and match'
approach of trading spaces also does not work well. Usually resorts
reserve the best time slots for paying guests rather than trade with you.
Almost always the resort is still in competition with you, offers free
dinners, can show units any time. Think about it, a 200-suite development selling at 50 weeks each needs to find 10,000 buyers! They will be
selling units against you forever. If you need to buy one, get a used one.
Chances are you get it at half price. Better yet, don't buy it at all.

The Vacant Land Buyer
The vacant land buyer is a pure investor. He's not interested in anything but profit. He is interested in two main positions. First, are the
clock and the calendar together. Is the inflation factor likely to make
the property more valuable with the passage of time? Secondly, is there
something he can do to create a profit independent of just waiting for
the price of the land to go up?

If he's buying the land to hold for sale to a developer, then he's a
vacant land buyer. If he himself is going to be the developer, then he is
wearing two different hats – but until the land is ready for development
he is not wearing the developer's hat, he wears the vacant land buyer's
hat until that time comes. Development is also in another part of the
book.

So let's talk about buying the land and waiting to see it go up in value.
Most of the time there is no conventional financing available for vacant
land. You either pay cash for it or get the seller to carry back the paper.

Like any other commodity the only two things you need to have in
order to be successful are: the money to do the deal and an accurate
opinion of which way the market is going.

As a general rule vacant land, if you only look at the land, reflects
inflation. But there are other factors that can bring you out way ahead
of just the appreciation from inflation.

1. Buy big and sell small. Large acreage often contains a number of
smaller, separate titles, which can be split off and sold separately for a
profit. For instance, an old abandoned townsite might be on the market

as one block, but be registered under literally dozens of titles. Assuming the place is accessible and reasonably pleasant, these narrow town lots are perfect for RV owners tired of having to pay camping fees every time they head out.

2. On a slightly larger scale, the land might have recreational sub-division potential. Check with the local authorities in regards to the access, sewage/septic field requirements, minimum allowed lot size and so forth. Be mindful that while some regions are easy winners for this type of product, other areas are a tougher play. Time it right and you can make lots of money. Time it wrong and you won't.

3. Buy an axe, buy a ratty looking piece of land with potential and then clean it up. People and plots; first impressions make a big difference. Pick a weekend during fall or spring when the woods are dampish and the fire hazard low, go in with your family, remove the underbrush, limb the dead bottom branches off the trees, burn the trash (keep the fire small and manageable) and open the place up to make it "park-like." It's surprising how much can be done in a couple of weekends and what a difference it makes on the resale.

4. Hire a backhoe and do a big-scale cleanout. As the demand for timber grows, more properties are being privately logged. Once the trees are gone and the timber-profit realized the owner often will sell the cleared land for cheap. Properly cleaned and re-seeded with grass (which makes for a dandy deer habitat) or replanted with trees with perhaps a pond dug out or augmented, the value can be cost-effectively enhanced for relatively cheap. It can take real effort, but such land remediation represents a real opportunity for profit.

5. If you've bought in the path of recreational growth you are going to prosper when it comes

6. You can buy vacant land with timber on it and in many cases you can log that timber and retrieve your purchase price from the timber. In fact, we recommended to our subscribers in 1994 to buy 160 acres parcels in the $25,000 to $50,000 price range. Often even some 20 acres in usable timber paid for the whole property.

The vacant land buyer is looking for profit, for something to take off the land. In addition to timber there can be hay and sand sites. Storage facilities can be a very profitable factor. In certain regions where residential/commercial construction is on the rise, gravel beds are another concrete profit possibility.

He also benefits from the huge trend for people to own properties away from the madding crowd.

The vacant land buyer usually has to deal in longer time segments than the investor in developed real estate. But if you buy a piece of property that has already been logged and is in second growth say after 6 or 7 years, you re-seed it and thin it over time and let the clock and the calendar and Mother Nature do the work for you. Go camping on it once a year for 20 years and at the end of those 20 years you're going to find out where the expression 'happy camper' came from.

Buy a piece like that for your grandson or your son at birth and long after you're gone they will be lighting candles in front of your portrait on the anniversary of your passing. Today's 160 acre piece with solid fir is worth about $1,000,000 plus. But also the more inexpensive filler woods that grow faster are worthwhile investments.

One small word of warning here. Once you own some timber that can be logged you are going to be approached by people who are going to want to cut it down for you. You'll be presented with all kinds of scenarios.

For example, a friend of mind owned such a property and wanted to build a road and a logger said to him, "Let me cut down the trees that have to be removed to facilitate the building of the road and I'll take out one or two along the side of the road and all I want is the timber and I won't charge you anything for clearing the trees off your roadway."

Permission was given and the logger went in and cut the trees off the roadway. The next time my friend went up to look at his property he was shocked and dismayed to find that the "few trees along the side of the road" turned out to be every stick of wood on his property. The place was as bald as a prairie.

If you ever have a logger cut any trees, make sure you're dealing with a reputable person and make sure everyone is singing from the same hymnbook.

As with everything, it helps if you know what you're doing. There are all kinds of experts available to consult with you. What you've got to watch out for is that your consultant isn't trading one of his problems for your cash.

The vacant land buyer, more than any other kind of real estate investor has the best advantage from the clock and the calendar. He's holding his property with the least trouble and at the least cost and as time passes even if there is no monetary inflation, population pressure will make the land more valuable. Add to this the factor of some kind of a 'cash crop' and it's an even more attractive situation. The vacant land buyer has also benefited from a huge inflow of foreigners and the general trend of people wanting a piece of the green. We see this trend continue. This is also a great way to create a portfolio of high interest rate first mortgages. Since financing is difficult, buyers do not balk at a 12% - 14% first mortgage rate. You can have your RRSP invest by granting these mortgages, you are in first position and you are in great return territory.

The Seeker of Escape

Call him the rat race escapee; call him the seeker of paradise, a New World afficionado. He sees himself as quite daring and is full of excitement as he enters the New World of out-of-town investment. You'd be excited too, if you were stuck behind a desk all your life and spent a few days sniffing the air of a potential new life. But never make the mistake that this person wants to rough it. He may say that he does, but what he really wants to do is see the cows but not smell them … and of course he needs his sushi.

He and his family have been driving real estate values skywards in the most unlikely places. Yes, you will find some of them in resorts as well, but mostly they look for a place that offers amenities, a 'small town feeling' and a new life.

More and more we see the phenomenon of people taking stock of their situations and deciding that life in the big city isn't really what they want. They look at the rat race and it becomes abundantly clear that the rats are winning, so they make some decisions.

Rather than continue with all the stress and all the worry, and rather than continue to see the quality of life being eroded more and more by the pressures of modern day life in the big city, they decide to do something about it.

And if what you're looking for is a slower pace, then the small town has that to offer you. But there are other factors than the slower pace. There can be better areas (we're speaking of business here) of growth with less competition. Usually the new immigrants to a country congregate in the big cities and the competition for business and jobs is greater in those cities. In the small towns you can find opportunities that don't exist in the big cities.

At one time or another almost everyone dreams of making the

move towards less stress and a more leisurely life style. Today we are seeing more and more people actually turning the thought into action and making the transition.

Naturally, no matter where you go, civilization is going to be snapping at your heels. McDonald's, the big box stores, the super stores of all kinds are going to know where you are and as soon as there are enough of you there they are going to plunk down one of their stores right beside you.

As a matter a fact, as an investor you should get on the mailing list of big box retailers like Costco, Wal-Mart and the like. Where they pick a small town so should you. It is a great indicator that the people living there are in the 35 - 55 year range. No white hair brigade for these big boys. After 55 you already own all the hammers you need.

If the decision to move is made a little later in life, you want to be a little closer to a lot of the big city things whether they be entertainment or medical services or anything in between.

But one thing is for sure, with the growing awareness of what it takes to live longer and healthier lives; we are going to see an increase of people heading to small towns.

The Offshore Buyer

In 1995 we featured a story "The Cariboo where the deer and the Germans roam." It was easy to see that offshore investment in farms and ranches – particularly the nice pieces – were snapped up by European and American buyers. The coast of British Columbia as well as Nova Scotia has many instances of prime properties snapped up by offshore investors.

Some simply want to park money, others want to escape where they are from and most enjoy the low prices and 'get away lifestyle' that is offered.

Generally, the Chinese buyer is not among the seekers of the 'far away' places, he rather goes to 'way down downtown', although a number of developments have been financed in Ontario, BC and Alberta in smaller towns. Japanese buyers have been huge buyers of resort type real estate for many years, but the turmoil back home and the enormous real estate crash to boot has spooked them. They are not prevalent any more. The recreational offshore buyer in 2000 and beyond likely comes from the US and Germany. The EURO is not well liked by the average German (said one German buyer: "Ozzie, how would you like it if they took your Canadian dollar and called it an AMERIO … but not to worry, it will be based on the economies of Mexico and Brazil." That's how the average German feels about having his 'hard' mark tied to France and Italy). So more will come. By the way, the best place to sell property to them is the internet. (See Chapter 20.)

The Kookhead
Every once in a while you find an organization that believes the end of the world is near and they and their dried food and machine guns are looking for a hideaway. They want limited access, hidden away and safety. Needless to say, you can't buy any property to flip to them exclusively. There are too few of them. But if you have a 'far away dog' somewhere, this is a great group to sell to for maximum profit.

Now, last but not least, we come to the last category of out-of-town buyer, the opportunist. This is the category that you and I fit into.

The Opportunist
The word 'opportunist' has somehow gotten itself a negative connotation. I've never understood why. After all, an opportunist is a person who finds an opportunity that no one is taking advantage of and simply takes it. My favorite quotation about opportunity is from Napoleon who said, "I found the crown of France in the gutter, and I picked it up with my sword." The opportunist looks at all the above buyers and asks: "How can I get there first, buy and sell to them when they come looking?"

If you wish to benefit from investment real estate out-of-town, there are some rules you've got to follow.

Here is what you want to watch for and watch out for:

If you want to be where the 'seeker of peace' wants to go, pick a town that has a better than average growth rate. Your StatsCan office offers you a growth rate chart. Look at it. How is it doing? You certainly want one that is growing. If the population is shrinking, you'll certainly be able to buy property cheap but for very good reasons.

Pick a town that has a special reason to grow, such as a new highway or new industries. Be careful of single industry towns, particularly towns depending on forestry, mining and fishing. You will always have to make a judgment call, because if something happens to affect that industry the town could go from growing to shrinking almost overnight.

All Canadian towns in Canada must be able to make the shift from resource based economies to an agricultural or tourism based one or die. Look at some of the agri-tourism areas in the wineries or other tourist based areas.

Pick a town where the property is relatively inexpensive. There is a correlation between low prices and growth potential. You get more growth appreciation in the lower priced areas.

Pick a town where there is a good employment base. That's where your tenants are going to come from. If you want to find out the type of people moving into a town, get the school age enrolment growth rate. This is often an early indicator of future growth. If elementary school registration is up by 10%, there is a message there.

Keep a close watch on vacancy rates. If there is too much supply of rental product on the market, you're going to have to compete with the other vacant properties for tenants.

And, of course, the basic principle that you make your most money the day you buy the property applies. And the rule of thumb of – Buy Local/Sell Long Distance – also applies.

What this means is you yourself have to go to the place where you are buying and you have to locate a quality Realtor and personally do the shopping around. The difference between doing this and buying a unit at long distance from some syndicator can be as much as $20,000 or $30,000. So when you buy, buy from the same perspective as the local. And you'll be amazed how many times you can come from the outside and buy something that the locals don't see simply because they are so familiar with the market that they are not looking at it closely enough.

That's when you buy. But when it comes time to sell, you want to sell at long distance. You want to expose your product to the big markets. You use the multiple listings and the internet or our own *Jurock International Net* at www.JUROCK.COM … okay, okay.

Certain facilities and amenities contribute to the profitable investment experience for the out-of-town buyer. It bears repeating that lakes seem to have a certain magic of their own. There seems to be something left over from our primitive origins that draw us to the lakeshore. If there is a lake and if there is a road to that lake, then that property is going to increase in value over time.

Rivers have a special appeal. Proximity to a river is always desirable.

Oceanfront property is another example of the lure of the water. People will pay almost anything to have that ocean frontage. A good example of this is the oceanfront properties at Malibu Beach in California. Every few years a storm comes along and wreaks havoc and the people just rebuild and wait for the next disaster but it continues to be some of the most expensive real estate in the world.

And, of course, there is the magic combination of Ocean and Island or Lake and Island. When you combine the mysterious appeal of the water with the isolation of the island you get a most appealing combination. This is the one place where more than any other you have a no-lose situation. Providing you don't pay too much in the first place. Actually, you can pay way too much and eventually the clock and the calendar will correct your mistake. That is simply because there are more people that want it than there are sites to satisfy the need.

What you want to watch out for are situations where the prices in the recent past have gone up so high, so fast, that the properties have become fully valued or over valued. Then, as a straight investment, it's not a good idea to buy at this point.

Views get translated into money when it comes to real estate. If you doubt that then build the same home in West Vancouver, BC and Swan River, Manitoba and see which one will bring you the highest price.

Climate is another important factor. Climate doesn't just mean sunshine and warm weather. We have a large segment of our population that likes nothing better than to go up on a snow-covered mountain and hurtle down at breakneck speeds while balanced on two thin pieces of wood. I'm one of them. Skiing and winter sports as we have said before are a very big attraction.

As with everything else in real estate investment you have to do your due diligence. It's always important but when you're buying property out-of-town it's even more so.

~

In Essence

The herd instinct is always at work in the real estate investment world.
Due diligence is more important when you're on unfamiliar ground.

When you go into a new area you are competing with the people who live there who have the advantage of local knowledge.

The further out you go, the cheaper the land.

Chapter 22

MANAGEMENT

Good management techniques won't make bad people good but it will make them behave better.

Okay, we've spent 21 chapters trying to figure out what is the best thing to buy. Once you've finally figured that you have all your ducks in a row you pull the trigger and, 'Bam!' you've bought yourself a real estate investment. Now that you have it. You've got to manage this investment until you sell it.

The when, where, why and how much of that sale have very little to do with the management, but are rather aspects of the various investment decisions that you have to make. Management is the living with the investment in that period of time between the purchase of it and the sale of it.

I'm going to assume that the readers with large or very large properties and portfolios either have professional managers or have already learned the basics by trial and error. This chapter will be mostly for those smaller players or for those just starting out. Hopefully, you will find here a point or two that will save you from making an error or two while undergoing a trial or two.

And who knows, maybe even the sophisticates will pick up a point or two or be reminded of something that they have forgotten or are neglecting to pay attention to.

And, we're going to talk exclusively about income producing property – something that is rented or leased to the end user. If you have raw land, there isn't much to manage except to look at it every once in a while to make sure that a band of itinerant tinkers haven't set up a permanent camp there. Same thing applies to timberland or natural resource land and that's not the kind of management that we're going to talk about.

So now you've got it. If it's already rented all you have to do is keep a watchful eye on the property and the tenant and make sure that you're charging enough rent. You do this by knowing your market. Then all you have to do is keep breathing in and out and allow the tenant to amortize the property for you.

If the property is empty when you take title to it or if it becomes vacant afterwards, then you're going to have the job of getting it rented. For the sake of discussion we'll assume for the rest of this chapter that you're renting a single-family residence – either a house or a condo or an apartment. There are differences for different kinds of property but the principles are the same. You'll put up a sign and put an ad in the classifieds and in the local weekly paper and sooner or later the phone will ring and someone will want to see the place.

Treat your rental like an open house 'for sale'. Advertise that it will be open – by appointment – between 2-4 PM. This will allow you to gather names and applications. Then after the open house visit the prospective tenants where they live now … a real eye opener.

If your place is still occupied, it will help to be on good terms with the tenant who is moving out. It creates a better atmosphere and he will be more cooperative and have the place looking better whenever you show it.

When you're showing the property, point out the benefits and tell them which faults, if any, you intend to correct, i.e. carpets, painting, etc.

Use a rental application and have them fill it out. You need references that you can check and you have to be sure to check them. Don't be timid about this. The only people who are not anxious to give you their references from places that they lived in before are people who have something to hide.

When you check with other landlords remember that you are talking to a real estate investor just like yourself and you can be very confident that the information you're going to be getting will be valid information.

The better class property you are renting, the more vital it becomes to get the credit information and do a comprehensive credit check. If you don't pay a lot of attention to this step, you're going to be very sorry. The time to solve any credit problems that you might have with a tenant is before you let that tenant rent. You're better off to have the place stand empty and lose a month's rent than to let a deadbeat in.

You also have to decide what your policy is going to be on offers or counter-offers when it comes to the asking price for the rent. For the most part it's best to accurately determine what the fair market value is for the unit and have that as a firm price. If a prospective tenant won't pay that price and you agree to a lesser price, then you will have a serious problem with that tenant when you try to raise the rent. You are starting out on the wrong foot.

If it's a matter of them not being able to afford the rent, then again, you're better off waiting for someone who can afford it. Especially when you can expect that the first time they suffer any financial reversals it's going to be reflected in their ability to pay the rent. It's better to cut off these problems before rather than after they've moved in.

If however, the market is tough and you are competing for tenants, be innovative. I generally found it easier not to lower the rent but offer real inducements. If your unit has a rental value of $1,000 but higher vacancy rates made the competition lower their rents to say $900, leave your rent at $1,000 but offer one month free rent for this year and – if necessary next year. You are actually better off by $300 per year and when the market turns, you don't have to raise the rent. This works very well, as you can advertise '2 months free rent'. Also, note that you want to give the free month in the twelfth month each year, thereby assuring you have a tenant for 24 months. The key is to be innovative and draw the maximum response to your ad to select your best tenant from. Never give the first month free … particular in your ad as you will attract every deadbeat for miles around … always the 6TH, 8TH, 12TH month.

There is also the concept of 'rent-to-own'. Sometimes you may wish to sell, but the market isn't that great or you have a long-term tenant that would like to buy the property. Your tenant may say: "Look we'd like to buy this house but we have no cash down payment, please sign over the house and we'll pay you the downpayment in three years." Depending on the market condition and the financial shape you are in, this may sound like a good idea; after all you have known the guy for a while. But, never, ever sign over your property with 'no money' down to anyone. Buy yes, sell no. Times change, circumstances change. The tenant loses his job, follows the lure of the wild, discovers the joys of his secretary and there you are. To repossess a property where the buyer had no original equity is costly and time consuming.

But what you can do is to offer your long-term tenant or really anyone else a similar deal. Let's say the house is valued at $100,000, the rental value of the property is $1,000 per month.

Offer your tenant a 'rent-to-own' deal that is structured this way. Your tenant pays the $1,000 a month, plus $200 extra. You then give him the option to buy the house with a fixed contract due on a fixed day on which he has to exercise the option. The accumulated extra $200 per month will be applied in total against the down payment of the property.

Here, the contract would be written with an option for 30 months, at the end of which the tenant can buy. He now has $6,000 of which he can use $5,000 for the down payment. He can get a CMHC first mortgage for the rest and has an extra thousand for the transfer costs and fees. The beauty is that if he does not exercise the option for any reason, his extra monies are forfeited. After all, you effectively took the property off the market for him. If he buys, fine, you have a sale at a price you wanted in the first place but couldn't get any other way. If he doesn't, you have an effective 20% rent increase. And yes, use a lawyer to draw up the option. Everything in writing is the only good policy.

So make sure that you use a rental agreement. If you don't have your own, there are standard forms you can use. The most important factor is to have everything in writing. Having things in writing won't make bad people good and won't make good people better, all it does is delineate the parameters of any legal action. You never want to take legal action if you can possibly avoid it. But a strong rental agreement allows you to make convincing threats.

Let's talk about how much. Sometimes it's hard to know what is the most you can charge without negatively affecting the rentability. It's better to be a few dollars below the market rather than a few dollars over the market. If you're even one dollar over the market, your unit won't rent and if you're raising the rent of an existing tenant, they'll move out.

So it's important to keep surveying the neighborhood to know what comparable units are renting for because these comparable units are your competition and an accurate assessment of this competition is going to tell you what you can charge.

Next, you have to decide what you're going to allow and what you're going to prohibit. Children and pets are the main factors here. Children

246

and pets are hard on property. While there are always exceptions, at the end of a year's tenancy a piece of property that had kids and pets will be worth less than the same property that didn't have kids and pets. If you permit them, you're going to have to allow for this. I'm not making a recommendation because I think it's an individual choice. Personally, I like kids and pets, and I have rented homes to large families with few problems. Just be aware and take extra care doing your due diligence. The important thing is to know that they cost more and allow for it, otherwise it's going to be like contributing to a private charity.

You've heard me say over and over that you make your most money the day you buy the property. There is a parallel to that in renting property. You save yourself the most trouble the day you decide not to rent the property. Ideally you want to nip all the problems in the bud and have all those problem people take their problems somewhere else. That's the ideal. That is why I recommend that you visit tenants where they live now. That is particularly useful if you are renting a free standing home to a family with kids. How do they treat the property they are in now? Do not let the urgency of getting the first month's rent covered govern your actions. Tenants will be at their absolute peak behaviour when you first meet them. Follow the steps outlined and you will have a lot less grief.

In the real world every once in a while you make a mistake and let a problem person in. When that happens you have to deal with it right away. With property management, problems do not get better and they don't go away by themselves. They get worse and they multiply. So you have to deal with problems right away. This is a classic example of 'the first loss you take is always the smallest'.

This means if you have a no pet rule and they get that cute little kitten that is just too precious for words, you have to be the villain. If you don't, the next pet might be an eighteen-foot boa constrictor that will escape and curl up behind the dryer in the laundry room and put that nice little eighty-three year old widow on the third floor into near cardiac arrest. (I only mentioned this because this actually happened to a friend of mine.) Or, if next month's rent is due on the last day of this month and it's a day late, you better be the villain because next month it will be five days late and so on and so forth.

My late-rent philosophy is this: People have to make a conscious choice as to who they are going to disappoint when it comes to being late with money. They will invariably disappoint the nicest person because this is the easiest and most pleasant course of action. I arrange things so that the last person on their list of people to disappoint is me. I suggest you do likewise. (If you get nothing else out of this book, this one paragraph gives you your money's worth.)

But the best-laid plans of mice and men, etc. Every once in a while the dice are going to fall the wrong way for you because they fell the wrong way for your tenant and late rent is going to turn into no rent and you're going to have to get them out of there. This is where it helps if you have a good relationship with them and it can be kept friendly. If it can't, you've got to go through the eviction process. Avoid this if you can but if you can't, do it as quickly and as expeditiously as possible.

You hear all sorts of horror stories about people who rented to a motorcycle gang who completely trashed the property before moving out. That's why you want to be careful at the beginning. If you were careful in the beginning, you will have a minimum of problems at the end.

When your tenant does move and if there is a damage deposit involved make sure you inspect the premises before you return the damage deposit. Also, don't return any deposits until they have completed the moving out process.

When you buy one or two investment properties out-of-town it is very important to hire a property manager. All the joy of ownership goes out the window, when tenants/landlord relationships go sour. In fact, it is the single most important consideration when buying rental property.

I have owned my share of rental properties and have both good stories and absolute horror stories to tell. The good news is that you can avoid the horror but you need to be good. Good at being a manager that is. Often we mix up our objectives when we try to manage our rental property ourselves. We want to increase the value of our property, we want a tenant to pay our mortgage, we want to be loved by the tenant and we want him to pay on time every time and we want him to take care of the property better than if it was his own. Yeah, well I have news for you. You'll get some of these some of the time, but not all of these all of the time. The worst one here is wanting to be loved by your tenants. You can't be, you are at odds. He wants to pay as little as possible with you shouldering all of the upkeep of repairs, including window washing, you want him to pay as much as possible and cut the grass too. End of Love.

Property management can make or break you. This is where lots of people fall down, more than anything; it will test your ability. Unless you actually live within easy reach of all of those far-flung revenue properties, you're going to be relying upon someone else to manage things. If you've got trusted tenants, be thankful ... but don't be complacent. If you're buying a unit in a multi-unit revenue property, be darn sure the prospectus and related documents ring true. Sometimes a combination of hidden deferred maintenance and a matter-of-fact management company which would 'rent to anyone' can end up cracking many an investment egg. Property management is a business. If you can't treat your property management like a business, get a professional who can. Think about it. The average investor owns his property 6 years. The average single family home rental value in Vancouver is $1,500 per month, $18,000 per year or a cool $108,000 income. This is serious money. To be managed seriously. Property Management means: writing ads, handling inquiries, showing property at night, collecting rent, unfriendly tenants ... it all spells personal involvement and free time encroachment.

So, unless you know what you are doing, hire someone qualified who will also give you great service.

A good property manager doesn't take the first yokel that wants to rent the place. He has a plan of action to get tenants, he has a clearly itemized – who is responsible for what – contract with his owners and one with his tenants. He must have a reviewable business plan. Ask your manager for his.

What does a 'quality service' oriented property manager do, anyway?

He has: a *written* budget outline; income projection; timely collection of rent; expense control; establishing rental value; clean, simple accounting; maintenance.

He also has to show you the *operating procedure* he employs for maintenance (ongoing action or re-action to problems as they occur only), repairs (ditto), safety and security issues (spelled out, how, when, who?) and insurance (enough, all eventualities covered, etc.)

You should also *inspect the property* with your manager together and meet the staff he employs (you may like him but shudder at the employees). What's his regular (weekly, daily, monthly) inspection routine?

Understand the *scope of his authority*. Does he hire contractors to do the work? Does he advance funds? Does he use rental income to place ads or bill you? Does he make his own repairs? What is the track record? Who can you call to verify?

Do this all upfront. Have a *written understanding of your relationship* – small building or large – and you have a basis to measure actual performance against promised performance.

After you've hired a professional manager you then have to manage the manager. You've heard that "the price of liberty is eternal vigilance." The same thing goes when you hire a manager, you have to be eternally vigilant so you'll know when he's stopped doing what he's supposed to be doing as soon as he's stopped doing it.

When you look at vacancy factors in a certain geographical locale as it pertains to a certain type of accommodation, you would be well advised to believe the numbers and set aside the necessary reserves. Over the long haul you will experience the average vacancy factors. If you're lucky and you don't, then you can add those reserves to the net profit when you sell the property. Until then, you have it as a very necessary cushion.

A final word about management – the better you or your manager perform the management functions the more you will gross and the less you will spend. And of course, whatever you don't spend is what you get to keep. After all, that's the reason we play the game.

~

In Essence

The best time to solve a management problem is before you let that tenant move in.

A strong rental agreement allows you to make more convincing threats. There's a saying that if you can do it then it's not bragging. The same goes for the rental market – if you can get someone to pay it, then it's not too much.

A professional property manager is essential for out-of-town properties.

Make sure you are the last person on your tenant's 'who are we going to disappoint' list.

Chapter 23

INCOME TAX

If you have the soul of an accountant, but not the personality that you need to practice accountancy, then a career with the tax department should be perfect for you.

There are a hundred people I can think of who are better equipped to write this chapter. Every tax lawyer knows more about taxes than I do. Every accountant knows more about taxes than I do. You could open the yellow pages at random and stab down your finger and probably hit the name of someone who knows more about income tax than I do. The only factor that qualifies me to write on this subject is that I hate paying taxes as much, or more, than any other person on the face of the earth.

Everything there is to say on the subject has already been said. "Only a damn fool pays income tax!" – Bernard Baruch. "Don't give money to politicians. It only encourages them!" – Will Rogers. "You might as well pile your money on the table and set fire to it!" – Anonymous. It isn't likely that I'm going to come up with anything new.

But then again, I don't really need to come up with anything new because when it comes to taxes we are already preaching to the converted. I have yet to meet anyone who thinks that taxes are too low or that if the government only had some more money they could do more good things, especially because they are doing such a good job with the money they are getting now.

For those who are reading this for advice, I can't tell you what to do or how to think. You have to decide that for yourself. However, I can tell you how I think and I can share some of the experiences with you that people have shared with me.

First, let's deal with the philosophy of income tax. The idea all got started when two families got together and decided to put a protective fence around their huts. The dominant male said, "I'm going to be in charge of building this fence and maintaining it but I don't see why I should have to pay for it myself so everybody protected by the fence is going to have to kick in his share so that everything will be fair." And everybody kicked in his share and everything was fair. Of course, it was necessary to give a name to this share and because it sounded more like a tax than anything else they'd ever encountered, they decided to call this payment a 'Tax'.

Then one day the dominant male thought it would be a good idea to put up a statue to himself and so the tax had to be increased to cover the cost of the statue. People complained that the dominant male was spending money on statues when there were people starving who could make better use of the money so the dominant male had to send over a policeman to bop them on the head until the complaining stopped. Naturally, the cost of the policeman had to be covered by an increase in taxes.

There were usually two kinds of people in the village; those who had property and who made money and the other kind who had nothing and needed things. At first the dominant male made slaves out of the people who had nothing and this was tried for a few thousand years but the trouble with slavery is that after a while slaves get cranky with being slaves and they rise up and make things inconvenient for the dominant male and things have to be sorted out all over again. It's a lot like kicking over the Monopoly board and having to start the game all over again. Nothing much changes in the long run but it is messy and it aggravates the dominant male.

Then some genius discovered that economic slavery was way better than the kind with whips and chains. Oh sure, they still had periodic revolutions just not as often and not as severe. But this same genius discovered that, 'The power to tax is the power to destroy – and the power to destroy is the power to rule!' Which is what everyone was looking for in the first place.

They decided to enslave the productive segment of society by taxing them just enough to keep the government going and yet not so much that they would rise up in armed revolt. It's like fishing with a cormorant. A cormorant is a bird that is great at catching fish. What you do is catch a cormorant and tie a string around its leg and put a ring around its neck and let it sit on the edge of your boat. When it sees a fish swim by it dives down and swallows the fish – at least it tries to but the ring around its neck keeps it from swallowing the fish all the way. Then the fisherman pulls on the string and hauls the cormorant together with the fish back into the boat. He reaches into the cormorant, retrieves the fish and perches the cormorant on the edge of the boat until the next fish swims by and the cormorant does it all over again.

Every once in a while the fisherman removes the ring from around the cormorant's neck and the bird gets to eat a fish. That way he stays interested in the game. The fisherman is either going to eat fried fish or roast cormorant and the cormorant knows this. Everyone in the equation is properly motivated.

And here we have very accurately described the relationship between the productive taxpayer and the taxman. If you're happy with the way things are, then skip the rest of this chapter. If you'd like to have more money to spend on yourself, all you've got to do is figure a way to send less of it to the tax man and that will do it.

Most sensible people agree on the same things. Certainly we have to have roads and schools. We must have police and probably even an army. Widows and the aged must be cared for and orphans must have milk. The only area of disagreement comes in determining what is the best way to accomplish this. There is a school of thought that says that if you let people who make money keep that money and allow them to use that money to make more money then the standard of living for the whole country will be higher. Then there is the school of thought that says if you give all the money to the government they will use it to create a heaven here on earth. The answer, of course, lies somewhere in-between but probably a lot closer to the first than to the second.

People who pay the least taxes and therefore keep the most of the money they earn for themselves are the people that consider themselves to be at war with the tax department. The best weapon you can have in this war is a constant awareness that the war is going on. This requires a shift in attitude. Instead of a 'We're all in this together' point of view you have to have an 'Us and Them' point of view.

This doesn't mean you're going to be a bad citizen. It just means that you're not going to pay any unnecessary taxes. The operative phrase here is 'unnecessary taxes'. Judge Learned Hand of the U.S. Supreme Court said that it is a person's right to arrange his affairs so as to pay the least tax possible. The operative phrase there is 'the least tax possible'. Or it is tax avoidance whenever possible. Never tax evasion.

If you think that the less money government has, the more efficient they are going to be then you have a duty as a good citizen to give them as little money as possible. Politicians spend your tax money because their success is measured in whether they get re-elected. They spend your tax money in order to buy your vote. If you don't think this is the reality, then you should be drawing pictures with a crayon and affixing them to the side of the refrigerator with a magnet. Bureaucrats spend your tax money because their success is measured in the growth of the number of personnel and the size of the budget of their bureau. Each year has to be more and bigger than the previous year. And any of their budget that is not spent is returned to the treasury and that amount is deducted from what they are given for next year's budget. Can you guess what they are going to do with any money that looks like it might be left over? As you can see, the course of your duty as a good citizen is clear.

Every dollar you don't pay tax on is really one dollar doing the work of two. It's like a free dollar. What you should do is every time before you earn a dollar you should consider if there is a way to take that dollar as anything other than income. Every time you spend a dollar you should consider if there is a way to make that expenditure deductible from your income. You do that every time – with every dollar.

Some take the approach that what they want to strive for is to get as close as possible to making every breath they take tax deductible. If they buy a stick of chewing gum they give half of it to a prospective client so they can write it off. They have a home based business so they can write off a portion of their house. They have a ten-year-old clunker that is the family car and their home based business provides them with a Cadillac Eldorado for their business calls. They save every scrap of paper and document every transaction in their diary for that fateful day when the taxman decides to audit.

You might as well be aware of the reality and regard yourself as being at war with the taxman. There is no way you can buy his love. Nothing you do short of sending him all your money is going to satisfy him. You are better off to have that dollar in your pocket with the tax man facing the task of getting it rather than the dollar being in the pocket of the tax man and you faced with the task of getting it back or failing that, faced with the task of getting along without it.

The key, particularly for the real estate investor is to have a sound system of record keeping right off the bat. If you are properly documented and have a logical rationale for even an aggressive tax posture, you will not present an attractive target to the taxman. Remember that the taxman is running a money factory and every department and every person in every department has to produce a certain amount. If you are not an attractive target, they are going to pass you by and concentrate on someone that they can beat up more easily. But even if they decide that you are an attractive target, they have to beat you before they can collect.

When it comes to being a target you want to be as unappealing as possible. Skunks and porcupines know what they are doing. You don't want to be a do-it-yourselfer when it comes to tax. The tax department loves to deal with amateurs. It makes their work so easy. But being well documented and having a good tax professional standing between you and the tax department makes you not nearly as appetizing as the amateur. The very important operative phrase here is 'good tax professional'. The taxman, like all of us, is going to follow the course of least resistance. So your objective should be to offer as prickly a target as possible. However, remember that being well documented is more important than the letterhead of your tax professional. However the larger the portfolio, the larger ' brand name' should be your accounting firm.

If you worry about audits, you will not be, if you have your 'ducks in a row.' You shouldn't care about audits because everything you do is going to be defensible and well documented. You are avoiding, not evading. I know people that feel, if they are not being audited once in a while, they are giving the tax department too much money.

I know someone who received his tax return requiring a healthy amount to be remitted to the taxman along with the bill from the tax preparer. He said to his tax preparer, "You don't seem to understand. I have money for income tax; I have money for your fee; I don't have both." The tax preparer recalculated the numbers and the tax return was almost nil and his bill was the same. It all depends whose ox needs goring the most.

You can be as creative as you want – within reason. I heard of a cab driver that claimed his uniform as a cost of doing business. The taxman disallowed the deduction because he needed clothes anyway. The next year the cab driver claimed the cost of his uniforms but this time he put it down as 'seat covers'. No problem.

Another chap was in the seminar business and was always elegantly attired in very expensive tailored suits, which he deducted as an expense. The taxman denied the deduction because the suits could be worn for non-work activities. The next suits the man had made were constructed without any pockets. No problem.

In the real estate investment world there are a hundred things to know about write-offs, taking appropriate deductions and submitting taxes. We mentioned that your rental property has to have a 'reasonable expectation of profit' sometime in the future, or your deductions will get gored. You could be liable for a myriad of things. Here is were you need professional advice. Your business plan makes it easy. Go see the professional, tell him or her. "This is what I want to do, how best do I position myself before I start?" and you will be as tax-effective as possible.

It's all a matter of how creative, how well documented, and how logical your premise is; assuming, of course, that you're working within the framework of the laws as they exist. Everything else being equal, the person who is the most aggressive will pay the least tax.

∽

In Essence

The power to tax is the power to destroy – and that's the good news.

The people who pay the least taxes and therefore keep the most money are the people who treat the tax department as the enemy.

The good citizen has a duty to give the government as little money as possible.

The taxman sometimes loses – which indicates that religious people might be right.

Chapter 24

WHAT TO BUY *&* WHAT NOT TO BUY

Trust in Allah, but tie up your camel!

During some 6 years I have published a highly detailed 16 page monthly newsletter and a weekly 2 page fax service to several thousand subscribers. I hold 6 in-house subscriber seminars and am a hired speaker at over 100 events per year. I analyze, I debate, I write and I talk giving detailed analysis on any and all aspects of real estate investment. But in the end it always boils down to this: "Okay, okay, Ozzie, I understand, but now tell me what should I buy and where? Give me the short summary of the principles. Exactly please!"

We all run busy lives, we understand we ought to do more due diligence, but events take over ... we live our lives constantly reacting to situations; it's difficult to catch a breath. In the end we like someone to tell us what to buy and so I will.

However, I do not know when you will be reading this. The 'you' from the future may find a different world with different circumstances than the one I am writing in today.

In 1993 we advised our subscribers to 'head out-of-town' and identified a number of small towns in Canada. Among them we recommended Courtenay. Vacancy rates there were falling, big retailers were moving in and the population was growing. In fact, Courtenay by 1996 had recorded the highest population growth in BC. Yet, by the summer of 1994 we placed Courtenay on 'investor alert.' The same good reasons still applied for buying there, but it had become visible to all and sundry. Developers were now moving in by the droves, building, driving up land prices, with the result that prices for condos almost doubled. For us it was time to leave. Since I am a frequent guest on Michael Campbell's great "MoneyTalks" show, I had mentioned Courtenay on the show in 1993. For years after – and when Courtenay experienced price reversals in 1997 and 1998 – people remembered only that 1993 radio show. My subscribers and I were long gone.

The same went for recommendations we made at Whistler. While we very leery about some investment property at Whistler (see Chapter 21) we recommended Whistler for years. Strong population growth, rated as the number 1 ski resort in the world, huge capital investment – all solid reasons to invest. However in February 1997 we placed Whistler also on Investor Alert. Overbuilding – available room nights were projected to soar from 1.2 million to 2 million and no amount of visitor growth would, in the short run, sustain value increases. We forecast 20% price increases in Toronto in 1996, 10% for Calgary in 1997 and 1998 and to 'only buy the deal of a lifetime in Vancouver from 1995 to 1999'. Yet, by the time you read this we probably have changed direction again and an outright buy or sell signal has been given to our subscribers for these markets.

In the eighties it used to be so easy to buy property, if you paid too much for it, you just bought it too soon. Inflation bailed you out. In the new millenium it won't be quite that easy. Some property classes will rise in value while others fall at the same time in the same marketplace. Some real estate values in some parts of Canada will never recover, others will continue to soar. One thing is for certain things will continue to change. Caveat emptor.

Some nuts and bolts first:
1. As an investor in a new home you need to buy at least 12% below the market. Take a $400,000 home, add GST at $28,000, land transfer taxes of $5,000 (or so – varies by area) and $14,500 in commission when you sell it. You need to sell the property for $447,500 just to break even. And that does not count the legal title transfer costs.
2. As an Investor in a used home you have GST but everything else stays the same, you still need to buy below the market.
3. In most markets in Canada sales volume in the first 6 months is 60% of the volume of the last six months. Remember that when you sell, it is better in the spring.
4. In most major markets in Canada prices in any cycle peak during the first half of the year – usually in May and drop for that cycle in the

December - January period. When studying the comparisons be careful who is comparing what time period to which point they are trying to make. Often the best time to buy is in the low cycle, opposite when you sell. Yes, there are exceptions.

5. *Prices start rising in small towns and northern towns usually after the winter goes and contract lower after the snow falls.*

6. *For the smaller investor single family homes have outperformed townhouses and condominiums every time and for every market.* No matter which city we look at, Vancouver, Toronto, Calgary, Edmonton. Over time single family homes bring greater price appreciation. It is in the land. Canadians still like a place to put their barbecue. Townhouses also usually perform better than condos but not as well as single-family homes. This may change in those cities where the proportion of condo to single family home sales crosses 50%. In Edmonton and Calgary the condominium portion of the market is below 18% with 72% of the sales found in the single-family home sector. In Vancouver, however, more than 50% of all sales are now condos. Wherever the greater number of people want to trade price, appreciation follows.

7. *Ground-oriented townhouse type units generally outperform high-rises condos.*

8. *New condominiums depreciate. Used condominiums appreciate.* Unless you buy in high inflationary times. Otherwise – it's a truism.

9. *Don't pay too much for higher floors in a high-rise.* If a building is 25 stories high, unless you own the penthouse, don't pay more for 'view'. Once you are 'in view' – say, on the twelfth floor, don't pay any more for a suite located between the 12TH to the 24TH floors. You will not get your money back. We have seen developers add $2,000 per floor 'because you get better views', but it is money wasted for you the investor. Once you are in view, resale buyers will not pay the extra money to be a little higher. It does not matter to them.

10. *Resort properties do well in an upper-end resort.* If there is only a parking lot and a lift, it may be a great family place to go to. But price appreciation is much slower.

Myths

1. *You make a lot of money buying foreclosures.* No, you don't. It is tough, it is tedious, and the courts always side with the owner. It sounds sexy, but it is an investor graveyard of time and effort wasted. I have seen very, very few foreclosures work for the investor.

2. Tax sales are a big money maker. No way. A real fad (in the mind of some – fanned by late night U.S. TV shows). There are very few tax sales investors that are consistently successful in big cities. Probably none. There are some out-of-town properties that get sold in the boonies ... and for a good reason – no one wants them, even for the taxes owing. In the United States, the law is much tougher on people that do not pay taxes, liens and judgements. We have featured Washington tax sales a number of times in our newsletter. In the US it works, in Canada it does only rarely.

3. Cities with Government as the major employer experience fast growth. In fact we predict the opposite. We placed Edmonton, Ottawa and Victoria on Investor Alert in 1995 for that reason. We voters are so disenchanted with government that we want them to downsize. Downsizing means fewer employees. Fewer employees means properties are sold. Result, falling market. But things change, once cities are finished downsizing and prices have fallen, there will be a great upside for other fundamental reasons. The only exception may be in cities where land settlements are paid in cash and administered by a native band. For a while they will become the major employer in town.

4. A good location outweighs the timing and trend identification. Never. A good location helps, but you always make more money faster if you get in at the beginning of an up-cycle or where you identify a new trend.

What To Buy?
1. Your own single family home

2. Single family homes with basement suites anywhere

3. Used downtown condos in a major city, with view, on water, park. 2-5 years old without GST

4. All waterfront, river, lake, ocean, it will always appreciate within its timing cycle.

5. Major resort properties with unlimited personal use

6. Mini warehouses for an investor and as an owner With the greater trend to self-employment more and more small companies look for their own space. Look for suburbs or cities where they allow a larger component of office space (more than say 15%) in an industrial warehouse. Buy individual units or if you are larger, buy an existing industrial park, spruce it up, get more and more office space converted and keep it ... or strata title it for sale.

7. Mini-storage parks With some downsizing by families and the trend to move out-of-town, mini-storage parks are increasingly attractive. A strong real estate play, good cash flow and overhead.

8. Trailer Parks are always good cashflow and there are never enough.

9. While REITS *are still in a buying mode, helping to drive prices higher, buy small apartment buildings or strip shopping centres.* Competition will drive up values far beyond underlying revenue streams. Watch for falling stock markets.

Where?

1. Consider Casino towns. Where casinos are located in better towns with strong capital investment, more employment tourism, etc. will lift values generally.

2. In some downtown markets like Vancouver used condos were discounted by up to 40% under $160 per foot.

3. Single family homes with basement suites A home that sells for $110,000 with a $5,500 downpayment can bring a rental income of $1,000 from the main floor and $300-$400 from the basement. With payments of under $800 per month, cash flow is considerable. This is available usually in smaller markets with strong employment and population growth. But some cities in 1999 still qualify – Edmonton, parts of Calgary. You can build a large portfolio with little cash.

4. Small towns in Alberta, BC and Ontario with the pre-requisites of:
    a) Population Growth same or better than provincial average;
    b) Vacancy rates are below 4% or getting there;
    c) A reason to grow, new highway, new employment;
    d) Good prices;
    e) Good Property Management is available;
    f) You can buy with low downpayment and yet have good cashflow;
    g) It is not a one-industry town;
    h) University or college towns with character.

What Not To Buy

Whatever I put here, someone will argue that he or she, Aunt Harriet and Uncle Tom made money buying these, but remember we talk about the greater number of people here.

1. In resorts:
    a) Time-share units are not real estate.

b) Limited personal use units unless there is nothing else and you just gotta be there.

c) Hotel type limited use units

2. *Out-of-town*

    a) Without the above proven principles, many small towns will never have price appreciation.

    b) Deals without proven property management

    c) Out-of-town deals that do not cash flow

3. *Limited Partnerships you can't get out of*

4. *For now, in 1999, we tell our subscribers not to buy property situated on, abutting or located in an area where you have to drive over Native Land to get to it.* Either fee simple or lease land. Some resort property owners have seen the values of their land depreciate by 50% because of roadblocks. Owners with native leases in place in major cities face huge increases at renewal time. Finally, in a few places, bridges that give access to fee simple land have mysteriously burned down. On balance – remember we are talking to an investor – while there is turmoil and more ahead, stay away from Native Land investment. If this doesn't worry you, check to make sure that the development you wish to buy in has a head-lease in place with the Department of Indian Affairs in Ottawa. Otherwise no laws apply to you. There is little protection. We also have seen a number of strata title properties where the Real Estate Act Part II does not apply, again not consumer friendly – no recourse.

5. *If you are living in a Chinese area, you may want to consider the question of good Feng Shui.* I know, I know, depending on where you are when you read this, you think I have gone bonkers. But if you reside on the West Coast with many new immigrants you would be well advised to note a few basics.

The Chinese exponents of Feng Shui believe that where you live and how you allocate and arrange the elements of your home or workplace can significantly affect the harmony of your health, wealth, and happiness. By acknowledging and augmenting the all-pervasive life energy, or *Chi*, you can affect the whole tenor of your well-being. Simple things like improperly placed furniture, incorrect color schemes, and elemental conflicts (i.e. having the 'water' – refrigerator – next to the 'fire' – stove) can create factors that impact negatively on your life. So, if your likely future buyer is of Chinese descent avoid:

1. *A straight road leading directly to the home*, with people coming and going, or a small stream flowing in a straight course, from it will dissi-

pate the good influences.

2. *Avoid building* at the junction of a T-street or at the end of a cul-de-sac because these locations are on the receiving end of the straight-flowing Sha. A dead-end street traps the bad Sha.

3. *The front entrance* should not face the upstairs stairway.

4. *The front door should not have a view of the back door.* The through hallway is a no-no.

5. *Heavy beams* in the recreational room are a burden and interfere with Chi. There are many more. Numbers matter. The number 8 is lucky the number 4 is not and so on.

Is this all? Of course not, the market changes. If and when inflation returns, visibly returns, you may buy anything located anywhere and do well with it. Until then, look over some of the suggestions and pick your best bets.

∼

In Essence

Single family home investment has outperformed all other home ownership classes for the small investor.

Foreclosures are hard work, tax sales are fads.

Buying in a small town can be profitable if you follow some principles.

Waterfront, river, lake or ocean will always be valuable.

Chapter 25

WHAT TO DO WHEN THE RAINS COME

History has a way of repeating itself – especially the bad parts.

This chapter is about an aspect of the real estate business that you almost never hear discussed and that you almost never read anything about – and that is what to do when the bad times come. Any darn fool can survive good times. There's no trick at all to that. What separates the grown-ups from the children is how you handle the trouble.

The problem here is that it's almost impossible to get experienced at handling trouble to the point where you are adept at it. The reason for this is that in real estate investment when you get into trouble you lose money and losing money has a traumatic effect on most people. When it happens there is that tendency to take whatever money you have left and get out of the game. However, if you lose all your investment capital and don't have any more chips to play with then you're automatically out of the game.

Therefore, if you're going to learn about this at the point where it's going to do you some good, you're going to have to benefit from the experiences of people who have already walked the road. If possible, this is not the kind of thing that you want to learn first hand.

Besides, who wants to take lessons in failure? Nobody wants to learn about failure. What everybody wants is to learn about success. For success we know what we have to do. We have to seek out successful people and get them to tell us their secrets. It stands to reason that the same thing would hold true if we wanted to know about failure. We should seek out people who have failed and get them to tell us what went wrong. But human nature being what it is you will find that people who have failed, find there is not too much call for their consulting services. Go to the library and look at all the books they have on success. You wouldn't live long enough to read a fraction of them. Try to find something about failure. The selection is not what you would call really extensive.

There is a wonderful book about the legendary developer, William Zeckendorf called *Zeckendorf*. The book starts out with him having gone broke and the furniture movers under the directions of the receiver are carrying his office furniture out to the moving vans. He persuades the receiver because there is a glut of unoccupied office space in the area and because used office furniture has practically no value, to put the furniture back, reconnect the phones and allow him to occupy the offices until he can get back on his feet.

Zeckendorf did get back on his feet and went on to complete many great projects and won for himself a star in the walk of fame for real estate developers. (Okay, okay, I know there is no such walk of fame – but there should be!) But it's a real shame that we will never know the name of that receiver who had the imagination to listen to Zeckendorf and the courage to use his own money to reconnect the phones in the office.

It's really too bad that they don't teach this anywhere in the schooling process. You can go out there and get a mountain of formal education. You can get a Masters of Business Administration, you can get a Bachelor of Commerce degree, you can study for years and years and not one of those textbooks and not one of those professors are going to tell you what to do when you find yourself in trouble that you can't get out of.

Bear in mind that we are not concerned here with how to avoid trouble. We've been talking about that since the beginning of the book. Here we are only concerned with what to do when all the avoiding hasn't worked and we actually find ourselves in the glue.

Okay, when we talk about trouble, just what is it that we're talking about? We are talking about anything that is going to cause you to lose money. This trouble is going to come from three major sources. They are:

1. Things you do to yourself.

2. Things other people do to you.

3. Things that just happen, like earthquakes, depressions and bad luck in general.

The best kind of trouble is the trouble from things you do to yourself. The reason for this is that as soon as you recognize what's happening you have it in your power to stop doing whatever it is that is causing the trouble. Most of the time this won't help because the mistake has usually been made and what you are going to suffer is the effect of the mistake. If, however, it is an ongoing thing then you might have it in your power to do something about it.

For example, you might decide that there is a market in providing rental accommodation to biker gangs. So you go after that market and you rent one of your houses to a biker gang and the first thing you know they have painted it purple and the front yard is littered with old motorcycle parts and they are not paying you any rent. So you have to evict them and cover over the purple paint and get rid of the junk and start all over.

Before you had the actual experience the idea of the biker gangs seemed like a good one. It appeared that you could ask a higher rent and there wasn't much supply available to them so you'd be able to have the market pretty much to yourself. But once you had some actual experience with them the idea didn't seem so attractive. So you would stop doing what it was you were doing and go in a different direction.

The second category is where other people do things to you. You might go into partnership with someone and their job is to look after the property management duties. In this scenario they are the ones who decide to rent the property to the biker gang. All the results are the same but the difference is that there is someone else to blame – or is there? It all depends where you're measuring from. Is it his mistake for renting to the biker gang or is it your mistake because you selected him for a partner or gave him the responsibility for making the decision? It's the age old question of where does the buck stop?

The amount of trouble is the same. And – the person who pays is the same. You.

The third category is the one that is usually the most expensive and yet it is the one that is easiest to bear. In case this seems like a contradiction in terms, let me explain. In the third category which can be described with the catch-all label of 'bad luck' we don't have ourselves to blame and that's what makes it the easiest to bear.

Let's say that the government decided that they wanted to pass a law that said that you had to rent your property to biker gangs and there was nothing you could do about it. This would leave you no choice but to shake your fist at the sky in well justified rage.

An inordinate amount of sheer bad luck comes to us from the government. Now, there is the school of thought that says that people get the kind of government they deserve and if your government is perpetrating things on you, then in the final analysis it is your own fault. Your own fault, because you didn't get up off the couch and campaign successfully to put better people in there, so please shut up and stop complaining. That outlook does not give a whole lot of comfort to someone caught up in the coils of some mindless, faceless, brainless and heartless bureaucracy.

As any developer will tell you: any one of them can ruin you. The tax people, the environmentalists, securities regulators, inspectors at city hall, the fisheries department, the zoning, the by-law inspectors – any place where you give authority without personal responsibility you are going to create the potential for some investor to run into a brick wall that didn't exist when he left for work that morning.

If you can't do anything about it, then the source of your difficulties doesn't really matter. In all cases the causes, the costs and the consequences are all the same. The only difference is whose fault it is. It is, of course, little comfort to anyone who finds themselves in trouble to learn that it doesn't matter whose fault it is.

I once overheard a conversation at a car repair shop while waiting for my car. The service manager was explaining to a customer why the mistake they had made was not their fault. The customer's response was, "Look, I pay for my mistakes. If you have someone who pays for yours, please tell me who it is so I can continue this conversation with him!"

That's why, if you're the one who has to pay, it doesn't matter whose fault it is.

So let's move on to how do you know when you're in trouble? Simple. You know you're in trouble when you've got more money going out than you've got coming in – or, when the property is going down in value – or, when you have amounts that you need to pay but the money isn't there ... or all of the above.

The warning signs will eventually manifest themselves and when they do here's what you do about them. And pay careful attention here, because this is one of the places where the time you've devoted to reading this will be especially well spent.

There are three rules that are carved over the portals that lead into the Ozzie Jurock College of Knowledge. The first we've already dealt with and that is: *you make your most money the day you buy the property.* The second is: *forget about location, location, location,* and the third is a companion rule to the first and it is just as important: *the sooner you take a loss, the smaller it's going to be.*

While your business plan stated that you weren't concerned about making a capital gain, but wanted someone else to pay down the mortgage, you might argue that you'll outwait the bad times. If things go seriously against you then you had better sell. Serious means, three out of five units are empty, you simply do not have the wherewithal to subsidize the units. Or you thought your timing was good and you were in an up cycle, yet the market is still going against you. No recriminations. Things change.

The big trick is in recognizing it as soon as it occurs and then having the wisdom and the courage to take the necessary steps. This is where human nature is our worst enemy. We run into what I call, 'emotional cost accounting'.

People have two different approaches to losses. The realists figure a loss occurs when it happens. Let's say you buy a stock on Monday for $100. On Tuesday it's worth $90. The realist would say that he lost 10% between Monday and Tuesday.

The 'Emotional Cost Accounting' person would say, "I paid $100 for this and as long as I hold it in my portfolio and don't sell it I will not have actually suffered any loss."

The difference between these two approaches are how they affect a person's course of action. The realist is in a position to recognize the loss on the first day that it starts and if he sells the stock on Tuesday then his loss is limited to 10%. The 'Emotional Cost Accounting' person takes comfort from his delusion that the loss hasn't happened yet and he props this up with the hope that it will come back. He feels in his heart that this investment now 'owes him' $10. He will look you in the eye and with a straight face he will say, "I can't sell this stock until it comes back to what I paid for it." And he sticks to this position even if the stock drops from $90 to $10.

The realist gets to take the $90 he has left and uses it to make back the $10 that was lost. The 'Emotional Cost Accounting Person' is riding that investment toboggan as far down as it will go.

The stock could go off the board, the company could be delisted, the entire board of directors could be sent to jail and the 'Emotional Cost Accounting' person would keep those stock certificates in his safety deposit box where they would be discovered when the box is opened up to get out the will for the executor.

Whether it's bad luck or bad judgment the results are always the same. The only difference is going to be in the amount of remorse. But the sooner you recognize it the sooner you're going to be able to exercise whatever damage control is possible.

Damage control is the name of this particular game. One of the drums that we beat on constantly is the importance of a written business plan. If you have a detailed written business plan, constantly update it, and consistently keep measuring your progress, you're going to know as soon as it is possible to know when you are not meeting your benchmarks. You're going to know as soon as it's possible to know when changes occur that are going to require your attention.

Maybe knowing in time will not make the problem any easier to solve but it goes a long way towards minimizing the damage.

A friend of mine once spent a summer when he was at university as the director of a day camp. He tells me it was the most stressful job he ever had. There were 42 six-year-olds and all he did all day was count from one to 42 – over and over again. When they were on the playground, at the beach or in the park he counted over and over again. Whenever the total was 40 or 41 everyone went looking for the missing kids. Once they found them he would go back to his counting.

The same principle can be applied to your investments. The closer you keep your eye on them and the more you measure them against your written plan the sooner you are going to know when things go wrong and the sooner you are going to implement damage control. The sooner you start looking for the 'missing six year olds' the better off you're going to be. This will always translate into dollars in your pocket.

Everyone's circumstance and situation is different. One person might be investing a portion of his RRSP in first mortgages on residential income producing real estate. Another person might have taken his life savings and mortgaged the family home in order to do a recreational land subdivision. If things go wrong for the first person then he is going to suffer a slight dent. If things go wrong for the second person, he is going to be wiped out. In both cases the earlier the problem is recognized and the sooner damage control is implemented the less will be the damage.

There will come a time when the trouble is severe enough that you are going to have to get some help. When the wolves start to snap at your heels is when you have to interpose some intermediaries between you and the people who are harassing you. Your accountant, if his expertise is in this area, can buy you time and breathing room. If he's not experienced in this area he's not going to be of much help. Same thing goes for your lawyer. And your lawyer is important to you during the bad times because he can create the most time and the most breathing room for you. The difference between negotiating for yourself and having a lawyer negotiate for you is like the difference between chicken salad and chicken manure. If you've had both experiences then you know what I mean. If you haven't had both experiences then you better take my word for it. If you don't, you'll wish you had. That's why your choice of these professionals at the outset is so important.

Now, I don't have any personal experience with this, but at their very worst things will be so bad that you will have to play the bankruptcy card. For this there is no question that you are going to have to employ the services of an expert. There are all kinds of ways to go bankrupt. I have seen two partners go bankrupt in the same deal. One of them did it the wrong way and wound up losing everything that was possible to lose including his wife. He wound up living in a bachelor suite. The other did it right and managed to keep his house, his vacation place, his boat and a couple of very expensive cars. That his marriage stood up under the strain might just have been coincidental – who knows?

What explains this wide disparity between the two? One had good advice and the other had bad advice. One acted in time and the other didn't. One thing is for sure, if you have to push the bankruptcy button the difference between losing less and losing more is going to be in the quality of the bankruptcy lawyer that you use.

Let me give you this piece of advice about bankruptcy – if it has to happen, the sooner the better. Any stalling that you do is dead time out of your life. Whatever money you're going to be able to salvage will be salvaged just as well no matter when you act. The money in the 'estate', as they refer to whatever is left, will usually, in a business continuum, be eaten up by the lawyers and the accountants. They have a vested interest in stretching things out as long as possible. You have a vested interest in getting things over and finished as soon as possible.

The reason for this is that until it's over and done with you can't get on with your life. I know a person who dragged out his bankruptcy for three and a half years. In that time the lawyers and the accountants made a small fortune. The creditors got less than they would have if things hadn't been delayed so much. And the person going through this bankruptcy procedure was in limbo for three and a half of what should have been the most productive years of his life. If you ever find yourself in that position, don't you make the same mistake.

It's important to bear in mind that the only thing we're talking about is the loss of money. Since they did away with the debtor's prison, the only thing they can take away from you is money, property and things. As long as you don't make yourself sick over it, you're going to come out the other side in one piece and you can make it back.

Even if you can't survive financially, you want to do the best you can to survive psychologically. Most people, when they lose most or all of their money treat it as if it's the end of the world. And for most of them it is. It all depends on your perspective.

Everybody has their own way of dealing with these matters. As we said earlier, the problem is that nobody ever goes through real trouble of this kind often enough to get any good at it. So the way you react and the way you deal with it is going to be dictated by the kind of personal philosophy that you've developed.

I know many people who have 'gone broke' several times. They share a lot of the same qualities. The principal ones are optimism and resiliency. A person who goes broke once and then quits is easy to understand. What's a little more difficult to grasp is how a person could fail more than once, start all over again and continue in the game.

Some of these 'repeat offenders' have been people that would not inaccurately be described as 'experts'. The outsider looking at this is tempted to ask, "How can an 'expert' keep going to the well and keep breaking his pitcher?"

The answer is that while I know of many experts who have had repeat failures I don't know any expert who had the same kind of failure twice. There are many who've had repeat failures who didn't make any mistake at all but merely experienced bad luck.

If you play the game often enough, it is not unreasonable to expect that you might run into some bad luck.

When we say 'bad luck' what is it we're talking about? Let's take for example the leaky condo crisis of British Columbia. Let's say you're just an average investor and you decide (before any of this leaky condo business bursts into the newspaper scene) that you're going to buy a condo as an investment. It's nice and conservative as an investment and it has the advantage that some years down the road, after your kids leave home, you might want to sell your house and move into this condo and all in all it makes a lot of sense.

So do you plunk down your money and become the proud owner of a condo? Not so fast! We are prudent investors. We do all kinds of investigating. We check out the neighborhood. It's good. We check out the past history of the builder and the architect and the developer. All good. We check the Realtor and how much of the project is sold. It's good – as a matter of fact 90% of the units are sold. We do all the comparisons and checking that we can think of and all of our answers are positive. So we are satisfied and then and only then do we plunk down our money and become proud condo owners.

The day after they cash our cheque someone in the building reports a leak. Then another and another. There are strata council meetings. People thump on the table and beat their breasts and fingers are pointed and committees are appointed. And after a while it turns out that the building is leaking like a sieve and once the water gets in it can't get out. Everything is going all moldy. Pretty soon the numbers start coming in on what it's going to cost to fix and the amount is more than we owe on the mortgage.

We have to think in terms that our money is irrevocably lost. Did we do something wrong? No, as a matter of fact we did everything right. The only mistake we made was not to own a crystal ball with which to read the future. This comes under the heading of plain, ordinary, garden variety bad luck.

But we are just Joe Average. What has this got to do with experts? Down the street from us there is another project just like ours. Same architect, same builder – the only difference is that this project came along three months behind ours and now with all the bad ink in the newspapers about leaky condos the developer can't sell any of his units. His lender gets tired of waiting for the construction loan to be repaid so he forecloses and because the developer, as a matter of course, signed a personal guarantee he is going to wind up bankrupt. Did he make mistakes? Only the one about not having the crystal ball.

Did he go broke ten years ago? Yes. Was it the same thing? No, it was totally different. Interest rates doubled overnight and the ostrich consumers stuck their heads in the sand and didn't buy anything for six months. Again he was part way through a project, the lender got tired of waiting and foreclosed. And again he went bankrupt. But he wasn't alone. He had a hundred other developers for company. Does this mean he should get out of the real estate investment business?

Let me illustrate with the story of the man who worked for the circus cleaning up after the elephant. Every day he would come home reeking from the elephant dung. His wife wouldn't let him into the house until he had taken off all his clothes in the garage and hosed himself off. One particularly hot summers day he arrived home particularly ripe from his days activities. His wife was putting some things away in the garage – she took one look and one smell and something snapped. "For Goodness sake," she said, "why don't you find some other line of work?" "What?" he answered in astonishment, "and give up show business?"

Most of the professionals and experts that I've come across feel the same way about real estate investments. They feel it's like show business – only better.

In summary, what is really important here is how soon you recognize the problem, what you do to mitigate the effects, how you salvage what you can and how you do as much as you can to preserve the relationships you're involved in. You can always get more money – and even if you can't, it's really not important. Family and friends are what's really important.

~

In Essence

You're in trouble when you have more going out than you have coming in. The way of Zen tells us that the longest journey begins with the first step; in the same way the serious trouble begins with the first loss.

The sooner you take a loss the smaller it's going to be.

Don't delude yourself into thinking that the loss hasn't happened just because it hasn't shown up on your balance sheet.

Don't lose sight of the fact that it's only money. Even if you can't salvage the property and the things, you can salvage your relationships.

It's never too late to start again.

Chapter 26

EPILOGUE

They always say that time changes things, but you actually have to change them yourself. – ANDY WARHOL

I've gone across the whole spectrum of the real estate investment business. I wish I could tell you that you now know everything but the fact of the matter is that I've just scratched the surface. Yes, I have touched on the major categories but I haven't dealt with anything in any real depth. In order to do that instead of twenty-six chapters there'd have to be twenty-six books.

But what I have done is described the field of study and I have pointed out some of the directions where you have to focus your attention. And I've told you some things about this business that you won't find written down anywhere else.

If you are a beginner or if you are a sophisticate or somewhere in between, you should not read this book once and then put it on the shelf. Keep it near your desk, or by your bed, or in the bathroom. (Yes, I know, I'm giving my critics an opening with that last suggestion.) You'll always get something new with each reading. It will bring to mind things that you've overlooked and remind you of things you have forgotten.

Just reading the chapter headings will tell you, by categories, the scope of what there is to know. Reading the little squibs at the beginning of each chapter will give you an overview of my slightly skewed philosophy. And reading the 'In Essence' tags at the end of the chapters will give you a distillation of what's in the book.

It took me a lifetime to learn what's in this book. A lot of it I learned from personal experience and by doing. But most of it I learned from the examples of others. Those who traveled the road ahead of me. The latter is, without question, the most effective, efficient way to acquire knowledge. How many of us despair while we watch our children busily reinventing the wheel and making all the mistakes we made while we sit on the sidelines in frustration knowing that we have all this wisdom to impart to them if they would only avail themselves of it.

It wasn't until I sat down and edited what I had written here that I realized the scope of what there is to know. One of the cornerstones of the human experience is that, "There ain't no such thing as a free lunch." Actually there is one exception to that almost universal truth. There is one kind of free lunch. When you learn from someone else's experiences and mistakes – that's a free lunch. This book is a whole menu of free lunches and I'm grateful for the opportunity to pass them on.

I've been a one-man real estate operation and I've been president of the largest real estate brokerage company in Canada. I've had a chance to observe every kind and degree of success and every kind and degree of failure. I've taken what I consider to be the important elements of these observations I've put them in this book along with an attempt to explain why and how they happened.

You could read this book once a year for the rest of your life and every time it would be brand new. That's because every time you read it you're going to be a different person.

If I was going to teach a young person some of the things that they should know about real estate investment, the following are the points I would stress. Common sense will tell anyone that they are valid but common sense won't tell you how important they are. Only experience will do that. We'll give the following the title:

Some Of The Things You Should Teach Your Kid About Real Estate Investment:

About 10% of what most people do is 'action' and the other 90% of what they do is in reaction. People let circumstances dictate their reactions and they feel that are doing 'the best we can do at the time'. While I believe that people have a lot more choice if they only sat down, planned more and reacted less, life for most people means being stuck in a rut.

But even if we only act from choice in that 10%, let's make sure that those 10% of our activities are all 'action'. This is where the 'free will' comes in. My advice to you is to direct all your 'action' to activities that will make you grow. At the end of twenty years you want to be that person with twenty years experience, not the person who has had one year's experience twenty times.

The basics aren't difficult to grasp. At the core of everything is the premise that you make the most money the day you buy the property. Then to this you add:

1. Asking the necessary questions;
2. Seeking out the required answers;
3. Interpreting the information you get from those answers;
4. Taking the necessary actions.

Listen to the answers. Be a good listener. God gave you two ears and one mouth for a reason. Don't assume anything. Always look for win/win type of situations.

Your timing is important. You want to be selling when others are buying and buying when others are selling. Part of this is because the public is always wrong and part of it is because you always want to be either buying or selling into the biggest market possible.

Another reason timing is important is because the real estate market is like a duck flying through the air. When duck hunting one has to lead the duck. You have to shoot ahead of the duck so that you allow for the distance the duck is going to fly while your shotgun pellets are getting to him. If you don't, you'll always be shooting where the duck was, not where the duck is. Same thing with the market. It is always changing. Nothing ever stays the same. You have to know what's happening with those aspects that involve your properties. If you don't, you'll pay in real money for that ignorance.

This applies whether you are a big investor or a small investor. There are all kinds of differences between the big investor and the small investor but the cost of ignorance is the same. It is a matter of degree not a matter of kind.

The small investor has the advantage of flexibility. The large investor has the advantage of muscle. It's like tennis. Play to your opponent's weakness and try to get them to play to your strengths.

Regardless of your size one of the most important factors is understanding yourself. Understanding yourself can turn you from a small investor into a large one.

The new millenium is all about building lasting quality relationships.

You build them if you are a strong 'winner type' personality.

People are attracted to a winner. Have passion and enthusiasm. 'Enthusiasm' comes from the Greek and means the 'god within'. Don't have any doubts about you, the product or service you offer and the real estate you own or want to own.

A good axiom to remember: *one per cent doubt and you're out*. I find that there is benefit in reading biographies of self-made men. Men like Napoleon Hill and J. Paul Getty. You're always going to get a point or two of extremely valuable information but the real value is the inspiration that you can get from the example of their courage and their dedication.

I've read a lot of biographies of second and third generation multi-millionaires and don't find them nearly as inspiring. After all, it's tough to turn the clock back and arrange to be born into a wealthy family.

You should paste the following on your bathroom mirror so you can see it every morning. 'There are only three ways to lose money in real estate – Greed, Ignorance, and Bad Luck – and if you combine all three you can really accelerate the process.'

There is nothing more important than putting your personal real estate investment plan into a written form. The written personal real estate investment plan will, at the beginning of your career, help you delineate what kind of a player you are which, in turn, will help you determine what kind of games you play.

Write things down; develop a plan of action. Commit yourself to it and go do it. Perform to the plan. A plan allows you to measure your results. A plan allows you to walk away, if the opportunity doesn't match the objective. Remember the three words 'Commit, Perform, Measure'.

A very important aspect of this is for you to be able to accurately gauge what your risk tolerance is.

And here's a most important point; risk tolerance doesn't exist in a vacuum. By this I mean that your risk tolerance doesn't mean just you. If you're married, you and your spouse are a combined entity. If you are as brave as a lion and your spouse is as timid as a mouse, then the investment posture has to be adjusted.

Notice that I did not say that one of you is going to have to change. My experience has been that by the time people are old enough to have some money to invest in real estate they are too old to change. Sure, there are exceptions to the rule but the vast majority of times it's true. Therefore it's the investment posture that has to be adjusted. The most practical approach is to adjust your investment approach to the lowest common denominator of risk.

Twenty years from now you'll be celebrating some landmark anniversary with a big cake instead of communicating through your lawyers about those late alimony payments.

The written personal real estate investment plan will also help you define what your expectations are. If you have a step by step achievable plan, you have a much better chance of knowing whether that plan is realistic or not.

Robert Burns said, "A man's reach should exceed his grasp else what's a heaven for?" What we're looking for here is that happy balance between ambition and prudence.

Another of the main benefits of the written plan is that it maps a route from where you are to where you want to be. By doing this you will be able to pinpoint what your next step is. If you have a clear understanding of what your next step is then you only have to work on one thing at a time. By definition you will always be working and directing your energies exactly where you should be.

When you have people do things for you, you have to watch to see that they are doing it; but after they've done it, you have to make sure they did it right. 'People do what you inspect and not what you expect.'

If you don't, then you may have to do it yourself.

It's very important to know that the money you don't lose is twice as important as the money you make. If you start with a dollar and make another dollar you will be one dollar ahead. If you lose that dollar, then you'll have to make two dollars next time to be where you should be. If it's twice as important, then it deserves twice as much care. It doesn't matter how many good deals you say no to as long as you don't say yes to a bad deal. After all, the very best way to deal with trouble is to stay out of it.

Never lose sight of the fact that when you're acquiring a piece of property the asking price represents one thing and one thing only; it is the 'absolute wildest expectation of the seller'. The only thing it should represent to you is that this is the vendor's way of telling you the maximum that he will accept for the property.

Also, be aware that the 'seller's market' is a myth. There is no such thing. The buyer is the one who always sets the price. Always. The only thing the seller gets to decide is whether there's going to be a transaction or not.

In any negotiation the person who cares least is going to have an advantage, a large advantage.

If you are winning the negotiation, make sure you allow the other person to save some face. I have seen buyers make offers and get them accepted immediately. Were they happy? No, "I should have offered less," or "I wonder what's wrong with it," was the more likely reaction. So, if you like an offer and are ready to accept it, as is, wait awhile, tell a fight story. Understand human nature. Always, if you can, create the illusion of a win/win situation. Sometimes it's better not to try to wring the last dollar out of the negotiations to get the deal done or you'll negotiate yourself right out of the deal.

The best tool that you can have in the negotiating process is knowledge of the market combined with knowledge of the negotiating process. It doesn't do you any good to be an expert in one if you're ignorant in the other.

Beware of the villains. No matter what kind of a horror story you hear about what happened to someone in a real estate investment you can be secure in the knowledge that something worse happened to someone else and something even worse than that can happen to you, if you're not careful.

Finally, beware the naysayers. The world has changed and is continuing to change; the new millenium seems a frightening place ... but so were the eighties and the seventies and the sixties. In 1961 not one house sold in the suburb of Burnaby. In 1969 I couldn't give away brand-new $19,900 full basement homes, in 1974 the U.S. stock market crashed by 40% and the gloom descended on Vancouver's housing market. Headlines were "Realtors are prowling like hungry tigers," "Real estate prices will never recover again." In 1981 and 1982 real estate values did crash by 45% in 18 months. 5-year mortgage terms were written at 16.5%. In fact, all of the eighties featured 5-year mortgage terms at an average interest rate of 12.45% and never once never less than 10.75%. In 1988 the end of the real estate world was predicted following the 1987 stock market crash. In 1995 and 1998 the doomsayers used demographics as reasons not to buy a family abode. The baby boomers won't buy any more, they cry.

Had you listened to all the doom and gloom of 1961, 1974, 1981, 1982, 1983, 1986 and 1988 and not bought a house you would have done a serious disservice to yourself and your family. If you had listened to the demographics argument in 1995, you would have missed the 20% house price increase in Toronto and the 9.5% to 20% house price increase in most major cities in the U.S.

Of course, this is a New World. You have to apply some new principles. Get some unbiased advice, listen to where the naysayers come from. Make some intelligent decisions. Discard some of the old standbys. I can boil down this book to this:

"There are no good or bad markets, only good and bad deals."

I have seen the absolute worst deals in the so-called very best markets (i.e. some condo hotels in Vancouver and at Whistler in 1980, 1995 and 1996) and I have seen the very best deals in poor markets. I have listened to the gloom and to the boom. Every year for 30 years somebody tells me that there are too many Realtors in the business, that no one can afford to buy anymore (yep, they said it in 1969 too) and then they say: "I wish I had bought 10 years ago..."

Good times, bad times. There will always be the gloomsters. Don't become involved with them. Prices rise on properties in places where people want to live. Real estate ownership is the greatest wealth builder for individuals of all time. It always has been and it always will.

Those are some of the more important points to impress on your kid but first make sure that you have impressed them on yourself. There isn't any big secret to making money in real estate investment. There isn't even any big trick to it.

All you have to do is possess the relatively ordinary qualities of hard work, ingenuity, resourcefulness and care. And then you have to put those qualities to work.

I wish you luck in your adventures.

THE MAN WHO THINKS HE CAN

If you think you are beaten, you are;
    If you think you dare not, you don't;
If you'd like to win, but think you can't,
    It's almost a cinch you won't.
If you think you'll lose, you're lost,
    For out in the world we find
Success begins with a fellow's will;
    It's all in a state of mind.

If you think you're outclassed, you are;
    You've got to think high to rise.
You've got to be sure of yourself before
    You can ever win a prize.
Life's battles don't always go
    To the stronger or faster man;
But soon or late the man who wins
    Is the man who thinks he can.

WALTER D. WINTLE

INDEX

About the Author

Ozzie Jurock is president of Jurock Publishing, Jurock New Media and Jurock International Net.

Vancouver magazine ranked him among the 45 brightest people in Vancouver, BCTV features him every Wednesday on the News Hour and for *Business in Vancouver* he is a real estate columnist. He has written hundreds of real estate articles and several thousand people have subscribed to his monthly and weekly newsletters – *Jurock's Real Estate Investor* and *Jurock's Facts by Fax*.

But he is not just talking about real estate. He is living it. He has sold, bought, owned and managed it. Ozzie Jurock served as the past president of Royal LePage (Res.), the past chairman of NRS Block Bros. As well he managed real estate companies in Taiwan, HongKong and Tokyo. He has served on the boards of the BC Real Estate Council, the Vancouver Real Estate Board, the UBC Real Estate Research Bureau and the Quality Council of BC among others. He is also a Fellow of the Canadian Real Estate Institute.

His busy life found him elected president of the Canada Taiwan Trade Association, serving as a judge for the Ernst & Young Entrepreneur of the year award but he still finds time to hold over 100 speeches a year.

Ozzie Jurock is known as one of Canada's leading business motivators. His investor outlook conferences attract audiences of over 500 attendees every time. There is only one reason: Ozzie Jurock delivers more than he promises.

He and his wife, Jo, currently live in Vancouver, Canada.

This book was designed by Robert Carlson and Albert Liao at Jurock New Media in Vancouver; researched and edited by Sam Allman; printed and bound by Hignell Printing in Winnipeg.

Type: The text face is Minion, designed by Robert Slimbach, and released by Adobe Systems, 1989. Cover text is Minion and Univers, designed by Adrian Frutiger and released by Monotype, 1957.

Paper: 60 lb #2 offset

Products and Services from the Jurock Group of Companies

∾ For Corporations & Executives

- Keynote business motivational presentations
- Keynote economic & real estate forecast presentations
- Keynote internet outlook forecasting
- Keynote internet practical applications
- Real Estate sales & motivational training
- Real Estate management training
- Real Estate business consulting
- Executive planning & strategy sessions
- Quantity discounts on books, tapes, business plans & other materials.

∾ For Investors & Individuals

- *Jurock's Real Estate Investor* monthly newsletter
- Jurock's weekly *Facts by Fax*
- Jurock's weekly Hotline
- Ozzie Jurock Real Estate web site: WWW.JUROCK.COM
- Investment strategies & services
- Books
- Motivational tapes
- Real Estate outlook tapes
- Special Real Estate action "how to" reports in hard copy or on disk

∾ Web Development Services

Jurock New Media
- Award winning web design
- Powerful web site hosting
- Web site marketing

- Database programming & Integration
- Java programming
- CGI scripting
- Intranet design & implementation

∾ JUROCK INTERNATIONAL NET

- Jurock.com on-line business directory
- Properties for rent & for sale
- Recommended Realtors & firms
- New Real Estate developments & investment deals
- Legal & financial firms
- Expert advice & predictions
- Shopping
- Interactive Real Estate bulletin board
- Interactive Business bulletin board
- Monthly & weekly guest columns by Canada's leading writers
- Weekly news
- Travel services

Jurock New Media - over 600 Canadian and American Corporations chose us to design and launch their web environments.

Jurock New Media - Winner of the 1998 Sales & Marketing Award by Sales & Marketing Executives of Vancouver

In Canada call toll free: 1-800-691-1183
From the United States call: 604-683-1111
Fax: 604-683-1707
Email: info@jurock.com

Visit *Jurock International Net*: WWW.JUROCK.COM
Visit *Jurock Products and Services*: WWW.E-MONEYWHEEL.COM
Visit *Jurock New Media*: WWW.JUROCK.NET
Visit *Jurock 'Media Kit'* for advertising: WWW.JUROCK.COM/MEDIAKIT/